J. Bell.
M Co

EVER BY MY SIDE

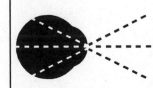

This Large Print Book carries the
Seal of Approval of N.A.V.H.

EVER BY MY SIDE

A MEMOIR IN EIGHT ~~ACTS~~ PETS

DR. NICK TROUT

THORNDIKE PRESS

A part of Gale, Cengage Learning

GALE
CENGAGE Learning™

Detroit • New York • San Francisco • New Haven, Conn • Waterville, Maine • London

GALE
CENGAGE Learning

Copyright © 2011 by Dr. Nicholas Trout.
Thorndike Press, a part of Gale, Cengage Learning.

ALL RIGHTS RESERVED
Thorndike Press® Large Print Biography.
The text of this Large Print edition is unabridged.
Other aspects of the book may vary from the original edition.
Set in 16 pt. Plantin.

LIBRARY OF CONGRESS CATALOGING-IN-PUBLICATION DATA

Trout, Nick.
  Ever by my side : a memoir in eight [Acts] pets / by Nick
Trout.
    p. cm. — (Thorndike press large print biography)
  ISBN-13: 978-1-4104-3618-4 (hardcover : lg. print)
  ISBN-10: 1-4104-3618-7 (hardcover : lg. print)
  1. Trout, Nick. 2. Veterinarians—United States—Biography.
3. Human–animal relationships. 4. Veterinary
medicine—Anecdotes. I. Title.
  SF613.T76A3 2011b
  636.089'7092—dc22
  [B]   2010050118

Published in 2011 by arrangement with Broadway Books, an imprint of
the Crown Publishing Group, a division of Random House, Inc.

Printed in the United States of America
1 2 3 4 5 6 7 15 14 13 12 11

For Pauline, Duncan, and Fiona

CONTENTS

7

AUTHOR'S NOTE

For more than twenty years I have worked as a veterinarian, blessed with the responsibility of caring for sick animals and in doing so, granted unprecedented access into the unique and powerful bonds between humans and their pets. In my professional life I am constantly striving to make a connection with owner and animal alike and it is always a delicate balancing act. I want the other human in this our triangular relationship to realize that I am sensitive but not too sappy, that I am intrigued but not prying, that I can be objective and scientific but more than prepared to share my own experiences and philosophies. Most of all I want them to see that I understand why they seek my help. I know what motivates their desire to restore their pet to full health. I know what an animal can do for a lonely soul, a family, a broken heart, and an angry state of mind. I know the power of the stuff

9

that cannot be put into words and I won't ask them to try, because I want them to understand that I get it.

I imagine my life has been similar to those of most people — stuff happens, we make choices, we take a certain path, and many of the decisions we make depend upon the lessons we learned along the way and how we interpreted their meaning. To my way of thinking it's like bumper stickers on the back of a clunker — you choose the stickers that reflect your personality and the more you accumulate, the better the guy driving the car behind gets to appreciate the kind of person you really are. I've been fortunate enough to spend most of my life around animals, the creatures I have come to think of as my own pets. Each and every one of them has played their part in bringing me to this point. In their own unique way, they have all donated a bumper sticker or two, their message catchy, simple, and above all else, honest.

This book is based on my own recollections of these personal pets (and many more besides) with occasional input and insight from members of my family. In some instances the names and identifiers of individuals central to the story have been changed to maintain anonymity. The result is perhaps less memoir than discerning retrospective, as I take an opportunity to relive a few of the defining moments throughout my life in which animals took their cue, stepped up, and gave me a chance to appreciate a different perspective. This is my attempt to show them off and share their subtle, startling, and inspirational lessons, which have played a small but vital part in helping to shape the person you see with the stethoscope around his neck. As you read on, I truly hope my interpretation of their significance will resonate, will induce a knowing smile, a nod, and maybe a wayward tear, as you too recognize the powerful benefits of the animals in your own life.

■ ■ ■ ■

PART ONE
UNION JACK

■ ■ ■ ■

1.
THE DEFINITION
OF DIFFERENT

I wish I could tell you I have enjoyed the company of a dog or a cat every day of my life, but it's simply not true. In fact, my earliest appreciation of pets in any form did not occur until I was four and, even then, was limited to my grandmothers' dogs.

My mother's mother possessed a white male toy poodle named Marty. From the start, Marty made it abundantly clear that he had no patience for small curious hands, except perhaps as chew toys. Venture into his territory, that is, anywhere within an invisible fifty-yard perimeter of my grandma's house, and he would come at you, bouncing forward as if his legs were little pogo sticks, emitting a bark that could crack bulletproof glass, before scurrying away to safety behind grandma's ankle, only to repeat the process over and over again until he finally ascended into her arms. From this lofty position he could look down at me

15

with an expression that said "If you bother me, I will make you pay in blood and tears."

Marty was not even a year old and his presence had already negated what few pleasures there were after a two-hour car drive to visit my grandma.

"Sit you down while I put the kettle on," Gran would say as everyone rushed for a vacant seat in a game of musical chairs that invariably left me with the sofa where Marty had settled. Curled up on the middle cushion, Marty would emit a throaty, malicious grumble if I so much as inched toward the ends of the couch.

There was also the smell. The entire house reeked of the only food Marty deigned to consume — sausages! I never once saw him eat regular dog food. And I'm not talking about classic British bangers. Marty's delicate mouth and discriminating palate preferred, no, insisted upon, a small, hand-crafted breakfast sausage from a local butcher that had to be fried, allowed to cool, and then carefully chopped into congealed mouth-size pieces. At some point during every visit Gran would excuse herself, go to the kitchen, take up a position next to the stove, and disappear into an oily cloud as she seared sheathed meat that crackled and spat in her direction. I would look over at her and she would smile the smile of old people everywhere, content to check off another comforting chore in her daily routine. Meanwhile Marty might squirm a little on his throne and sigh, not out of boredom, but approval, pleased the hired help was doing his bidding.

Neither my grandma nor my parents ever suggested Marty and I become acquainted or that Marty become socialized around children or that he be reprimanded for his bad manners. Perhaps I couldn't be trusted not to pinch, yank, rip, or snap as I did with most of my toys. Perhaps they didn't want to take any chances. Whatever the reason, I kept my distance, painfully curious to discover the feel of his hypoallergenic, steel-wool fur but convinced he would practically explode if I so much as touched him. After a while, I lost all interest in Marty. What was the point? How could I have a relationship with an animal who might as well have been behind bars in a zoo? I couldn't understand what anyone saw in a pet you couldn't, well, pet.

On the other hand, my grandmother on my father's side had a placid female Dalmatian named Cleo and to my delight (and no doubt to the delight of my mother), they occupied a small bungalow next door to our house. In contrast to Marty, Cleo could be completely trusted around children. She was tolerant and forgiving and endowed with seal-pup insulation that possessed a certain . . . give, similar to a Tempur-Pedic foam mattress. Cleo never tired of me petting her, happy to relinquish her short, fine hairs to my sticky palms, which would soon resemble a pair of black and white mittens. I could fall over her or fall into her and she would either lie there and take it, indifferent to the contact, or rise quickly to her feet and find somewhere else to lie down, as though she was sorry for getting under foot rather than angry at being disturbed. At the time, my little sister, Fiona, was too small to play with me, so I was thrilled to share our backyard with a big old spotty dog who never once regarded me as though I were a tasty hors d'oeuvre.

To fully appreciate the bond that formed between me and Cleo, you have to understand our shared interest in swallowing inanimate objects and to help you do so I must mention a chilling yet formative recollection from my childhood.

Late one night, barefoot and immersed in oversized cotton pajamas, this four-year-old boy stood alone in the kitchen having snuck out of bed in search of a snack and a glass of milk. I have always been partial to yogurt, methodically working my way to the bottom of the carton, scraping every last pink glob of strawberry-colored additives off the plastic and onto my spoon. Even now I can recall the feel of that particular spoon, cool and smooth and small, like a silver christening spoon, satisfyingly tinkly on my deciduous teeth and almost weightless in my mouth. With the yogurt gone and my mind in a dull and dreamy state, I began playing with the spoon in the back of my mouth, appreciating the metallic sensation way back on my tongue and how it was possible to push it a little farther and induce gagging, a sharp and forceful contraction deep in my belly — until somewhere just beyond this point, the reflex of actual swallowing took over, involuntary and, to my horror, completely irreversible. I felt the tiny handle leaving my fingertips and slipping from my grasp, and suddenly, like the yogurt, the spoon was gone, disappearing deep inside my body.

When I felt it go there was no pain or discomfort, only the rush of fear that I had done something very wrong and, perhaps more important, impossible to justify. I mean you don't just swallow a spoon by accident. What was I going to tell my mum and dad? I fell on a spoon while my mouth was open! I was so hungry I ate my yogurt, spoon and all!

I waited for a few minutes and nothing happened. I had a drink of milk and nothing happened. I didn't feel any different. If I jumped up and down nothing rattled inside my body, nothing tickled or poked through my skin. In the end, instead of confessing my sin to my parents, I decided to wait and see what, if anything, happened and besides, I was tired, so I went back to bed.

At this early stage of my life, I'm not entirely sure I could make any connection between what went into my mouth and what came out the other end. All I knew was that by the next morning I still felt fine. No one seemed to have noticed there was anything missing from the cutlery drawer and so I decided to keep my acquisition of a foreign body a secret, comfortable with the notion that the little spoon was lost inside me, hidden somewhere dark and warm and safe, not causing me any harm, inert and happy to simply hang out. It was not until I was thirteen years old, and clearly not much wiser, that I feared my secret would be revealed.

In trying to define my early teenage stature, some might use the word *lean* out of kindness. Truth be told, I was a scrawny whippet of a boy. I was, however, blessed with a semblance of speed, a characteristic that did not go unnoticed by our school sports teacher, Mr. French.

"All you have to do is catch the ball and run for the line."

Sounded simple enough, but his synopsis of what would be required of me as a winger on our school rugby team failed to do justice to the rough and tumble of what the game meant to boys with far more muscle, spite, and testosterone.

I like to remember the critical moment in terms of the dying seconds of a crucial game, perhaps a grudge match against local rivals or a match to claim a league championship title, with time running out and one more try needed to win — me making an impossible catch, a shimmy left, a fake right, defenders falling at my feet as I charged for the line, rugby ball tucked tight and safe in my chest as I leapt over giants and landed for my winning points just as the final whistle blew. What actually transpired was that I caught a ball in the middle of the field and hesitated, and in a moment of panic half a dozen boys jumped on top of me, frozen mud on the right side of my body, hundreds of pounds of grunting, writhing, sweaty bodies on my left. Something had to give as a result of this mayhem and unfortunately that something happened to be my breastbone.

I'd be lying if I said there was an enormous crack akin to a shotgun blast. In fact I got up and carried on playing. All I noticed was an increased difficulty in breathing and by the end of the game it was obvious that this was more than a general lack of physical fitness on my part.

And so I found myself in an emergency room hearing a young doctor suggest that I get a chest X-ray and realizing that for the first time since swallowing that fateful spoon, I would be the recipient of a test that would surely unmask my embarrassing silverware secret.

"You know, Dad, I think I'm feeling better. It's probably nothing," I said to my father, convinced that after all these years the spoon was somehow still sitting in my stomach or casually leaning into the side of my esophagus, minding its own business.

When the doctor emerged with the images, I braced for the ramifications of their peculiar and unequivocal revelation.

"Well, guess what I found hidden in his chest?"

I knew it. The X-ray machine was just another type of camera and I knew how a camera never lies.

"See this dark line, here. That's a crack, a fracture. Your son has broken his sternum."

I looked at the black-and-white film for myself, not at the break, but all over the image, looking for something metallic, white, and vaguely spoon shaped. But there was nothing.

It wasn't until I studied biology in school and ultimately medicine at college that I realized the stupidity of worrying over a chest X-ray. They would have had to take an X-ray of my lower abdomen. I'm sure this is where that pesky spoon is still lurking to this day.

But let's get back to Cleo, to the two of us in our backyard, my green universe, playing endless rounds of fetch with her favorite ball.

For a while the game proceeded as expected — slimy ball, painfully short throws from an uncoordinated little pitching arm, patient soft-mouthed dog politely performing retrieval exercises. Then I noticed something long and thin and obviously amiss dangling from the base of Cleo's tail and trailing behind her. She took a time-out, intermittently squatting, straining, and dancing around as if she had a length of unshakable toilet paper stuck to her foot. She was visibly upset and unable to continue our game. If I had to put an emotional label on her behavior I would say she appeared to be embarrassed.

Concerned and curious, I ran to the house to fetch my father, insisting he come and check out Cleo.

"Look," I said, all business as I pointed toward the aberration. "There's something up her bum!"

Dad greeted Cleo with a pat to her head before shuffling around behind her, nodding his agreement.

"It's okay, son. It's one of Gran's old nylon stockings."

I was puzzled and a little upset.

"Why would Gran stick a stocking up Cleo's bum?" I asked.

"She didn't," said my father.

"Then who did?" I said.

My father hesitated, deliberated, and ultimately opted for a time-honored adult approach to my line of questioning, that is, he ignored it.

"Let's just give Cleo a few minutes in private. See if she sorts herself out."

Dad took me by the hand and we backed

24

off, retreating several yards before he squatted down by my side and whispered,

"We'll watch her from here."

"But why is it coming out of her bum?" I whispered back.

He considered me with what I would later recognize as a mixture of pride and frustration for being such a relentless little bugger when it came to my wanting to figure out the ways of the world.

"Because she swallowed it," he said, trying his best to tamp down the curt edge creeping into his voice. "Because Cleo likes to eat things she shouldn't. Things that aren't good for her. Things other than dog food. Things like Gran's underwear. But don't you worry, no matter what your Cleo eats it always comes out the other end."

Here was my first lesson in basic gastrointestinal physiology, that according to my father, what goes in, must come out. Of course I was potty-trained and more than capable of taking myself off to our bathroom alone, but this was the first time I recall a clarification of the cause-and-effect relationship between ingestion and elimination. What I really needed to know was whether, during inappropriate dining, Cleo had ever swallowed a spoon. If her current discomfort was anything to go by, surely I would have noticed when a firm metallic object found its way out?

My father must have misread the confusion and anxiety playing across my face and tried to placate me by adding the word "Eventually."

It didn't work.

We waited for what felt like three hours but was probably more like three minutes and watched as Cleo spun around and around, scooting her rear along the grass in vain, clearly becoming more and more frustrated.

"I've got an idea," my father said, standing up and heading back toward Cleo. "Go grab her ball."

I did as I was told and reported for duty.

"Now, when I'm ready, I want you to throw Cleo's ball as far away as possible."

I didn't understand.

"Why?"

"You'll see," he said.

Another adult response all inquisitive children despise because obviously I didn't see and that was why I was asking the question in the first place.

"But I can't throw very far."

My father insisted that this wouldn't matter (alternatively, he may have said, "Just shut up and do as you're told") and stood a short distance behind Cleo after placing me and the ball in my hand at her head.

"Hold on a moment, son," he said, watching and waiting as Cleo forgot about her troubles, focused on the ball, and tried to anticipate which way it would go.

At the time I never noticed how my father was placing the sole of his shoe firmly down to the ground, pinning the trailing end of the wayward hosiery in place.

"Now," he shouted, and with concentration and enough fierce determination to produce a little grunt as I bit down on the tip of my tongue, I released the airy plastic ball from my hand like a shot put, and it landed about three feet away.

Not far but far enough for Cleo to pounce forward, retrieve the ball, and leave the stocking behind, lying on the ground.

Cleo acted as if nothing had happened and plunged right back into our game, dropping the ball at my feet, ready to go again. Just once, she glanced over her shoulder at my father and the stringy, discolored length of nylon before focusing on me, as if she seemed disturbed by what he was doing, as if she would rather he pick up whatever it was that had become stuck to his foot because it was disgusting.

Although I like to chalk this up as my first,

if indirect, canine medical intervention, I should point out that this approach to treating Cleo's protruding foreign body may have seemed rational but was totally inappropriate. My father should have left well alone and sought veterinary advice. What if the stocking had been lodged in Cleo's small intestines? What if the nylon had cheese-wired through her guts? Fortunately, as it turned out she was lucky, perfectly fine, ready to graze her way through my grandmother's lingerie once again. It would be decades before I saw the error in our approach to her predicament.

All three of us walked away from the incident as though nothing much had happened. At no time did my father and I dwell on what we had done, on how our ploy had brought about Cleo's transition from anxious and uncomfortable to oblivious and happy to play. He never paused to ruminate on the moment when the seed of possibility was firmly planted, to recognize the first inkling of his son's interest in helping sick animals. Within seconds Cleo and I had returned to the carefree rhythm of fetch and my fickle attention had moved on, my pitching arm quick to tire, boredom setting in, and a more pressing question racing to the forefront of my mind.

"Mum," I shouted, "when will dinner be ready?"

Being around Cleo was great. She was the perfect playmate. I think the best way to describe our relationship would be to say that I was like a smitten grandparent with my first grandchild — I got to enjoy all the fun stuff, but at the end of the day I could walk away. And when I did tire of canine company, searching out other kids in the neighborhood, Cleo never complained or bore a grudge, happy to pick up wherever we left off on my timetable and not hers.

I should mention that this was England in the 1960s, an era when children led "under-scheduled" lives, kicked out of the house at eight o'clock in the morning, only allowed back in if there was no more daylight, you were suffering from clinical dehydration, or you had sustained an injury requiring nothing less than a blood transfusion or surgical removal of an appendage. Exiled kids, forced to use their imagination, tended to gravitate toward one another, mergers leading to friendships and the emergence of something we were all proud to be a part of — a gang.

Across our street and a few houses down lived Timmy and Keith Toenail. Timmy was a terrier of a boy: squat, scrappy, and determined, cursed with disobedient locks of tightly curled platinum blond hair, making him look a bit like Shirley Temple in *Heidi*. He and his older brother, Keith, demonstrated all the physical similarities of brothers like Prince Harry and Prince William, that is to say they were both male and that was about it. Keith's hair was jet black, overly conditioned to a greasy shine, and meticulously maintained in the style of a German World War II infantryman's helmet by his doting mother. Unlike his younger brother, Keith was prone to tears and a trembling lower lip, a feature accentuated by an overbite that would forever vex his orthodontist.

Across the street and one house up lived a girl several years my senior. Her name was Amanda Ravenscroft and she was my first crush (after the cartoon character of Daphne on *Scooby-Doo,* of course). Amanda was tall, blond, and muscular. She favored braided pigtails that made her look as though she had just stepped off a conquering Viking ship.

For the most part our playtime together was predictable, rotating between cops and robbers, cowboys and Indians (the term "PC" had yet to be coined), and, of course, "war" (we always fought "the Germans," not "the Nazis," since England lacked a significant Germanic component to its general population). Amanda's maturity made her leadership material and on the whole the rest of us were putty in her hands, as easy for her to manipulate as a group of dolls at a tea party. Strangely, every plot she concocted seemed to include a damsel in distress, Amanda happy to step into the role, living a little fantasy, no doubt enjoying the fierce competition among the three of us boys trying to come to her rescue.

When we tired of make-believe, we would break out our bicycles and tricycles and the four of us would prowl the nearby streets in search of adventure. On one memorable day, we hit pay dirt.

It was Amanda, leading our formation, who made the discovery, noticing something white and writhing tossed into the bottom of a hedgerow. I heard the squeal of her brakes as her bike clattered to the pavement and she dismounted, and watched as she retrieved what appeared to be a dirty old pillowcase.

"Look what I've found," she said, raising the bag in the air like a trophy.

And even before the rest of us had peeked inside, it was obvious what she had discovered given the chorus of muffled cries coming from inside the case.

"Kittens," Amanda proclaimed, as though the hapless threesome who finally caught up to her might need help identifying the four angry newborn mammals crawling over one another.

It was a good job there were four of them — one all black, one all white, one black with white patches on his paws and chest like a tuxedo, and one white with a black swatch under its nose like a mustache. We all knelt down, formed a circle, and passed them around among us, constantly changing our opinions as to which one was the best, the strongest, the runt, or our personal favorite.

I wasn't used to cats or, for that matter, any other life form that seemed so upset and vulnerable. Their pointy, triangular faces, their incessant mews, their perfect little paws and claws and plump bald bellies were so very different from what I knew because all I really knew was a dog named Cleo (to my way of thinking Marty the land shark didn't count).

"I'm calling this one Sugarplum," Amanda declared, cradling the all-white kitten in her cupped hands and rocking him or her back and forth.

"Then I'm calling this one . . ." Timmy hesitated, as if he had prematurely pressed his buzzer on *Jeopardy!* and didn't really have an answer for Alex. "Um . . . um . . . Blackie," he said triumphantly.

At the time this seemed perfectly appropriate and original.

"I don't have a name for this one," said Keith, holding little Mr. Tux, his voice trailing off in a manner we all recognized as a potential preamble to tears.

"Me either," I said, gently stroking the one with the mustache. Secretly I was pleased with the way our game of "musical kittens" had worked out. In my opinion, Poncho Villa was the best, the runt and my favorite.

Suddenly Keith laid Mr. Tux on the ground and made a lunge for Timmy's kitten.

"I want Blackie. Who says he belongs to you? Give him to me, he's mine."

Timmy sprang to his feet, pulling Blackie into the security of his chest as he backed away.

"Get off me or I'm telling Mum."

Ordinarily, especially if there was nothing much going on, Amanda and I might have looked on as the two of them got into it, Keith bigger and stronger, Timmy tougher and more resilient, their fights guaranteed to end in tear-streaked dirty red cheeks all round. But on this occasion, Amanda's maturity and wisdom were their undoing.

"Do you really think your mum will let you keep him?" she asked.

I wasn't sure whether the question was directed at Keith or Timmy, but Keith latched onto this perspective, shaking his head.

"Not after you killed our goldfish."

"Did not," said Timmy but without conviction.

"I know my mum and dad won't let me have a kitten or a puppy," said Amanda, wistfully. "I ask them every birthday and Christmas and they always say no."

Though no one turned to look at me or ask me directly, I felt as though I was the kittens' last hope of finding a home. The thing was I'd never really considered why my parents didn't have a cat or dog of their own. They both seemed to like Cleo, so what was holding them back? Maybe all I had to do was ask.

"I know," said Amanda, briefly offering Sugarplum up to the heavens before planting a kiss on the kitten's pink nose. "We'll go ask the Cat Lady what to do."

This should have been my cue to raise an

eyebrow and work a little apprehension into the reply "Cat Lady?" but Keith beat me to it.

"Do you know her?" he said, with the kind of veiled reverence normally reserved for celebrities.

"No, but I know where she lives and my dad's met her and I heard him telling my mum 'she's a little strange but well-meaning.' "

I had never heard of the so-called Cat Lady, making her no less mysterious than Bigfoot or the Wizard of Oz. And what did Amanda's dad mean by "strange but well-meaning"?

"Come on, it's just down the street," said Amanda, already ten yards ahead of us. "We can leave the bikes here."

So, armed with a kitten each, Keith still whining over being dealt Mr. Tux and the fact that none of us were prepared to swap, we marched off in the direction of a small cottage hidden behind a forest of vines and dense thorny vegetation. If we had celebrated American-style Halloween, this would have been the spooky house no kids in the neighborhood dared to hit up for trick or treat.

"What a pigsty," whispered Timmy as

35

Amanda knocked on the dilapidated front door.

At a downstairs window a shredded lace curtain fluttered and then a tiny woman appeared at the doorstep looking as if she had just got out of bed in her mauve bathrobe and matching slippers, even though this was the middle of the afternoon. She was not much taller than Amanda, but her skin was waxy and wrinkled, her gray hair stiff and lopsided, as if it had dried in a strong crosswind.

This is all the description I can offer because my eyes began to water, my vision blurred, and I had an overpowering desire to pinch my nose and run away, gasping for fresh air. The Cat Lady was careful to close the front door behind her, but she had already unleashed a pungent, toxic cloud of aerosolized feline urine into our environment.

To her credit and my surprise, Amanda managed to stay focused and told the story of how we found the four abandoned kittens in a pillowcase and how they seemed hungry and in need of food and shelter. In the meantime Keith looked like he might vomit, the nausea contorting his face fueling a giggling fit that his brother Timmy struggled to contain.

"We didn't know what to do," said Amanda, showing Sugarplum to the Cat Lady.

Now, some parents might be reading this and thinking an impromptu visit to a complete stranger with a local reputation for being a bit of a weirdo might not have been a particularly good idea. What if the Cat Lady invited us in and introduced us to her husband, the Big Bad Wolf? In fact, personal danger never crossed our minds. Helicopter parenting had yet to be invented and besides, the old woman's getup gave her a warm and cozy bedtime aura, as if she might break out the hot chocolate and tell us a story at any moment.

The Cat Lady kept her lips pursed, head angled slightly down, forcing her eyes to roll up as she considered the four of us through wispy gray eyebrows. We held our collective breath (primarily because of the overpowering aroma of cat pee), but she may have mistaken this for worry on our part over what she was going to do.

"Follow me," she said in a plummy voice that exuded military hustle, leading us down the side of the house — not through it — to a small backyard. There, inside a wooden shed (thankfully well ventilated), was a series of crates and cages containing a couple of older kittens and some adult cats. Everything was clean and orderly, plenty of newspaper and blankets to go around.

"Let's have a look at him," said the Cat Lady and held out her hand to Amanda, taking Sugarplum and inspecting his belly, his mouth, and his eyes. At the time I thought this was just another way of judging which one she would choose to be her favorite, but of course she was trying to get a sense of the kitten's age — whether it still had the dried and shriveled umbilical remnant of a kitten up to three days old; whether it had any nubbins of teeth coming in, suggesting a kitten about two weeks of age; whether, as was the case with our litter, the eyes were still shut.

"You can leave them with me," she said, "but I'm not promising anything, you understand. They're more than three days old but less than ten. A difficult age and a lot of work, but I'll give it a try. You never know."

One by one we said our goodbyes to the little creatures in our hands and entrusted them to the Cat Lady. We thanked her and headed back the way we came, ignoring any uncertainty about their futures. To our way of thinking, what could be so difficult? Don't you just give them food and water and watch them grow? The biggest dilemma was whether your mum or dad would let you do it at your house, not whether or not it could be done.

Looking back, I realize that no one earns the moniker Cat Lady by having one or two cats lounging around the homestead. How many cats does it take to go from cat lover to collector of cats? Six, a dozen, a hundred? When does devotion become obsession, become something compulsive, pathological, and terribly sad? All I can tell you is our Cat Lady may have benefited from opening a window or two, neutering all her male cats, and investing in a little Febreze, but from what I saw of her cat rescue operation she was no hoarder of cats. The animals out back appeared to be in good health and well looked after. I simply had no point of reference for the smell of tomcat pee in confined spaces.

To fully appreciate how good we felt that day, you need to know that we were a generation of kids who loved to visit our local movie theater every Saturday morning, basking in the opportunity to throw candy at each other, to stomp our feet to the rhythm of every chase scene, to watch a cartoon, a serial, and a feature-length movie that always portrayed kids our age as would-be heroes who got themselves into, and out of, a tight spot, beating the bad guys and living to play another day. Well, that particular afternoon, we walked away from the Cat Lady's house with a certain swagger, heads held high and big smiles all around, because for the first time in our lives, albeit with a quartet of abandoned kittens, and in spite of their uncertain future, we believed we got to right a wrong, just like our idols on the big screen.

Time has a knack for distortion — fogging the images from the past, making everything feel bigger than it really was, messing with the collage of mental snapshots pinned to the corkboard of our memory. So I have to believe the clarity with which I still see what took place on an empty beach pounded by an angry Irish Sea as a reflection of its enduring influence on me.

Like most kids, I was blissfully ignorant of my family's financial and social status. Now I don't want to give the impression we were *Angela's Ashes* poor or anything, but I never saw a banana until I was twelve and thought that trousers were meant to be worn above the ankles, and vacations were something you did for one day and always within driving distance.

On this particular day trip our normal family dynamic was upset by the addition of my grandma and more important, and to my dismay, her four-legged escort, the infamous and menacing Marty. Quite why we had to take the poodle with us on a car ride to a sleepy seaside town in northern Wales I will never know. What I do know is the six of us piled into our Morris Minor, Mum and Dad up front, Grandma in the middle between me and my sister, Marty perched on her lap. Nobody wore seat belts back then, so for several hours we were tossed back and forth and side to side on winding country roads, my father imperson-ating a British Grand Prix driver as we sucked down his secondhand cigarette smoke, wondering who would be first to claim car sickness. All the while Marty kept vigil, staring me down, defending his per-sonal space, offering me the occasional snarl and wrinkle of his upper lip, feigning in-nocence and doe-eyed stares every time I complained to Grandma. There's a reason why I have always found poodles to be one of the smartest breeds of dog.

When we got there we had a picnic on the beach, adults sipping hot tea from a thermos in plastic cups and commenting on the gritty sandwiches they had prepared, the ominous-looking clouds, and the threat of rain. There was the promise of ice cream later, but first my father had agreed to help Fiona build a sand castle. For some reason I was more interested in beachcombing, so my mum, Grandma, Marty, and I set off on a postprandial walk down to the water's edge.

This was autumn, off-season, chilly, and there were very few people out and about. The overcast sky blended into the ocean. We were wrapped up in sweaters and overcoats and the tide was way off in the distance, forcing us to head out across wet sandy flats if we wanted to get near the waves and the possibility of washed-up shells. Marty was off leash, having the time of his life, scampering around, quick and dainty, hopping from one tidal pool to the next. He didn't even mind that I was holding Grandma's hand.

At the water's edge it all happened so fast. The tide was still headed out, the surf crashing hard, frothy gray breakers with quite a pull washing over the sand. This was not swimming weather (in this part of Britain it rarely ever was). This was not even paddling weather, the water icy cold to the touch. So you can imagine our concern when one minute Marty was gaily dancing in and out of the lapping foam and the next he was gone, disappearing out to sea, swallowed by a wall of gray water, quickly ten, fifteen yards out and drifting still further away. He didn't bark — he probably couldn't from the cold shock stealing his breath — he just tried to paddle, head up, neck outstretched, looking in my direction.

There are several possibilities as to how this pivotal moment in my early life might have played out. For starters, I couldn't swim, so a selfless, heroic act in which I rescued a drowning dog as motivation for a career helping animals in need was never in the cards. Besides, I'm pretty sure my mother had not packed my inflatable rubber ring.

At this point you would be forgiven for gasping in horror if you feared the possibility that I was some sort of malicious Damien child, a furtive witness to poor Marty's exodus, seizing the opportunity to be rid of my nemesis and rival for Grandma's attention by squandering precious time pointing out a particularly fascinating variety of seaweed before offering an inquisitive but nonchalant "So, where's Marty?"

Don't worry, what really happened struck me as far more impressive and has nothing to do with guilt or the quest for redemption. Seeing Marty bobbing helplessly in the waves my grandma jumped into the roiling waters and began swimming out to sea.

Bear in mind, to my way of thinking, my grandma was at least two hundred years old and could hardly walk, let alone swim. She was fully clothed, not bothering to remove her coat or sweater or shoes. She just dove in like she was all lubed up for a Channel crossing and headed for the little white drowning rat bobbing up and down on her horizon.

For what seemed like forever, the angry waves mocked Grandma's rescue bid, pushing her toward Marty only to pull them apart at the last moment, until finally she had him in her arms, swimming back to shore and clambering back up the beach on all fours, Marty released into the shallows, able to break free, trot off, and shake himself down.

"What were you thinking?" my mum screamed, helping Grandma to her feet, taking off her own coat and putting it around her mother's shoulders. That classic cocktail of anger driven by fear had gotten the better of her. "You could have got yourself killed! And for a dog!"

Grandma was shaking all over, her false teeth acting just like those wind-up false teeth, chattering uncontrollably. We began walking back up the beach, back to the car, Marty staying right by her side, and I asked, "You okay, Grandma?"

She looked down at me and smiled one of the coy, conspiratorial smiles that she occasionally let me see, as though she knew she had been a naughty girl, but it had been worth it.

And right then it hit me that my grandma had actually put her life on the line for a creature sent by the devil to instill fear in children. I could have understood if this was Cleo, but this was Marty. What strange spell had this toy poodle cast over my grandmother?

What has stayed with me, all these years later, is my incredulity over an unthinkable rescue followed by a realization that something mysterious and powerful was at work between my grandma and Marty. Trudging through the wet sand, watching a mother and daughter together, their roles reversed, and a pathetic little dog, frightened of straying and consequently getting underfoot, I was forced to concede that Grandma must really love her poodle. Their relationship did not look like my relationship with Cleo and I couldn't imagine it felt anywhere near as good, but right then I realized that different is not the same as less important.

It had to have something to do with the same feeling that came over me whenever I hung off Cleo's neck after giving her a big hug. Or it could have been similar to how my neighborhood friends and I all felt after rescuing our bagful of discarded kittens. Whatever it was, I had witnessed one remarkable consequence of the warm, fuzzy, soothing sensation that could develop between certain animals and people, and this realization made one thing perfectly clear — I needed to learn how to swim.

2.
THE AURA OF DOG

My earliest attempts to acquire a pet of my own, of any type, were always met with some variation on a recurring theme. Dad was undoubtedly the softer target, and he seemed genuinely receptive to the idea, but every time I tried to pin him down he would say, "Go ask your mother," which I have come to understand is universal code among fathers for "I'd love to help, but when it comes to major decisions it is my wife and not I who actually wears the trousers in our relationship!"

Whenever I approached my mother, no matter how I phrased the request — piggybacked onto a stream of compliments, offered as barter for completion of chores, whimpered in a weak voice from a sickbed — her answer went something like this:

"Oh, Nicholas, don't be so silly. You can't even look after yourself let alone a pet."

Disappointed, eyes filled with tears, I

would trudge back to my bedroom, fall face down on my bed, and try to cry loud enough to be heard — kicking, thumping my fists, and wailing. No one ever checked on me to see if I was all right, except perhaps my sister, and only then so that she could savor my anguish or report back on the satisfactory state of my distress. Eighteen months is all that separates me from my only sibling and no matter how hard I tried — how much quality Barbie time we spent together, how large the stash of candy I offered in the bribe — Fiona seemed lackluster in her support for us getting a pet.

To be honest I didn't really care whether it was a dog or a cat. Either was as ridiculous as a rhinoceros to my mother, but my father did show a deliberately detached interest in the possibility of us acquiring a dog, so it was in this species that I invested my very best effort, pretty much exhausting every trick in the "How kids get what they want from their parents" handbook.

Having failed with temper tantrums I decided to move on to negotiations and deals, which, for most kids, equates to telling out-and-out lies. To a parental chorus of "Uh-huh," "Right," and "Of course you will," we kids promise to take our new pet dogs for walks, to feed them regularly and without needing to be nagged, to happily replenish their empty water bowl when necessary and, as though it goes without saying, to supervise their potty training. Naturally we have thought none of this through. We are convinced that our parents will be so bowled over by the shock of our gesture, so consumed by the decency in its intent, that one if not both will crack, guaranteed to hold this promise over us for the life of the animal, understanding that *they* will be the ones charged with all these tasks when the novelty wears off and the real work of raising a puppy begins.

This ruse was fooling no one, least of all my mother, so I quickly moved on to pouting, moodiness, and impersonating a Trappist monk for extended periods of time. I had just started kindergarten and the adjustment to school life was proving difficult. Surely, if I appeared increasingly reclusive and socially stunted, Mum might see the benefits of having a puppy in a new light. Sadly, for me, my mother seemed to welcome my attempt at isolation and indifference, but then, given her choice of career, I shouldn't have been surprised that she was accustomed to such tactics.

My kindergarten teacher was, to my dismay, disproportionately strict with me compared to my fellow classmates. She seemed indifferent to my academic effort and participation, constantly ignoring my raised hand. She never sent me home with a report card at the end of each term and if I ever misbehaved, ordered to face the wall at the back of the room, my threats to report her to my father were met with howls of laughter. Worst of all my parents appeared to be unreceptive to my distress.

"Oh, I'm sure it's not all that bad," said Mum, almost willing me to grow a British stiff upper lip and tough it out.

"But Mum," I whined, "I thought you loved me?"

My mother flashed me a perfunctory smile before being distracted by the culinary demands of mixing powdered potato with boiling water.

"Of course I do," she said, "it's just that at school, things are different. Now, be a good boy and go and set the table."

So I did, dispirited by my own inconceivable bad luck in having a mother who was not only a kindergarten teacher but was also *my* kindergarten teacher.

And so, faced with the unrelenting rejection of every reasonable ploy I attempted to obtain a puppy, I made the fatal mistake so many children turn to as a last resort — the desperate, always disastrous tactic of the ultimatum.

"If you don't let me get a dog I'm going to be the naughtiest boy in your class."

I think I stamped some authority on my bravado by folding my arms across my chest and delivering a firm nod of my head combined with a loud huff.

Tolerance finally gave way to anger and a stare with the kind of icy intensity that instantly broadcasts "You have gone too far."

"Nicholas. You are *not-getting-a-dog.* Do not ask me again."

This time my silence and the single tear rolling down my cheek were grounded in a new and unprecedented reality — failure.

Fortunately, at that age, all memory is pretty much short term and as soon as the potency of my mother's command had started to wear off, I again turned to my father to take up my case.

"Duncan, we can hardly afford to feed ourselves, let alone a dog."

It was bedtime and I was finding excuses to avoid heading upstairs, sitting in front of the TV, trying out "just one more minute" for the fourth time, when I overheard a whispered conversation in the kitchen.

"I know, I know," said Dad too loudly, before being reprimanded and continuing in a softer tone, "but I think this new job is really working out. I like training to be an electrician. I can see myself sticking with it, doing it for a living. People will always need their TV or their radio fixed and they're always telling me how the money's going to start getting better pretty soon."

There was a pause and I edged toward the kitchen door, drawn by the silence, hanging on this moment of capitulation, poised to run in, screaming, hands waving in the air, ready to join my parents in a celebratory group hug.

Instead I stared and although the words said it all, it was what I saw that found its mark.

"That's great," said Mum, but her flat tone belied any genuine enthusiasm. "I'm glad."

And in her eyes she couldn't hide the frustration and familiarity of having heard it all before.

Dad may have reeled from the blow to his ego, but I could tell that in part, he thought he deserved it.

He caught me standing in the doorway.

"Go brush your teeth and get into bed," he ordered, and then added, softening, "I'll be up in a minute to tuck you in."

I did as I was told and waited.

"Mum will never let us get a dog, will she?" I said as soon as he joined me.

Dad flinched, wanting to convince me otherwise but uncertain where to begin. He perched on the bed beside me.

"Your mother's just worried about money, that's all. Buying a dog let alone keeping a dog is expensive and it's not helped by me jumping from one job to the next. Just promise me you won't end up like your old man."

This was well-trodden territory, Dad rambling on about his misspent youth, his lack of high school qualifications and his desperate attempts to carve out a career path while starting a family. He had already told me the story of how he tried his hand at being a door-to-door salesman and a truck driver delivering toilet rolls (which I believe I was meant to find both amusing and demeaning).

"But now you are mending TVs," I said. "Now you have a good job. A job you like."

He eyed me with a sideways glance, instantly forgiving the sneaky eavesdropper.

"Let me tell you a story about when your mother and I were first married."

I grinned and squirmed in my bed, getting comfortable, savoring this unexpected extension of lights out.

"I used to play drums in a three-piece jazz band at some of the pubs around Liverpool."

"What's jazz?"

Dad looked displeased at the interruption. "A type of music."

"Okay," I said. But before he could start up again, I added, "What type of music?"

He inhaled, paused, and then tried to mimic a hissing rhythm leading the way for a rambling double bass.

It sounded awful but I affected approval.

"Late one night, we had already been playing for hours and I was asked if I was interested in making a little extra money playing drums at . . . ," he hesitated, wondering how best to phrase this next part. ". . . a different type of place altogether."

I frowned and knitted my downy little brows to let him know he would have to do better than that.

"It's called a gentleman's club. It's a place where certain women slowly take off their clothes to music while men watch."

Now he had completely lost me. For starters, at my current age, close proximity to girls, including my sister, fully clothed or otherwise, was unthinkable. Why on earth would members of my sex ever want to witness such a spectacle? Yuck! Double yuck!

With this troubling image trapped inside my head, he went on to explain how then, like now, he was desperate for cash, and though he was exhausted he agreed, finding himself playing drums in a dark corner of a smoke-filled stage on which a young woman was beginning to undress.

It is my understanding that the British strip clubs of the early sixties were relatively tame by today's standards, committed to the "tease" in striptease. Thus my father bore a heavy burden of responsibility, as his talents were essential for the appearance of modesty through the coordination between the artist and the man working the lights. He was told that at the climax of each act, the stripper would glance in his direction and this was the signal to begin his drumroll, building to a crescendo of crashing symbols coordinating with the briefest flash of naked female flesh before the lights went out to predictable groans of manly frustration.

We will never know whether this particular stripper was lost in the moment, oblivious to the lack of percussion during her grand finale, or whether the man on the lights believed she had made some special arrangement with the stand-in drummer. For whatever reason, my father, bless his soul, fell fast asleep, the lights stayed firmly focused on their target, and by the time the cheering audience had roused him back to consciousness, it was too late.

"They fired me on the spot," he said. "Insisted I leave immediately."

I could have requested psychiatric counseling over the news of this unfathomable form of entertainment, but I maintained a blank stare and pulled out the classic banality, "Is that it?"

Dad felt the need to clarify. You see, he hadn't been playing this story for laughs or in some naive attempt at male bonding long before I had much in the way of testosterone. He simply wanted to justify the skepticism I had witnessed in my mother. He wanted me to feel his humiliation through this low point, to justify her apparent apprehension to his claim of finding a career, and to better understand her reticence over our adding four more legs to the family. Throughout my life, one of the fundamental tenets of my father's style of parenting has always been to try to help me get it right, by pointing out where he had got it wrong.

"What I'm trying to say is it doesn't matter if you are a brain surgeon or a garbage collector. I just hope you will try your best. Fulfill your potential. That's all I will ever ask. Just try."

I smiled. There was always something so warm and comforting in this philosophy, because it felt forgiving yet attainable. Trying demanded effort without the pressure of expectation. So long as the intent was absolute, despite the results, there would be absolution.

I dutifully nodded my understanding and said, "So does this mean we're getting a puppy?"

In the end though, after all my begging and pleading, it came down to a factor I had never even considered — our neighborhood.

We lived on the outskirts of a wealthy city but on the wrong side of the tracks, in a suburb dominated by government-subsidized housing. I'm not saying I was from the projects exactly, but our house was flanked by some pretty mean streets, home to dispirited unemployed miscreants looking for trouble.

Early on, the word *prowler* was introduced into my vocabulary. Apparently there had been a series of break-ins at nearby homes. (My parents failed to inform me that our house was actually broken into twice —

what on earth were they after? My father's beloved lava lamp?) I was led to understand that "the Prowler" was a shadowy figure who wandered our neighborhood late at night, biding his time, poised to make his next heist really count.

Domestic alarm systems were in their infancy and Britain has no Second Amendment in its Bill of Rights, so the possibility of a four-legged security system began to get some serious airtime during dinner conversation.

"I'm just saying that a dog might be the perfect solution," said my father. "There's plenty of room in the backyard. I'd be the one taking care of it and all he needs is a big, booming bark and no one will think to come near the house."

I jabbed another bland wad of lettuce into my British "salad dressing," i.e., runny mayonnaise, and stuffed it in my mouth, chewing over my father's suggestion. Several points jumped out at me. First of all he said "he," a male dog, and all I really knew was Cleo, his mother's female Dalmatian. Would a male dog be different, less sociable, less playful, more domineering? And if he had to have a loud bark, what kind of dog would that be? I couldn't remember Cleo barking once, not even during our games of fetch.

Did my dad already have a certain breed in mind? Did he really want to keep everyone who wasn't in our family at bay? And what about my friends from across the street?

It would be some time before I understood the term *whipped,* but the expression on my mother's face almost dared him to go ahead, to get a dog and brace for the consequences. My mother rarely needed to use words; her sparkling green eyes said all that needed to be said.

So her surprise was no less than mine and my sister's when my father turned up with a great big boisterous teddy bear of a German shepherd puppy. Whereas our surprise turned into jubilation, my mother's was quickly surpassed by anger and condemnation. Forty years later I would discover that the puppy was obtained as part of a conspiracy between my dad and his mother, the two of them pretending to go off for a Sunday drive and secretly visiting a dog breeder. My mother was never consulted because after all our combined attempts to achieve a concession, she continued to refuse, even after Dad had played the canine security card. To this day he still believes she has never quite forgiven him.

Of course I was blind to all this matrimonial turbulence, breathless at finally having a dog that would actually live in and stay in our house. And what a dog he was, so different from Cleo, black and tan with over-sized ears, snout and, most striking of all, paws. His paws were massive, as though he had been born with the wrong feet, each one several sizes too big.

"What are we going to call him?" asked my father, reining us in when our petting became too exuberant, when the puppy became mouthy in his own defense.

This seemed like an easy question. For as long as I could remember, I was allowed to watch a children's television show on the BBC called *Blue Peter.* The show started in 1958 and is still running to this day, and it regularly featured the presenter's pets. At the time, each of the two male presenters had a German shepherd, one a female called Petra and the other a male called Patch. These were the only other German shepherds I had ever seen, so it seemed perfectly logical that all male dogs of this particular breed be named Patch.

"Patch it is," said my father, glancing over at my mother, hoping our elation might go some way to melting her icy reception. He was in the wrong and he knew it and having his son name the dog was the clincher. The naming of an animal is like an engagement ring, a betrothal. Once it has been offered and accepted, it's virtually impossible to take it back. My father had much work to do to mend the rift with my mother, but he truly believed he could turn her around, bring out the dog lover hidden deep inside her, and make her realize his sin was not selfish but motivated by a desire to invigorate and complete his family.

As Patch matured, his wooden-puppet puppy moves smoothed out, coordination, strength, and stamina setting in as he began transforming into a lean and muscular machine. During this time, his floppy ears finally decided to perk up, though the changeover was staggered, one ear up, one ear down for a while, giving him a goofy, slightly perplexed expression as my father worried whether or not he had been sold a lemon. When Patch finally had a pair of pricked ears, he was handsome, classically and beautifully marked and destined to be a big dog, a dog who would always garner respect and the label "formidable."

Early on it became clear that Dad and I were far more invested and interested in Patch than my sister or, obviously, my mother. Fiona was only a few years old at the time and she quickly discovered that this cute and cuddly fur ball called a dog was actually headstrong, independent, and inquisitive. Dolls and stuffed animals were a whole lot easier to play with — they were indifferent to dress up, they never lost the plot, and they stayed where you put them. And her tendency to scream when she ran around didn't help matters. What might have been a useful learning experience for Patch, accepting the unpredictable and shrill sounds of a child at play as another normal, nonthreatening stimulus, frequently turned into a chase in which he barreled into her and knocked her down. Looking back, my father realizes he missed a teaching opportunity for both dog and daughter. Consequently Fiona and Patch maintained a relationship that was more civil than genial. More forced roommates than family, they coexisted rather than engaged with one another.

My mother, on the other hand, had a cold facade to maintain. She had never wanted a dog and on some level having Patch around was always a reminder of a moment of weakness in her marriage, a sort of permanent scar left after a brief rift where trust and communication went by the wayside. Unfortunately for her, there were times when I could tell she actually enjoyed the dog's company. Patch would jump up on the sofa next to her, pad around, and lie down, his head on her lap, chocolate eyes meeting hers, daring her to resist his charm, daring her not to pat his head or stroke his velvety ears, and though she made a fuss, shouting, "Duncan, get this dog of yours off of me," she would succumb, passing a hand over his head or his bushy tail before he disappeared.

From time to time, when she thought no one was looking, I might catch her talking to Patch, engaging him in puppy banter and play, stopping abruptly and pretending to do something else if she discovered I was there. Her only concession to his merit in our household was her approval of the heightened security he provided by nothing more than his presence.

This apparent division of the sexes in our appreciation of dogs seemed to be written in our genes and, on the surface, gender-linked. I had been given my father's dog-loving DNA — fascinated by these four-legged creatures, drawn to them, thankful to have them around and part of my life. My sister, on the other hand, seemed to have received my mother's dog-aversive genes in her DNA — a take-it-or-leave-it attitude of "Share my space but don't get in my way or cramp my style."

Despite my personal desire for this dog to be "mine," it didn't take very long for me to realize that my relationship with Patch was not, and never would be, the same as his relationship with my father. When I watched the two of them together, Patch seemed more excited, more responsive and satisfied than he ever did around me. It was like the two of them were a couple of teenage girls who had shared their first sleepover — all inside jokes, secret signs, and an exclusive language only they understood.

At first, their rapport and the way Patch chose Dad over the kid whose crocodile tears helped secure his future with our family felt like a betrayal, like I was the friend who got him the introduction and now I was the one getting dumped.

"Why can't I hold the leash? How come Patch drops the ball at your feet and not mine?"

Briefly, this feeling of being used made me angry at my dad, but it was quickly replaced with another predictable vice — jealousy. Maybe, when I first suggested getting a dog, I should have clarified how this dog was supposed to be mine. He was meant to sleep at the bottom of my bed. He was going to learn my tricks, appear from nowhere when I called his name or whistled my special signal (assuming I eventually learned how to whistle). I would be the envy of friends, family, and strangers who marveled at our relationship, our silent bond and all the adventures we were having. Surely, it was only a matter of time before Patch caught his first bank robber or rescued me from a pack of wild hogs.

Fortunately, whimsy surrendered to reality. When five minutes and a handful of milk bones did not succeed in teaching Patch how to respond appropriately to my cocked-thumb-and-forefinger pistol and play dead, I began to see how much time and effort went into having a dog as a companion. My dad was the one who fed Patch first thing every morning, the one taking him for long walks, the one teaching him basic training skills. As far as I could tell, the two of them weren't secretly saving lives or solving mysteries and Patch hadn't learned to sing, let alone play dead, so I could forgive them their camaraderie, as long as I could still take the reigns when my schoolwork lightened up and the time was right for me. In the interim, I learned to accept the fact that my father had acquired a new shadow, no longer black but black and tan, and shaped like a dog.

One time, when Patch was still a puppy, I interrupted the end of a training session in the backyard. Dad waved me over as he was offering praise for a job well done and instead of the usual arbitrary belly rubbing, scratching, patting frenzy that normally ensued, he gently and methodically stroked specific areas of Patch's fur as the dog sat before him.

"We'll start with the face," he whispered, running his hand from muzzle to cheek, one side then the other, "then we'll go to chin, then ears . . ."

Patch turned to mush, uncharacteristically relaxed, as if my father were a gifted masseuse. Eventually he toppled over onto his side, the focus in his eyes all weak and wobbly, overwhelmed by the sedative power of his master's touch.

"And now we'll do feet," said Dad, kneading Patch's toes one by one, "we don't want him to be shy around his feet. Those big black nails are always going to need a trim from time to time."

I nodded my approval.

"And tail," he said, opening his palm wide, sweeping down the entire length, keeping the rhythm slow and even. Patch closed his eyes and appeared to fall asleep.

"And finally, I'll give him a scratch in his

favorite spot."

Dad moved to the thin turkey skin of Patch's armpits and worked his fingers, the dog letting out a sigh as if it was all too much.

This didn't seem right to me. Armpits were for tickling and other than that they seemed pretty much redundant. Patch wasn't squirming or giggling so where was the pleasure in scratching a dog's pits?

"How do you know it's his favorite spot?" I asked, hoping he would be forced to reveal another of their secrets.

Dad smiled.

"You only have to look at him to know. And think about it. It's one of the few places on his body he will never be able to properly scratch himself. He can't easily reach his armpit. He can't rub it against a tree. It's got to feel good me doing it for him."

My little fingers joined my dad's and Patch approved, adjusting his forelimb to put me in just the right spot. I looked over at my father as he raised an eyebrow, moving his own hand away as I continued to scratch, the transition seamless, Patch lost in tranquil ecstasy. It was my first and best lesson in animal handling.

My only genuine birthday party was compensation for the disasters of Christmas past. For a while there, I had been cursed, the victim of back-to-back catastrophes on what should have been the most important day of the year. Struck down by German measles when I was six years old and confined to bed in a state of feverish delirium, all I could remember was my sister's squeals of delight as she savored the limelight. The next Christmas promised to be the best ever, since Fiona and I had both been given our dream presents — identical big orange bouncy inflatable kangaroos, the kind you straddled and hopped around on. After no more than two minutes, I parked my new mode of transport near a gas fire, eliciting an impressive explosion and floods of tears while Fiona savored all her bouncy fun, affording me a pitying glance and a lazy royal wave as she hopped away. There would be no second chance, no replacement for me. My gift was intangible, boring, and a miserable reminder — a lesson in the value of taking proper care of my things.

So the offer to host an actual birthday party with cake and games and the promise of far more presents than I normally received seemed too good to be true.

"What about Patch?" said Fiona, obviously jealous and trying her best to scupper my prospects. "He'll scare people."

Mum nodded her agreement as though the women were once more united, naysayers using their indifference to Patch as an excuse to cancel.

"Don't you worry about Patch," said my father. "He's older and a lot less excitable than he used to be. I'll keep him locked up in our bedroom. It'll only be for . . . what . . . an hour or two."

I smiled, Fiona frowned, and we all waited for my big day to arrive.

When it did, I was rewarded with an enormous pile of gift-wrapped presents and the torture of my mother's insistence that I not open them until after my guests had left. The gang was all there — Amanda, Timmy and Keith, and a number of friends from school. With great enthusiasm we played "Simon says" and "Pass the Parcel" before chowing down on sandwiches and chips, blowing out candles, and getting chocolate cake all over our faces. I was too excited to think about Patch pacing overhead, eager to join in all the fun, in part because I never heard him barking or trying to scratch his way out of his confinement.

Eventually someone suggested we take the party into the backyard so that we could play blindman's bluff, which required more open space. Timmy volunteered to be "it" and put on a blindfold as we all circled, goaded, and teased, whooping and screaming with every failed attempt he made to tag us. I can still see him now, hands outstretched, groping and fumbling as the screams changed in an instant from delight to fear, merging into a unified wailing chorus as an enormous German shepherd burst from the front door and came bounding toward us.

To this day, Fiona denies any involvement in the affair, though her duplicitous and satisfied smirk as my mother vowed I would never have another birthday party made her seem a little too pleased. However it happened, Patch was on the loose and excited to catch up and join in all the fun. Bear in mind there were only two kids not screaming: me, because I knew there was absolutely nothing to fear, and Timmy, because he couldn't see what was coming.

If you're imagining a military attack dog taking down a hostile target then think again. Patch had become our family dog, desperate to be included, cantering around with a spring in his step, smiling, long pink tongue lolling out the side of his mouth. His biggest threat was his body weight and momentum, not his teeth. He wasn't barking or lunging or posturing. This may have been his turf, but there was nothing aggressive or territorial in his behavior. Still, when Timmy finally sensed something was wrong and took off the blindfold, I couldn't blame him for being afraid. Besides, the Brothers Toenail had little or no experience with pets except for a goldfish and we already know what became of him.

So Timmy took off after the other kids, headed for the bottom of the yard where there was a good climbing tree and the possibility of an aerial escape from danger. I made a grab for Patch, slowed him down, and Timmy made it, but not without claiming his bottom had come within a gnat's whisker of being devoured by the Hound of the Baskervilles.

Well, you can imagine the scene at the parent pickup, Patch's predatory attack the only topic of conversation among all the kids, my mother leaving my father to handle the situation, to apologize, to reassure. Irate parents whisked their offspring away while they bombarded him with questions. Didn't he understand kids were at higher risk for being bitten because they naturally vocalize and run, engaging an aggressive dog in a chase scenario? And just look at the dog, a German shepherd, and a male one at that, a

71

breed exploited for its aggressive behavior. Could he ensure that this never happened again? They certainly had one suggestion that would ensure it never happened again.

Thankfully, through a combination of groveling apologies, promises never to host a similar event (not that any of the kids would have attended), and poor Timmy having his bottom inspected in front of all of us by his mother, with not a scratch in sight, my father and Patch were reluctantly forgiven.

With everyone gone, I went back inside the house. Patch was outside in the backyard playing ball with my father, relieved to be burning off some energy, unaware of all the fuss. It didn't seem fair that he had been so misunderstood. He'd done nothing wrong.

I looked over at the pile of presents, looked out back at my father and our dog.

The presents could wait a while longer.

Patch's spirited antics at my birthday party persuaded my dad to be even more vigilant about keeping him away from strangers, precisely the opposite of what he should have done. But I do understand his intentions. Duncan had struggled through his twenties, finally starting to get his life in order, learning a trade as an electrician, loving it and hoping that one day he might be good enough to teach electrical engineering to others. In a small and simple way, Patch had played his part in helping the man settle, giving him structure and routine, making him set aside their exercise time, time well spent on reflection and contemplation.

More than any other breed of dog I encounter in my work, German shepherds seem inclined to gravitate to one particular individual in their pack. This relationship is special and they develop a unique chemistry. The dog is tuned in, checks in, relates to, anticipates, and connects in a manner altogether different from its behavior toward everyone else. Having locked on tight, the human who has earned a German shepherd's trust and respect will, in return, be rewarded with unquestionable and abiding loyalty.

Understandably, my father savored this unique bond, a relationship with a kindred spirit, so different from anything else in his life. Maybe he was afraid of everything he stood to lose if Patch misbehaved in public, frightening, let alone injuring, children. We could also blame his desire to nurture a dog who would provide security for our household; after all, his original sales pitch had been based on the dog's innate ability to deter the Prowler. What good was a dog that wagged his tail or licked the hand of every stranger who dropped by?

In the end, Patch's limited socialization skills made two distinct impressions on me — sometimes regret and sometimes pride.

Patch took his responsibility as the family bodyguard very seriously, on call 24/7, offering constant surveillance, prepared to protect and defend against any potential threat, no matter what form it might take. At that time, long before the advent of hybrid vehicles, Britain was inundated with one particular electric vehicle — the so-called milk float. Operated by a milkman, these pokey little trucks would glide around neighborhoods making their deliveries in the wee hours of the morning, taking away the empty bottles and replacing them with fresh milk just in time for breakfast. Generally, our milkman, George, did not conform to this disagreeable schedule, invariably pulling up after breakfast had been served, limiting my options to toast and marmalade. However, what he lacked in punctuality, he made up for in personality, a big smile permanently pasted on his face, always armed with a wisecrack, a joke, or a condemnation of the British weather. If I timed it right, I could meet him at the front door, where it was his habit to put down his milk, pick me up, throw me into the air, and catch me on the way down. It was all innocent fun, something that, according to my father, earned him the label "jolly." These days I would have been torn from his arms, and the poor man reported to his manager, and we'd be online trying to discover if George was actually a registered sex offender!

Once again, I'm not sure how it happened, but one morning I was in George's arms, about to take flight when Patch suddenly appeared at the doorway, alone, visibly perturbed, Mum and Dad nowhere in sight. I think I was dropped more than deposited on the ground, instantly replaced by one hundred pounds of snarling dog pinning George down by standing on his chest. My attempts to call Patch off went ignored, but they did attract the attention of my father, who soon was dragging Patch away by his collar, scolding the dog, and apologizing to George while searching the street and neighbors' windows for witnesses. Out-wardly, George made an effort to be under-standing but it was obvious from his face that he was no longer jolly. In fact I never saw him again. I don't know whether he changed his route or changed his schedule.

I do know deliveries of fresh milk consistently started arriving long before breakfast. But while it was unfortunate that we had to lose a convivial milkman because of Patch's lack of social graces, shall we say, his protective streak came in handy for an admittedly frail boy in a tough neighborhood.

Every morning I shuffled down the street to the nearest school bus stop in my school uniform. I may be biased, but for those of us who grew up as awkward, geeky kids, school uniforms were great equalizers among our peers, blazers and ties helping us try to blend in and remain anonymous. You never found yourself frozen in front of your wardrobe, trapped in a moment of deliberation, of troublesome color coordination, racked with the fear of lacking an appropriate designer label.

"No matter the uniform," said Mum, "uniformity makes you notice the character of the individual, not the clothes on their back."

Of course my parents did their best to neutralize these advantages. It's hard to avoid ridicule when they force you to wait at the bus stop wearing a crisp, oversized trench coat that makes you look like a cold war spy. And their faith in the respect and recognition afforded by a uniform extended to extracurricular activities. That was why I routinely found myself walking home alone from a local Cub Scout meeting late at night, sporting a cap, shorts, and colorful neckerchief. So you can imagine my concern one night when, with only yards to go before reaching the big white wooden gates that opened up to our backyard, I spied two kids, notorious bullies from school, emerging from the shadows and crossing the street to head me off.

To a nine-year-old kid, it can feel as though there is a fine line between being the subject of ridicule and being beaten up for looking ridiculous. And don't go badmouthing my parents for not picking me up by car. Back then, no one owned a minivan or spent their nights and weekends working as a chauffeur. So what if the neighborhood could be a little iffy. Everyone knew that if you were sensible, kept your head down, and didn't talk to strangers you'd be fine.

Carrot and the Slouch had other ideas, though.

I didn't know Carrot's real name but I knew enough not to refer to him as Carrot. He was an overweight redhead, relying more on fat than muscle to intimidate, always flaunting a lit cigarette as proof of his advanced maturity. His sidekick, the Slouch, was actually Simon Louch, a gangly kid with bad posture and a stutter that made him perfect for keeping his opinions to himself and simply grunting when Carrot sought his approval or disapproval.

"Isn't it past your bedtime?"

Carrot got the question off before the two of them reached me. I was pretty sure neither of them knew where I lived, but they stood between me and the white gates, blocking my path.

I didn't say anything, wondering if I could run at them, get past, and open the gate.

A cloud of cigarette smoke hit me in the face and I watched Carrot's smile fade in disappointment when he failed to induce a coughing fit. Those day trips trapped inside a car with my father's forty-a-day habit had to count for something.

"Where've you been?" Carrot asked.

I really wanted to look around for the hidden camera and say, "Where do you think I've been dressed like this, you big fat idiot!" but opted for a meek "Cubs."

Carrot nodded, flicked away his cigarette butt, and elbowed the Slouch.

"You pay your subs?"

"Yes," I said, thinking that since he had said "subs," short for "subscription" (dues), at one time or another Carrot had probably been a Cub Scout.

"Any left over or did you spend it on candy?"

This clinched it. Only an insider would know that the one upside to carving woodland animals out of bars of soap and trying to earn your first-aid badge was getting your hands on some seriously unhealthy candy at the end of the night.

"I don't have any money," I said, trying to sidle around them.

They saw the move for what it was and backed up all the way to the gate, trapping me on the wrong side of sanctuary.

The wooden gate must have given a little, emitting a slight creak as the Slouch leaned back into it, and that was enough. From inside the house, Patch, sensing a threat on the perimeter, let out a solitary but thunderous woof.

Carrot and the Slouch looked at each other, looked through the gaps in the gate, and saw nothing but darkness between the driveway and the house.

"You got a dog?" asked Carrot. He was truly gifted in the art of the redundant question.

"Yes," I said.

"What sort?" he said.

"Alsatian." (No one said "German shepherd" until the late 1970s.)

He scoffed and faked a wince of disapproval as though he was not impressed.

"They don't scare me," he said and the Slouch grunted his agreement that he too would not be intimidated by such a dog.

Carrot moved in close, close enough for me to smell his nicotine breath, and grabbed the front of my shirt in his meaty hand.

"He can't help you out here," he whispered, "so you best have some change left over to give me, or else."

The Slouch had taken his cue to muscle in closer, and just as he did, something big and angry slammed into the white gates.

Patch's bark exploded, as the gates bowed outwards, threatening to splinter. He stood tall on his back legs, with his massive paws leaning on the gate, head and neck lunging in the direction of my assailants. One second they were about to beat me up, the next they were gone, not just hanging back but vanished, disappeared, as if they had never been there.

"Good boy, Patch," I said, unlocking the gate, squeezing past him to get in, as he let out a brief series of "and don't you dare to come back" barks. I could tell he was pumped up, like a racehorse after a race, all pleased with himself, hackles up, pacing back and forth, letting the surge of adrenaline run its course.

I wondered if Carrot and the Slouch were still out there somewhere, watching me interact with the beast that had frightened them enough to make them run away. I hoped so. I hoped they could see how I may have been smaller than them but I was completely at ease around this intimidating creature. And looking back, this was a huge part of Patch's legacy for me. I may not have been his alpha dog, but I was a member of his pack and so we still got to spend a good deal of time together. It was this kind of effortless accrual of time, doing nothing in particular, simply sharing each other's presence, that let me feel "the aura of dog" — their mannerisms, their behavior and bearing, the everyday minutiae of integrating your life with theirs. It cannot be faked, this knowledge and appreciation of "dogness." You either get it or you don't. Thanks to Patch I was learning what it was like to be around dogs.

"Everything all right, son?" my father shouted from the back door.

"Yes," I said, patting Patch on his flanks and once more telling him he was a good boy. "Everything's fine."

3.
BLESSINGS IN CHILDHOOD TIME

All of a sudden, when I was about ten years old, my parents dropped the biggest bombshell of my young life.

"You're going to love it," said Mum, with the kind of artificial enthusiasm that makes all kids instantly suspicious. "New house, new school, new friends, and best of all we'll be just down the street from Grandma."

I've never been good at faking a hounddog look of desolation so I thought about my new proximity to Grandma's poodle, Marty, and bent my expression into a look of abject fear.

Dad mussed my hair and squatted down to my height to get a better read of my reaction.

"Don't worry, son. It's a nice neighborhood and best of all we're right next to a public footpath that leads to miles of open fields and woods. Patch is going to love it too."

I wanted to say, "That's great, Dad, and I'm sure Patch will appreciate the nearby recreational amenities but to be honest, this great outdoors angle isn't exactly sealing the deal for me."

It wasn't until I was standing in our new kitchen, surveying our backyard, that I realized why my father had felt the need to clarify Patch's new state of affairs.

Compared to his old backyard, a kingdom my little eyes saw as stretching to an emerald infinity, this new backyard would make Patch a veritable prisoner besieged on three sides by tall, creosote-stained fences, boxing him into a swatch of grass with just enough room for him to do his business and not much else. Playing fetch was out of the question, even when you took my limited ball-throwing skills into consideration.

"Dad, he's not got much room to run around in," I said.

My father winced ever so slightly, rolling his head from side to side, as if caught between a yes and a no.

"I think he'll be fine," said Dad, though he didn't look so sure. "You and I are going to have to do a better job of taking him for walks if he's going to get enough exercise."

I agreed, convinced these nearby hiking trails, wherever they were, had to be better than this snub to freedom and nature. We both seemed to know I had brought up something my father's conscience had hoped to ignore or overcome. For all the hypothetical pros in our domestic upheaval, the one family member who didn't have any say in the matter seemed to have been landed with a major con. And watching Patch sniffing and pacing out there for the first time wasn't helping matters. Patch seemed surprised by the brevity of his tour, the speed with which he had covered all the available space. He was a dog used to freedom, to surveying his domain by turning from side to side, not bouncing from one boundary to the next, forced to strain his neck upward in search of a glimpse of the world he used to know. I gazed up at my dad staring at Patch and later, much later in life, I would come to realize how the expression on his face reflected a sentiment my emotional palate was just starting to discover. I didn't know its name but I knew exactly where I had felt it once before. It had been during a school trip to our local zoo, staring at an animal that seemed so improbable on an unusually hot summer day — a polar bear. More than appearing to be uncomfortable, this impressive creature seemed so sad and frustrated, pacing back and forth in a space that felt all too small, his murky pool more suited to paddling than laps. There's nothing unusual about a kid getting all anthropomorphic in a zoo, but when it came to Patch, this nameless feeling seemed far more personal and disturbing, something close to what I might later come to think of as empathy.

Making Patch's precarious circumstances worse was the fact that our new next-door neighbor took an immediate dislike to him. Not that Mr. Peevish, as I will call him, singled Patch out in particular, he loathed canines of all shapes and sizes and he was particularly averse to any dog that, in his opinion, looked as though he could tear you limb from limb.

Sometimes, if I heard him in his backyard, gardening or mowing or plotting Patch's demise, I would take Patch out and make a point of fussing over him, brushing out his coat, roughhousing with him, hoping he might overhear how at ease a defenseless young boy was around this four-legged killer, hoping he might peek through a gap in the fence and see that Patch was really a big softy, all bark and no bite, or, as they sometimes say in England, "all mouth and no trousers"! I never envisaged the two of them becoming friends. I simply wanted to prove that Patch was not a mean dog, that with a little tolerance and respect we could all get along. But, sadly, as far as I could tell, Mr. Peevish never looked and he never listened. His mind was already made up. If there was ever the possibility of crossing paths with Patch when Patch was out on a leash with me and Dad, Mr. Peevish would visibly panic, as if calculating his odds of survival, all the while slowly backing up, Patch deemed no less terrifying than an escaped lion.

It seemed so unfair for Patch to be the subject of canine profiling. Then again, the Peevish disdain for dogs also included an adorable, submissive, perfectly affable two-year-old black Lab called Sam, who lived across the street. His owner, Martin, and my dad became friends, bonded by the universal camaraderie of dog lovers every-where. The same was not exactly true of Sam and Patch. Theirs was more of a grudg-ing respect — a brief circle and sniff, an indifferent and cautious "wassup," with an option for a little trash talk, and that was pretty much it. Their biggest battles were over who would be the last one to leave his signature over disputed territory like lamp-posts.

One thing I'll say for my father, what he

lacked in decent dog-training skills, he more than made up for in consideration for others when it came to Patch's etiquette in public. Martin, on the other hand, had no such qualms about letting people like Mr. Peevish know how he felt about irrational hostility to all canine companionship and Sam gave him the perfect opportunity to make a show of his irritation.

Sam's compulsion to one-up Patch in the battle for territorial marking got the better of him when one afternoon, long before leash laws and poop scooping, he slipped his leash, bolted across the street, and took the mother of all dumps on what he clearly believed to be our front lawn. I caught him in the act, all pleased with himself, scratching up stripes in the grass with his back paws before running back home.

Unfortunately his prank was flawed by one fundamental problem: the fresh turd sat in the middle of Mr. Peevish's immaculately manicured front lawn and not ours. Worse still, I was not the only witness to the crime. Within seconds of Sam disappearing into his home, Mr. Peevish emerged with a garden shovel, scooped up the offending item, careful to keep it at arm's length, walked it over to Martin's front door, and rang his doorbell.

Martin appeared at the door, joined by Sam, who politely sat by his side, attentive but chaste, affecting an inability to recognize his handiwork.

"I believe this belongs to you!" said Mr. Peevish.

Martin took one look at the steaming mound being shoved in his direction, saw his advantage and said, "Prove it!" before slamming the door in the poor man's face.

I admit it, a part of me enjoyed Mr. Peevish's moment of incredulity, his embarrassment as a car pulled into our cul-de-sac and the driver offered a friendly wave and an inquisitive "What you got there?" But when I stopped laughing, what remained was a man who would continue to condemn and seethe, and a need for me to understand that not everyone shared my point of view when it came to dogs. Putting all personal bias aside, Martin had been in the wrong. If Patch and Mr. Peevish were going to successfully remain in one another's orbit for the foreseeable future, Dad and I would have to work hard to be both responsible and respectful pet owners.

For some people, when it comes to their dogs, there's a fine line between devotion and raison d'être. Regardless of the label, all I knew was Dad kept his promise to Patch through a wholesome recreational alternative to a big backyard. Every morning without fail, they would be up at five, though I am led to believe the four-legged accomplice was the one who provided the alarm clock. Dad would don a waterproof coat and Wellington boots, regardless of season, and attach a leash to Patch's collar, and together they would set out for the fields and an opportunity to run free on more open land than Patch had ever known or could ever want for.

Accompanying them was unworkable for a boy who consistently struggled to regain consciousness before seven, but I might tag along for their evening walk, perpetually amazed by Patch's enthusiasm for the same routine, as though he had no idea where he was going and always thought that this time around would be a whole new adventure.

Of course we all saw through Dad's choice of off-peak hours. It was as if my father had confirmed something we had suspected for some time. Dad had given up trying to curb Patch's antisocial behavior. His solution was simple, some would argue lazy, but if nothing else, practical. If you can't stop the dog from behaving badly at least you can reduce the risk that he will get into trouble. Dad

89

had found a possible solution to a problem of his own making. He was trying to be responsible and, perhaps more importantly, he was trying to protect the dog he loved from being misunderstood.

The first time I joined them on their walk I discovered that Dad had also incorporated a backup security measure into their route. Within a few minutes of leaving the house we were lost in fields that consistently offered unencumbered vistas of the pathway ahead, providing plenty of lead time to grab a leash and call a name. There's no debating the fact that my dad did a far better job of teaching Patch to come when called than he ever did with me.

By the time we returned from that first walk, all my fears for Patch's mental well-being were allayed. I had watched him chase rabbits, explore a copse, leap over wooden stiles, and trot along, smiling, always slightly in the lead, his huge tail stretched out, down and low, bouncing with the beat of our footfalls. Neither my father nor I knew a thing about the science of animal behavior, but instinctively we both knew this was a happy dog.

When it came to the rest of Patch's well-being, there wasn't much to notice because there wasn't much that went wrong. These days, I often chat with dog owners who remember canine companions of yesteryear who similarly never got sick. They fondly recall a less complicated bygone era, governed by fewer conventions, when dogs knew how to be dogs, as though ailments and disease are disruptive innovations, like TV, rock 'n' roll, or the Internet. I have no proof that dogs were generally healthier a generation or two ago, but if they were, then Patch's good health was emblematic. Still, from time to time, we did take him to see a veterinarian and on one memorable occasion when I was eleven or twelve I asked if I could join Patch and my father for a scheduled annual checkup. Based on this experience, it is remarkable I would ever show any interest in working with animals again.

"Arthur suggested we get there early, slightly before afternoon clinics begin," said Dad. "That way we should get seen straight away."

I studied the man gripping the steering wheel as though our car had no brakes. Dad was a wreck, all clenched jaw muscles and white knuckles and a sweaty Nixonesque upper lip. Though he had kicked his cigarette habit years earlier I could still tell when a nicotine craving was rippling through his body and making him wide-eyed and jumpy,

91

as if he were fantasizing about lighting up and exhaling his mounting anxiety on a long and curly puff of smoke.

"Who's Arthur?" I asked.

"Arthur Stone, the practice's office manager. He's the gentleman who organizes the veterinarians and schedules the appointments and the farm calls. Coordinates the day-to-day running of the business. He's always been good to us. Understands how our Patch dislikes these visits. He tries to make them as painless as possible."

I didn't know whether our dog was feeding off Dad's negative vibe or had tuned in to the route he was driving, his innate canine GPS screaming, "Please don't turn left in two hundred yards because then I really do know where you're taking me!" but Patch stood on the backseat, refusing to lie down and panting excessively. He was a picture of apprehension and if my father had been a German shepherd, at that moment the two of them would have looked identical.

As we pulled into the small parking lot we both noted the presence of two other cars. I almost said something sarcastic about Arthur Stone being such a nice guy he was inviting lots of other anxious pet owners to turn up early, but kept my mouth shut as

Dad took a deep breath, attached a leash to Patch's collar, and headed for the front door.

I trotted along behind, like a reporter assigned to a combat unit in a war zone, trying to keep out of the way, maintaining a safe distance but still drawn to the action. I wasn't even inside the building when the first explosive went off. It started with the door swinging wide open on its hinges and Patch barreling into the waiting room, barking orders, instigating a pitched verbal battle with a defensive West Highland white terrier. I had time to see Patch lunging forward, the leash as taut as a bowstring, his front legs off the ground. Dad shouted over the din, apologizing to the Westie's owner, apologizing to a woman with a cat carrier on her lap, apologizing to Mr. Stone, finally getting the message that it might be best if Patch waited in the car rather than the waiting room.

I was still a ways off from perfecting a cocky adolescent sneer and pushing my luck with "That went well," so I said nothing as we did as we were told. I actually think I was too shocked and humiliated to speak. This was not the dog I knew and loved. Patch's obvious fear of all things veterinary had taken some of his disagreeable shortcomings to a whole new level. Dad had managed to keep him under control, but all we had done was enter the clinic's waiting room. What nightmarish transformation awaited us when the man in a white coat appeared? How would Dad be able to rein Patch in during an examination, let alone a shot? Then there were the other pet owners sitting quietly and politely, minding their business, right now shaking their heads, justifiably cursing the dog with bad manners and the reckless owner who had failed his dog with inadequate socialization and training. The three of us were sent to wait our turn in the car, where we sat like scolded children, certain we had not been forgiven even though we had said we were sorry.

The woman with the cat carrier emerged ten minutes later, walking quickly to her vehicle, key at the ready, as though this were not a parking lot in the middle of the afternoon but a dimly lit underground garage at midnight. I could tell she sensed the guilty threesome skulking in the nearby car though she never once glanced in our direction. She didn't need to — her bearing and pace said it all, a derisive "How dare you frighten my cat!"

I wondered whether Dad would abort the

mission if more cars started turning up, but they didn't and as soon as the little Westie emerged with his owner in tow, so did Mr. Stone, waving for us to come in, the coast clear.

Arthur Stone seemed to be enjoying himself. He was probably in his early sixties, heavyset, with cheeks that had succumbed to gravity a long time ago, melting into jowls that drooped over the collar of a brown plaid shirt and the knot of a brown woolen tie. He stood well back as he waved us inside.

"I'm sure you know the way, Duncan. First room on the right. Mr. Jones is waiting for you."

His voice was gravelly, his smoking habit betrayed by the small cardboard box distending his breast pocket. And his words were spiked with a mischievous edge, as if he knew sparks were about to fly and he was titillated by the prospect of watching the show from a safe distance.

Dad marched forward, keeping Patch on an extremely short leash. Waiting for us was a man with thick white hair and heavily tinted glasses. Back then, photochromic lenses were in their infancy — trendy, expensive, and extremely slow to change from black to transparent during the transition from sunlight to room light. This had the effect of turning Patch's doctor into a pasty English version of Roy Orbison. I'm not sure what I had expected. Up until now, the potential perils of such an encounter had been handled mostly by avoidance. For the first time in a long time, Patch needed to interact with a complete stranger. Maybe I had expected someone in a safari suit wielding a whip and a wooden chair.

"Come on in," said Mr. Jones, as though we just happened to be passing by. "I thought I recognized the sound of Patch announcing his arrival."

Patch completely ignored the polite banter and continued to rant, his volume all the more impressive in the confined and resonant space. Mr. Jones leaned up against his examination table, no more than ten feet from Patch's snout, talking over him, totally unfazed by his tirade, and suddenly I was faced with something completely new and unexpected: a stranger who was not the least bit intimidated by our big unruly dog. Maybe it was this abrupt contrast between a posturing dog and a reserved professional, but for the first time I felt truly embarrassed by Patch's behavior.

"Is this your son?"

Dad nodded and replied, "Yes, this is

Nick," but when Dad tried to smile he was betrayed by a grimace that said, "Can we please just get on with this?"

I said a meek hello and I saw Mr. Jones thinking about a formal greeting, hesitating, and backing off, since any attempt to shake hands would have forced his own hand into the strike zone, a maneuver guaranteed to produce the same response from Patch as dangling a T-bone steak in the air between us.

"Any problems since your last visit?" asked Mr. Jones.

"No. Not really," said Dad. "He seems a little stiff first thing in the morning when we go on our walks. Otherwise I think he's fine."

Mr. Jones nodded, scratching a note on an index card.

Patch continued to talk over their dialogue, but his listing of grievances began to slow down, becoming more muttering than shouting, the cranky gripes of an aging dog who resented being ignored. His posture had also changed, his hackles became less prominent, his ears flattened a little, and his tail relaxed into an enormous hairy question mark. Oh, he was still wired and Mr. Jones was obviously keeping his distance, but Patch seemed like he was prepared to

97

accept this state of play, this standoff — no fast moves and nobody gets hurt.

"I'm not sure I'm going to get to perform a meaningful examination," said Mr. Jones. "But I'm happy to try."

These days, this is precisely the kind of line I might employ, the "cover your ass" offer to wrestle with a powerful dog high on adrenaline while praying the owner has a modicum of understanding.

Dad did the right thing and shook his head, saying, "Might be best if you just give him his shot and then we'll be on our way."

To Mr. Jones's credit he managed not to look relieved or disappointed.

"Now, how best to do this?" said the doctor, more to himself, though this question had been foremost on my mind for some time. I didn't know a thing about veterinary medicine but I was pretty sure Patch was not about to sit still, roll up his sleeve, and look away when the needle pierced his skin.

Funny how sometimes the littlest details stay with you. I remember two posters pinned to the wall, one showing the anatomy of the dog, the other, the cat. All the internal organs were labeled and I wanted to find them fascinating and distracting, but the scrimmage that ensued kept vying for my attention. Patch seemed so afraid, completely unable to comprehend why he was being put through this ordeal, insensible to every attempt my father made to keep him calm. It was like my best friend was getting picked on by a gang of bigger kids in the schoolyard and I was standing there, watching it unfold and doing nothing to help. At the same time there was this overwhelming sense of frustration caused by our collective inability to convey trust and goodwill. I was too close to the action to feel this helpless.

Dad tried to place a leather muzzle over Patch's snout, failed, then tried to place it while offering a bribe in the form of a dog treat. Mr. Jones proposed a muzzle formed from a long single loop of bandage material, but it was like trying to lasso displaced air and moving teeth. My father recalled previous success with something akin to a "rabies pole," a long rod through which a thick, stainless-steel lanyard was passed, to be secured around Patch's neck in the manner of a snare. Fortunately, Mr. Jones had a better suggestion.

"Why don't you walk him out of the room and I'll carefully close the door on him, leaving his head outside so I can get to his backside?"

Frozen in fear, I stayed on the business side of the door, watching the action. Mr.

99

Jones worked quickly, offering me a wink and an "all done" as my father rode Patch's momentum from the jab, the dog scampering straight through the now busy waiting room and out to the car.

"You all right?" said Mr. Jones.

"Yes," I said, thinking how Patch's fur had masked the site of steel piercing skin, an observation that made me cower and look away every time I was the victim.

"You sure?"

Obviously my pallor had not convinced him.

"Don't worry," he said, "Patch will be fine. He's not the first protective German shepherd I've ever met and he certainly won't be the last."

I nodded, felt awkward, and made to shuffle out of the room.

"Here," said Mr. Jones, handing me a small dog biscuit in the shape of a bone. "For him, not you. Most of my patients prefer them to lollipops."

He pressed the biscuit into my open hand, while I offered a barely audible thank-you and ran out to catch up with Dad, who was paying his bill.

"Next time," said Arthur Stone in a polite whisper, "you might want to give Patch a little something an hour or so before he comes in. I can ask Mr. Jones for a prescription if you like. Make it a lot easier on you and easier on him."

Dad thanked him for the offer and after a few minutes Arthur returned with a small white envelope containing half a dozen bright orange tablets.

"Next time," said Arthur, sliding them across the counter and jutting out his chin, his chubby lips curved downward into the frown of someone who knows best.

Dad thanked him once again with an appreciative nod, but when he glanced down at me to say, "Let's go," I sensed he remained haunted by a mixture of skepticism and guilt for having nurtured a dog who required chemical sedation to come out in public.

To put Patch's antics in some kind of context, I can look back on my career as a veterinarian and realize that sadly, he would be right up there with my top ten all-time nightmare encounters. I'm no behaviorist but Patch seemed motivated by a dangerous combination of fear, dominance, and desire to protect his pack — me and my dad. Sometimes you can try removing the dog from the owner, but with Patch there would have been no separating him from those he was sworn to defend at all cost.

If I had been in Mr. Jones's shoes, I would have been rolling my eyes and shaking my head the moment Patch was out of my sight. It may seem inconsequential, but as an owner who acknowledged his pet's bad behavior, my father at least had one saving grace. An owner who appreciates there is a problem is always preferable to the smiling owner who quips as a pair of canine teeth sinks deep into your flesh, "Oh, yeah, I forgot to mention . . . sometimes he gets snippy!"

As I entered my teenage years, my inner nerd began to stir. I was the geek who craved a chemistry set (so long as I could try to make a bomb), was enthralled by any television show featuring Sir David Attenborough, and, though I dared not tell a living soul, actually enjoyed algebra. It became apparent that if I kept to the sciences and stayed far away from anything involving the English language, it was possible that I might just make something of myself. It was at this point that my father's inclination to coddle my academic efforts began to change. Don't get me wrong, my father's aspirations for his son were always well intentioned — consistent nudges interlaced with remembrances of his own failings in school, all aimed at preventing a similar calamity. But as I began to savor the feel of primitive peach fuzz on my cheeks and the first crack in my choirboy vowels, I noticed a shift in his focus on my scholarly success to bigger issues of career and even destiny. It wasn't long before the time-honored question, savored by so many parents and grandparents, finally emerged from his lips.

"So, son, what do you want to be when you grow up?"

To this day, I'm not exactly sure how I broadcast my curiosity about the life of a veterinarian, but my father jumped all over this spark of interest and soon arranged an intense one-day immersion program, at the very same practice I had visited with Patch years earlier.

Eager to make a good impression, I was worried that I would be perceived as an accomplice to Patch's bad behavior. I tried to convince myself that enough time had passed since the troubling encounter with Mr. Jones and besides, I was assigned to a different doctor in the practice, the man I would come to think of as our family veterinarian, Ryan James. I've written about this fateful day elsewhere, how James took an ambivalent schoolboy and somehow made him feel important, made him feel instantly and profoundly connected, and integral to his work of healing sick animals. The effect was both intoxicating and overpowering, though I cringed during my first few introductions to coworkers when Ryan said, "This is Nick. His dad brings in Patch."

My fear of being negatively associated with my pet's disposition was completely unwarranted. Sure, that one word, *Patch,* was all it took for some staff members, including Arthur Stone (whose initial failure to recognize me reinforced my conviction that I must be in the throes of a dramatic pubescent transformation), to give me a look that ranged from knowing to withering. And yes, Patch's notoriety may have been more Manson than Monroe and clearly he had made a lasting impression, with folkloric staying power. But, more telling than any unwanted recognition and in keeping with that wonderful day was the way in which neither my father nor I was ever made to feel irresponsible or negligent. Patch was never criticized for his behavior. He was simply another facet of the veterinarian's challenge, a difficult dog who misunderstood our intent. From that very first day I was already beginning to see Patch's societal failings in a different light.

As a parent, it doesn't get much sweeter

than having a child who believes he or she has found a calling in life. Aimless drifting, speculation, or passing interest is suddenly replaced by direction, motivation, and a clear-cut goal. For my dad, with his lifelong desire for me to discover a meaningful path, it appeared to be a dream come true. As evidence of his overwhelming support for my fledgling career path, he underwent a bizarre metamorphosis from which he has never truly recovered.

It began innocently enough with the sudden appearance of two new accoutrements for his walks with Patch. Both items consistently bothered me. They seemed so affected and unnecessary for a man about to turn forty. I'm talking about a flat cloth cap and a simple wooden walking stick. It was as if Dad sought an air of working-class practicality, a rural motif, despite his tendency to use the stick like a London gentleman uses an umbrella, snapping his wrists and striking out with the metal tip at every stride.

There followed the appearance of numerous James Herriot books conspicuously placed on bedside tables, kitchen counters, and sofa arms, spines split and pages well thumbed. And when my father sensed I was ignoring his bait, he switched mediums from paper to television, watching countless hours of the highly acclaimed BBC TV series *All Creatures Great and Small.*

"I don't think you've seen this one, son. I've recorded it, so no rush. Mum and I can wait until you're finished with your homework."

Eventually this sixteen-year-old boy gave in and one night I joined them on the sofa with Patch at our feet, stretched out across the carpet. I couldn't help but notice how the opening theme music seemed to cue up a sense of relaxation and contentment in my father and as the show progressed, I would glance over at him, studying his face in the flickering light, a witness to a phenomenon akin to hypnotism. The man sat mesmerized, entranced by the location and the characters, by the big moody skies and the even moodier big farmers. It was a wonderful show but for my father it appeared to be much more than entertainment. Sitting in front of the screen, the tired VHS tape rolling across the heads one more time, I would watch as his lips synchronized with the dialogue, as if he were participating in an evangelical service. Herriot's books had become his bible, the author's veterinary lifestyle revered like a new religion. As the hour-long period of worship drew to a close, I wondered if I recognized another possibility in his facial expressions. Was he daring to imagine a future for his son the veterinarian in the Yorkshire Dales? Was he mentally gesturing to the rolling landscape on the screen and saying, "This can be yours"? Or was his dream even more personal and intertwined, something more like "This can be ours."

I should not have been surprised when my father acquired a broad Yorkshire accent almost overnight. It is worth noting that the folks who hail from Yorkshire are a proud race of people. As Herriot is obliged to point out in his writing, they are suspicious and wary of strangers, a label applied to any man or woman born outside the boundaries of the largest Shire in England. They can make New Englanders look positively warm and fuzzy. My father was born in Zimbabwe, the only son of a Royal Air Force flying instructor, stationed in what was then Salisbury, Rhodesia, at the start of World War II. His pretending to hail from Yorkshire was like a Bostonian insisting he was a loyal and lifelong Yankees fan.

Armed with an incentive and a new vocabulary, Dad found the desire to mimic his hero from the Dales irresistible, and was eager to apply Herriot's rural terminology whenever possible. When friends called and I was busy doing homework they were informed that I was "out on a farrowing" even though I had never seen a sow in labor let alone assisted in the delivery of piglets. If I came home after curfew, he would inform my mother that I had been "out while all hours" and if I looked the worse for wear he would declare that I had "eyes like chapel hat pegs." He would say "t" instead of "the," "summat" instead of "something"; nothing became "nowt." On one occasion I asked if Fiona and I could go on a school ski trip to Italy and he replied, "I'm sure the world is full of wonderful places, and good luck to them that goes to see them, but just give me that parlor down at Mr. Dents and Marian behind the bar, the dominoes clicking and them logs roaring up the chimney, and you can keep all your Monte Carlos."

Sometimes I questioned who really wanted to become a vet the most and this led me to another logical possibility. Patch was a proven disaster around strangers and veterinarians, but what if his veterinarian was someone he trusted? Was Dad trying to cajole me into a profession for practical purposes, so he never had to endure the embarrassment of another veterinary visit with his unruly dog? Even if I was lucky enough and smart enough to become a veterinarian, it would be years before I was qualified to practice, much too far into the future to benefit Patch. Was Dad planning ahead, certain he would always have companionship with incorrigible canines?

While those awkward teenage years afford adolescents and their beleaguered parents an opportunity to discover a new and strained relationship, our bond to our pets remains an unwavering constant. In relative terms, Patch may have progressively shrunk in stature from when I was a little boy, but his presence was always inescapable and re-assuring. When I went to my first church hall disco, heard the opening riff to Lionel Ritchie's "Three Times a Lady," and plucked up the courage to ask a girl for a dance only to have her laugh at my effrontery, who was there for me to hug when I got home? After promising myself that I would never experiment with Southern Comfort again, on whose head did I lay my hand to ground me as the room continued to spin? And, in those days before cell phones and any semblance of responsibility, when I wandered home at two in the morning only to find my father sick with worry and waiting up for me, who understood my excuses and appreciated the sincerity in my apology? Patch and I had both grown older together, though, according to my parents, he was the only one who had acquired any wisdom. I never took him for granted; he just . . . was, amenable to affection so long as the contact was tough and manly. Patch didn't do "pet the dog" and on the journey into manhood, this kind of interaction suited me just fine.

Patch's morning stiffness, first reported to Mr. Jones all those years before, started to become increasingly problematic as he began to age. It took longer and longer for him to warm out of it and in the end he simply could not walk as far. He chased rabbits less frequently. He'd spot a bouncing white tail, mull it over, and decide to let it go, as if he had calculated the price to be paid for such bursts of energy was too high.

Hip arthritis was suggested to be the most likely cause (hip dysplasia, abnormal development of the hip joint, being rife among German shepherds of that era). Anti-inflammatory medications were prescribed, and back then veterinarians had very few options to choose from. Patch was put on a drug called phenylbutazone, a powerful pain reliever more commonly used in horses that went by the nickname "Bute." These little red pills worked their magic and thankfully Patch appeared to have none of the potential side effects of vomiting or diarrhea or signs of abnormal kidney function. He recovered some of his pep, his gait became more fluid, and once more the paperboy and the postman had to be alert to the possibility of a quick, mean dog defending our front door.

Patch must have been about twelve years old when he started to show signs of something more than just stiffness. As a clinician I see it all the time, particularly in older German shepherds, referred to me for chronic hip arthritis when sadly there is much more going wrong with their back legs. Oftentimes it is hard to appreciate the difference between muscle weakness secondary to long-standing hip issues and the emergence of a new, progressive deterioration in the portion of the spinal cord that feeds nerves into the hind legs. This neurological disease is called degenerative myelopathy and when it first crept into Patch's life it pretended to be another dimension of his ailing hip function.

"Duncan, has your dog been drinking your beer?"

The question came from my mother, and because she didn't pay as much attention to

Patch as my father and me it carried the weight of a fresh objective eye.

"Now you come to mention it, I see what you mean," I said, watching as Patch took a corner, perfectly coordinated on his front legs yet awkward and clumsy on his back, the paws crisscrossing over one another like the feet of a drunk trying to walk a straight line and miserably failing to retain his balance during a sobriety test.

Dad sought veterinary advice, but the progression of hip arthritis remained the prime suspect, the medical options limited and pretty much already exhausted. To this day degenerative myelopathy is a disease diagnosed by the exclusion of everything else. Definitive diagnosis in the living patient is only possible using one particularly useless test — microscopic evaluation of the affected part of the patient's spinal cord. There remains no specific treatment beyond dabbling in stem-cell therapy or homeopathic techniques. Then, as now, veterinary medicine hasn't got much to offer for the condition.

The worst thing about Patch's illness was the way it slowly but surely stripped him of his independence. To the best of our understanding degenerative myelopathy is not a painful disorder and to some extent, it is

112

this apparent absence of pain and suffering that makes it all the worse. It persuades us to become false optimists. We see a dog cleaved into two distinct halves — strong and healthy on the front end, frail and incoordinated on the back. His heart was perfect while ours were breaking. His mind was sharp and eager for normalcy, whereas ours were numb and frustrated. Perhaps as owners we should realize we have a problem when our minds are filled with the walks we are *not* taking with our dogs.

Patch began falling down, unable to scramble to his feet unassisted. Patch had always been larger than life, powerful and intimidating. Now his gait was clumsy, making him scuff the skin off his back paws with every step he took on concrete or asphalt, causing them to bleed. He would sit in the backyard, barking for help, unable to extricate himself from the bowel movement lurking below his tail. And as a final sign of Patch's infirmity, my most pathologically dog-fearing friend, Nigel, with uncanny self-assurance, began paying visits to our house.

Nigel claimed his cynophobia (fear of dogs) stemmed from a near-death encounter with a fiendish terrier when he was a little boy. Back then this was all I needed to know, the endless rounds of reparative plastic surgery and hours of psychological counseling something one could imagine but never dream of inquiring about. Decades later I discovered that his aunt's geriatric Jack Russell had merely growled at Nigel from afar when he picked up one of the poor dog's treats. Just the once! And there was never any physical contact! Now you have a sense of how sullied Patch's reputation had become. For years, when Nigel dared to visit, it was always a battle to apply a leash and drag Patch away from the front door. But Nigel's fear had begun to wane with the visible progression of Patch's disease and by now it was heartbreaking to have to take this poor dog's scrawny back legs like wooden handles and wheelbarrow him away to another room on strong front legs. Patch had done the unthinkable, he had become malleable, and wholly unintimidating.

Dad and I worked hard to keep the practicalities of Patch's progressive demise from my mother and sister, but there was only so much we could hide. I kept waiting for Mum to object, to be the voice of reason, but she looked the other way and she said nothing. Maybe she saw the pain and agony taking turns in her husband's heart. Maybe she was coming to terms with the amazing effect an unexpected and unwelcome dog was having on hers.

Sometimes it is not the things you do, but the things you don't do that leave a lasting impression. Though Dad and I believed we had done our best, we had essentially helped Patch, at thirteen, become a paraplegic. He had reached a point at which he needed a full-time nurse and the canine equivalent of a wheelchair. We both loved this dog but this dog was no longer the Patch we knew. Though it remained unsaid, I could tell Dad was battling a relentless undercurrent of guilt for having come this far. He knew he stood on the brink of a void created by the certainty of his best friend's demise. He could see it spread out before him — vast, dark, and unimaginably lonely. Fearing the future, he had clung to the now, the grim but preferable now, even though what he sought and the only memories he wanted to choose were lost in the past. It came down to whether he had it in him to do the right thing, to step into this future, face the fear of loss and embrace the promise of mercy for a friend trapped inside a dying body.

If I have one lasting and positive memory of that difficult final year in Patch's life it would be this. One night when I was heading up to bed I heard the television still on in the family room. I popped my head around the door and saw Patch lying in front of the sofa, dozing, with my dad lying down on the floor beside him. On the TV, Siegfried Farnon was giving James Herriot a dressing down about how he had handled the tetchy owner of a prized thoroughbred. Dad's choice of entertainment came as no surprise, neither did Patch's apathy toward *All Creatures Great and Small,* but Dad's posture, reclined on his side, hand cupped under head, elbow pointed to the floor, was most unusual. I stood there, silent and unnoticed. Dad was running his free hand over Patch's head and as I watched, he snuggled even closer, put his arm over the dog's big neck and gave him a hug.

The old Patch would have twisted out of the embrace, squirmed away, and come back at you with a mouthy "Give me a break! You goin' all soft on me!"

But not now. It was over in a matter of seconds, Patch apparently indifferent but tolerant, and what struck me, because it seemed so awkward and forced, was the unusual alignment of their bodies. When we as humans hug, whether we think about it or not, we have the potential to align our hearts. Subconsciously, in that brief moment, had my father found a way to truly connect with his dog?

When it finally happened, it came out of the blue, the news delivered in a phone call from my father while I was at school.

"I'm so sorry, son. The sores, the infection . . . I couldn't see him suffer anymore."

Suddenly my father was a little boy, tears and grief hacking his words into pieces. It was his seventeen-year-old son who held it together. There was nothing to discuss, nothing else that mattered. I told no one at school what I was doing or where I was going. I simply walked home because Patch and my dad needed me.

When I got there, the hole in the earth below a young apple tree was already taking shape. It was Mr. Jones, Patch's old veterinary adversary, who had come to our house and painlessly brought Patch's torment to an end. There had been no fight or confrontation, unambiguous confirmation that Patch was more than ready to go.

For a while, I helped my father dig. We worked efficiently and in silence as though this part of the project was all there was. And when the grave was ready we went about carrying Patch outside and laying him to rest. His favorite blanket, the one in which he lay, looked all wrong covered in earth.

"Thanks for helping me, son."

Tears were streaming down Dad's cheeks, but I held it together through a mixture of stubbornness, defiance, and teenage detachment. I risked a nod. Speech would have split me open.

As we stood there, side by side, staring down at the tilled soil, I thought Dad should and would say a prayer, but what he said, and all he needed to say, was "He was a great dog. A faithful friend."

4.
SEA CHANGE

I have known people who cannot do it over. Regular, everyday people who dare not acquire another dog or cat after losing the furry love of their life. I have argued with them, tried to convince them they are not being unfaithful, that no two pets will ever be the same, that a unique, capricious but equally magical relationship may unfold. Yet often these fragile souls would rather not risk any more heartbreak.

For a while I believe my father was one of these people. Possibly it was a mark of respect, akin to sitting shivah, a way to let the world know he was grieving a significant loss. He knew dog owners who were capable of getting a replacement puppy as soon as their steadfast companion began to wane, ensuring an overlap, a canine continuum. To him, this felt too much like buying a hot new car at the first sign your trusty clunker is beginning to break down. He knew of other dog owners who could lose their best friend and go straight out and get a new puppy, no problem. To him, this felt like the husband who loses his wife of forty years and at the next family gathering turns up flaunting a much younger replacement whom he introduces as his "soul mate." Dad wasn't being judgmental or suggesting that this approach demeaned the sense of grief. It was just that, as with so much else in his life, Dad had to go about healing on his own terms, even if I thought getting a new dog would cheer him up. Whether he still believed he had to atone for his underhanded acquisition of Patch and was daunted by the prospect of future negotiations with my mum, I didn't know. All I knew was our family was once more without a dog, with no prospect of filling the void any time soon.

This time around I did not badger my parents. Patch's absence was simply too big and palpable. Every day after school I would slip into the house unnoticed. No bark, no sniff, no cursory inspection, approval, and dismissal as our noble German shepherd wandered off to work on more important business. His water bowl sat on the kitchen floor, familiar and empty, and on more than one occasion I caught myself as I went to fill it up. No wonder I channeled my attention elsewhere, scoring my animal fix at Ryan James's vet practice.

Intoxicated by the buzz of that awesome first visit, I was eager to return and make sure the rush I felt working there was real and durable. What if I had been mistaken or gullible, easily disposed to a sense of wonder and adventure thanks to my father's brainwashing with the works of James Herriot? Perhaps more important, did I have what it took to become a veterinarian? Did I have the smarts, the stamina, the heart? All I knew for sure was that a place at veterinary school required higher grades than any other course of study, including human medicine, and that despite this ominous requirement, competition remained fierce.

When I confided this career possibility to my teachers at high school, they universally agreed that I had "as good a chance as anyone," but this felt more like "Why not apply, you've got nothing to lose" rather than a resounding endorsement of my academic aptitude. Part of me sensed their real interest lay not with me as an individual, but rather with me as a statistic, as placement of a student at veterinary school would be proof of their collective educational expertise.

In order to stand out from the crowd I knew I must demonstrate my desire to experience what it meant to be a veterinarian. And so, during every vacation from high school, I would try to hang out at our local veterinary practice for as long as they would let me, as desperate to prove my commitment as I was to assuage any uncertainties about whether this was really the vocation for me.

On that first day with Ryan James, when I had stood quietly by and watched a dog undergo a Caesarian section, a part of me had been pleasantly surprised at my own stoicism. But looking back, two singular events during my childhood had probably groomed me for a certain degree of composure in and around the operating room.

The first came courtesy of my sister, Fiona, when she was no more than three or four years old. If I wasn't playing with Patch or with my grandma's faithful Dalmation, Cleo, or the kids from across the street (pretty much in that order), Fiona became my foil, a rough-and-tumble playmate happy to rat me out to my parents when we moved beyond the "end in tears" stage of our games. She always embraced versions of tag or "You're It," alternating between smiles and maniacal screams as I chased her around our house. On this occasion, I had coaxed her to chase me, and hidden around a corner, in the manner of a Tom and Jerry or Road Runner cartoon, I stuck out a long leg over which she flew. I don't know why she didn't point the finger of blame in my direction. Perhaps it was the shock of how much blood was pouring from her head, making her look like a miniature version of Carrie on her prom night. Maybe it was a moment of amnesia coinciding with the impact. For whatever reason, as I bore witness to the deluge of what looked like bright red paint, somehow the guilt of what I had done helped me overcome any fleeting sensation of nausea or faintness. To this day I think poor Fiona believes the two-inch scar on the upper left side of her forehead was caused by accidentally tripping on a loose flap of carpet and landing on her skull.

My father was at work, so I was instructed to compress a tea towel into Fiona's brain, for I was certain that was what I was doing, while my mum drove us to the hospital.

Sitting alone on a plastic chair in the ER waiting room, I began to feel the regret and shame ebbing away, replaced by a growing confidence that somehow my heinous crime had gone unnoticed and would therefore go unpunished. And as my little feet began swinging back and forth, listening while poor Fiona howled from behind closed doors as each nylon stitch was placed across her wound, I had my first "note to self" moment, undeniable and to a certain extent, quite pleasing for a little boy — "I am disturbingly comfortable with the site of blood!"

In the second pertinent incident, it was *my* turn to have a run-in with a surgeon.

Like most mammals, dogs, cats, and humans are all bedeviled with a variety of useless or outdated organs. Anal sacs, for example, are an evolutionary remnant from the days of territorial marking, of scenting an animal's domain. Domesticity has rendered the anal sac pretty much redundant, but for many pet owners it can be the bane of their existence, emitting a foul discharge with a pungent, offensive odor as your dog rubs his bum across your living room carpet whenever friends drop by. Thankfully, we humans do not possess anal sacs, but then dogs and cats are spared the pitfalls of an appendix, a worthless vestige of our intestinal tract. As a churlish fifteen-year-old I discovered that the sole purpose of the appendix was to spontaneously become inflamed, making me throw up incessantly and reel from the pain whenever some klutz in a white coat poked the lower right quadrant of my abdomen and asked, "Does this hurt?"

With the exception of those who show their cats and dogs, most pet owners understand that a sterile surgical field necessitates the disappearance of a whole lot of fur and fluff. Depending on the location of surgery, the same also applies to humans, though I was surprised as I lay in my hospital bed — hungry, my mouth parched, waiting for my date with a scalpel — when a cheery young nurse popped her head around my door and informed me, "Someone will be by in a while to give you a shave."

I smiled and nodded my appreciation, thinking it was too bad this kind of attention to detail never made it into the newspapers when the pundits disparaged Britain's system of socialized medicine. How very civilized, almost decadent, of them. Using just the right amount of pressure with my fingertips I could definitely discern sufficient stubble on my cheeks to make it worth their while. Then it hit me. The nurse wasn't referring to the twenty seconds of spa treatment needed to remove my sparse, downy whiskers. This was a warning of pending baldness for my nether regions.

These days I would argue that with appropriate draping, such a violation was unnecessary, but at the time I was a self-conscious teenager consumed with the concept of a stranger, possibly of the opposite sex, possibly attractive, scrutinizing, let alone touching, let alone shaving, my particulars. The ordeal was fraught with ways in which I might embarrass myself.

I wonder whether the nurses do this sort of thing to get a kick out of torturing adolescent boys, planting the seed of fear and watching it blossom before sending in a woman old enough to be my grandmother with the businesslike efficiency of a gentleman's barber on a busy Saturday morning.

Wheeled down to the operating room for my appendectomy, I smiled as the overhead lights whizzed by just like they did in the movies and before I knew it, I was being invited to count backwards from one hundred while something liquid was pumped into a vein in my hand. The competitor in me wanted to get further than anyone before me, to unnerve the anesthesiologist, forcing anxious looks toward his colleagues as I effortlessly rattled off "forty-four . . . forty-three . . . forty-two," but my speech slurred in the mid-nineties and as it did, they pounced. If what happened to me happens to my patients then we have to improve our anesthetic protocols because I can still remember "feeling" the sensation of being intubated, of having a speculum shoved down my throat and a plastic tube rammed into my airway. It lodged in a place where it should have made me cough, and I still had enough presence of mind to realize that I couldn't cough — in fact, as hard as I tried, I couldn't breathe. My last conscious thought was that this was what it must be like to suffocate.

When I woke up I was back in my hospital bed, a string of drool hanging from the corner of my mouth, a dull muscular ache on the right side of my belly. In the following week I made two useful discoveries that would forever heighten my sympathy toward fellow surgical patients, be they human, feline, or canine. First, it is worthwhile making a neat and cosmetically appealing job of the surgical closure. Though I was comfortable staring at the slice in my flesh, I was bothered by the sneering lips of my incision, which were crooked, weepy, and bruised, the stitches irregularly spaced. Second, never underestimate how much a pet wants to scratch an incision and, to a greater extent, the area of skin that was shaved. For all the stabbing pain every time I sat up, the unrelenting itchy prickle of my fresh Brazilian was almost more torturous.

Of course my positive veterinary experience had not been a fluke. Arthur Stone was as affable and accommodating as always, finagling a way to help me hang out with the veterinarians, especially Ryan James. Never one to miss a teaching opportunity, Ryan would pull me away from the walls when I was trying too hard to be politely inconspicuous. He would insist I help hold a dog, restrain a cat, palpate a mass, take a listen with a stethoscope. He forced me to interact. He allowed me every opportunity to hear what he heard, to feel what he felt, relentless until I got it, until he could see it in my eyes, watching me catch the exact same bug that grabbed him when he was my age.

In the meantime, there was a strange turn of events taking place back at the homestead. In the immediate aftermath of Patch's death, the notion of getting another dog had been unthinkable, the subject taboo for my grieving father. For nearly a year, you could sit on our sofa and not have a mohair like coating on your clothing when you stood up. You could nonchalantly stroll around our backyard indifferent to your footfalls and friends even began to call for me by ap-

128

pearing at the front door rather than using the telephone. But, over time, I began to eavesdrop on conversations that told me Dad was coming back, recapturing his desire for a dog, my mother forced to reassert her original proclamation — "No more dogs!" Having to concede the word *more* meant acknowledging her past failure to prevent such a transgression, so, to provide extra menace this time around, she often tossed in a sentence or two that included the word *divorce.* Then the unthinkable happened.

"Mum's beginning to weaken," said Dad in a whisper over the cup of tea he was handing over as a bribe to get me up and out of bed for school. "Don't say a word, but I think we have a shot at getting a dog."

The combination of shock and disbelief made his request easy to carry out. I was careful not to leak my information to Fiona, fearful the womenfolk had laid a trap for us dog lovers, poised to expose and crush our pent-up desire for the return of canine company. I was careful not to weaken and let my mother catch me wearing a knowing smile, and any covert communication between my father and I during this period of delicate diplomacy was done far away from prying eyes and sensitive ears. We dared not risk a raised brow, a wink, or a nod. Mum needed to save face and cave on her terms.

The announcement, when it came, was delivered by both parents and shrouded in secrecy. Yes, we were getting a dog. No, it wouldn't be another German shepherd (no one needed to clarify this decision — for all of us, there would only ever be one German shepherd in our lives). Yes, it would be another male dog, and no, we would just have to wait and see.

I tried to coax a hint out of Dad but to no avail. All I knew was my father appeared to be supremely happy but was sworn to silence, and a significant clincher in the deal involved his submitting to my mum's choice of breed.

I hardly had a chance to point out that Mum, by her own admission, knew little about the characteristics of different dog breeds before things went from merely bizarre to almost unbelievable.

A countdown had begun, our unidentified dog set to arrive in under a week. Mum was at work when a gaggle of breathless kids converged on her kindergarten classroom, grabbing her by the hand and insisting she come with them. There, with her head firmly wedged between the metal railings that formed a perimeter fence around the front of the school property, was a forlorn and defeated black puppy, restrained as effectively as a prisoner in a medieval stock.

This should have been the point at which Mum passed the buck, yielding to colleagues who were forthright doggy types, but she stepped up, gently coaxing the poor dog's head free, picking her up, and carrying her into the school.

Her kids did exactly what I would have done at their ages, they embraced the rescue mission and their role as saviors, doting on the frightened dog, fetching her water, raiding their lunch boxes for bits of sandwich.

"Is she a Labrador, Mrs. Trout?"

"She looks that way to me," said Mum, though later I found her short on alternative suggestions of breeds for dogs that were black. In her defense, she did pick up on a critical inconsistency. "But this tiny white spot on her chest, this doesn't look right." The puppy had no collar and no form of identification, and none of the children in her class had ever seen it before.

The dog-resistant Mum I knew took the reins, driving the puppy over to the nearest police station and depositing her with an unsympathetic sergeant. Standard protocol dictated that the abandoned bitch would be transferred to a local dog pound. There she

131

would be assigned to death row, her sentence commuted for just seven days, after which time, if she remained unclaimed, she would be put to sleep.

By the end of the afternoon, another woman entirely placed a phone call to my father. This woman may have looked and sounded like my mother, but she had to have been abducted by dog-friendly aliens, her brain fried, and the circuitry completely rewired.

"Duncan, do you think we could have another dog?"

I wonder if my father questioned who was on the other end of the line, whether he dropped the handset, and how long it took him to regain control of his vocal cords.

"But . . . we're already committed to a dog."

"I know, I know," said Mum, "but I want you to see her."

This they did, visiting the pound together after work. At the back of a damp and chilly concrete cell sat a tiny black puppy. It wasn't the gentle whimpering that got to Dad as he picked her up. It was far more subtle. In her eyes, worse than dejection, more cutting, was a look of resignation, hopelessness, and acceptance of her lot.

Dad turned to Mum, cradling the puppy

132

in his hands.

"We must have her," he said, with a familiar, fierce determination that always bordered on tears.

Mum nodded, the smallest upturn at the corner of her lips all she would concede. Skillfully my mother had engineered an encounter between her sensitive husband and a dog in need knowing full well how it would play out. By leaving the final word with my father, she was now able to step back, divorced from the consequences, all the while ensuring, to my delight, that "her will be done."

Only then were Fiona and I apprised of this new development.

"But Mum," whined Fiona, "think about all that lovely crap covering the backyard, and two sets of sharp puppy teeth trashing your new furniture, not just one."

I braced for my real Mum to wake up, to snap out of it, but she shooed the notion away as though it were ridiculous, saying, "By this time tomorrow, she'll have been claimed, and your father's notion of two dogs will be forgotten."

I glanced at my dad, who seemed more than happy to take the fall. Fiona, on the other hand, huffed her disapproval and went off to tease her hair, or listen to Duran Duran or hunt for her missing *Dynasty* shoulder pads. I decided I would take a peek inside our medicine cabinet to try and discover what wonderful medication my father was using to poison his wife's mind. I didn't know how it was happening, but my dog-resistant mum appeared to be succumbing to the inevitable power of the dog-loving DNA I had glimpsed from time to time when she was around Patch.

Twenty-four hours passed and no one had come forward to claim a little black dog. I knew this not from my father, but from my mother, who quickly gained notoriety with the kennel staff at the pound for her persistent and anxious phone calls inquiring after the puppy who got her head stuck in the school railings. They should have waited a full week to make sure there wasn't someone out there hunting for a lost Lab mix, but after five days of my mother's badgering, they could stand it no more. The lost puppy was signed over to my mum and rode to her new home content on Mum's lap as my father drove, a huge grin plastered on his face.

My father named her Bess after a famous black horse, Black Bess, the trusty steed of one Dick Turpin, arguably the most notorious highwayman in English folklore. Mother had been correct about her breed after all: black Labrador with a hint of something else, a dash of hound, a smidgen of terrier.

These days, I could have swabbed a little DNA from the inside of Bess's cheek, submitted it to a laboratory, and discovered with roughly 90 percent accuracy which different breeds contributed to her genetic mix. I have read that this knowledge can give an owner valuable insight into a dog's behavior or predisposition to certain diseases and anomalies but to be honest, most of the owners I know who have forked over the cash for this simple test do so out of curiosity, to discover their pet's ancestry.

On only one occasion have I been truly impressed by the power of this genetic tool. A client visited me with what appeared to be a pit bull that had a lameness problem. The dog was fantastic, your typical friendly, rough-and-tumble "pitty" who would not hurt a fly, let alone a human, let alone a child's face.

"Not everyone shares my enthusiasm for pit bulls" said the owner. "Many of the households in the neighborhood have small children and a number of the parents got together to complain about my dog, saying the breed couldn't be trusted, that it was only a matter of time before one of their kids was attacked."

"That's ridiculous," I said. "You could say that about any dog in the wrong hands."

"Yeah," said the owner, "I'm telling you, if you put her in a ring with a rabbit my money would be on the rabbit! But I didn't want them coming back at me, so I decided to try something I wouldn't have ordinarily considered — genetically testing my dog to discover what she's made of. And here's the thing. She may look like a pit bull and she may act like a pit bull, but according to her DNA test she's actually a cross between a mastiff and, of all things, a Dalmation. You should have seen the neighbors' faces when I showed them the official report."

But I digress, because back then, all you had to do was trust the experience of your veterinarian, and as far as Ryan James could tell, Bess was simply a Lab mix, the "mix" component open to interpretation.

"One good thing going for a Heinz fifty-seven," James would later inform me, "is the benefit of hybrid vigor."

"Hopefully," said James, "Bess will have all the good breed traits and dodge all the bad. Part of the fun of having a mix is not knowing exactly what you're going to get."

Where there was ambiguity when it came

136

to heritage, nothing was more indisputable than the puddles of urine and tiny poops abandoned in bizarre locations and the lost sleep due to nocturnal puppy whimpering. By the time my mushy, sleep-deprived brain was remembering not to walk around the house in bare feet, it was time for Mum and Dad to collect Bess's canine companion. They disappeared one Saturday morning, maintaining their contrived shroud of mystery to the bitter end.

They would concede only one detail, that they would be gone for at least five hours, giving me more than enough time to ponder the possibilities. For a split second I thought about discussing the matter with my sister, inviting her to make a prediction. Then reality kicked in. Fiona would rather discuss the finer points of calculus or debate symbolism in the novels of Thomas Hardy than speculate about canine matters. And so, as the arrival time approached, I sat alone in our living room, little black Bess pooped out (literally!), curled up and sleeping on my lap, the two of us wondering who and what was about to become her new BFF.

Based on my mother's recent purchase of royal blue wall-to-wall carpeting for several rooms I couldn't imagine it would be a dog with a tendency to shed, a dog with a long fur coat of a fair color. Mother had weakened over a black dog with slick short hair reminiscent of an otter. Surely she would lean toward something similar?

I wondered whether she would go for a small dog, following her mother's penchant for a toy breed. By now Marty had to be about fifty-three years old (okay, sixteen) and he was still going strong. Either he was the Benjamin Button of poodles or my grandma had been pulling off the old goldfish stunt, trading up for a look-alike, keeping the same name and hoping no one noticed. My mum's cousin Pat bred and showed Tibetan terriers. These are fantastic little dogs, full of vim and vigor, but somehow I didn't see a small breed of dog in our future. If Bess was going to be approximately Labrador in size, I didn't imagine Dad striding off to the nearby fields with anything that could wear a pink bow in its head, needed a coat in winter, and could dress up for Halloween. Dad had been enjoying this game. I didn't believe he would act that way if he wasn't extremely satisfied with Mum's choice.

When the car pulled into the driveway, Mum emerged clutching something swaddled in a plaid blanket, tucked tight into her body, as though she half expected to get jostled by paparazzi and needed to ensure the creature's anonymity.

"Fiona, they're back," I shouted upstairs, not even expecting a reply and therefore surprised to hear feet bounding down the stairs as she ran to join me.

I opened the door for them and stepped back, Dad beaming, Mum behind him, turning slightly away from me and my sister as she tried to heighten the tension. It was like watching an *American Idol* finale and there's Ryan Seacrest flaunting the sealed envelope with the winner's name at the camera and you just want to slap him upside the head, grab the envelope, rip it open, and find out who won.

Bess was in my arms, lost to a place where well-fed fat bellies and sleep rule. I watched as my mother crouched down and slowly lowered the contents of her blanket (which I noticed were covered in patches of milky puke) to the carpeted floor.

"Here you go," she said, beaming in a way that was so surprising, so unexpected, it was all the more affecting. "Here's Whiskey."

And out trotted a golden retriever.

Whiskey was male, twelve weeks old and, to my way of thinking, more blond than golden. He too was christened by my father, on the basis of his most obvious traits.

"He was soft, gold, and had plenty of spirit."

Unfortunately, the term *spirit* was being applied to behavior that most people would define as destructive or willful. Whiskey was endowed with a dangerous combination of good looks, rolls of squishy, cherubic puppy fat, unlimited tail-wagging charm, and a drive that kept him pushing forward, stopping at nothing when it came to inappropriate chewing, brawling with Bess, and general domestic destruction. He quickly asserted himself as the alpha to Bess's beta, and you can get a sense of his curb appeal if I tell you that at our first meeting even Fiona rushed forward, picked him up, and cradled him in her arms, applying a lipstick bindi, a red third eye in the center of his broad golden forehead.

Hindsight is like an annoying colleague who always speaks up after the fact, tapping you on the shoulder with a cocky smile, a knowing look, and the phrase "Told you so." Hopefully we learn from hindsight for the next time because, by definition, the time for its usefulness has already passed. Now, having spoken to a number of animal behaviorists, I know that some of Whiskey's "spirited" personality traits were related to his age at the time of his adoption. Bad habits in puppies can already be deep-seated at eight weeks. They are by no means irreversible, but by twelve weeks the window of opportunity for meaningful correction is already beginning to close. These days, it's unusual to pick up a puppy as late as three months from a reputable dog breeder. My father, a man with a less than stellar track record when it came to dog training and socialization, was already, unwittingly, behind the curve.

Whiskey required constant puppy patrol. We always had to be ready with a paper towel, and alert to possible household hazards — electric cables, telephone cords, VCR tapes, potted plants, the list goes on and on. Sure, I did my share of prying tiny teeth off chair and table legs, fed Bess and Whiskey, and shooed them into the back-yard, eager to gush over a timely and ap-propriately placed bowel movement, but I was distracted by the academic demands of high school, given what I would need to achieve in order to have a shot at veterinary school.

"Feel free to give Bess or Whiskey the once-over whenever you want to get some practice," said Dad. This was the first time he had used the term *once-over* and it would not be the last. I think Dad put it out there as something I might enjoy doing, good preparation, a useful learning experience. But part of me felt as though I now had an obligation, a new role to fulfill as his personal veterinarian. I had observed Ryan James performing his ritualistic physical exam dozens of times and Dad glowed as I tried to mimic his routine. I didn't own a stethoscope, not that I would have known what I was listening to, but I could pry open their mouths, squeeze their bellies, and bicycle their limbs. Bess and Whiskey were in perpetual motion, running, squirming in my hands, resistant and mouthy. I didn't know what I was doing, what I was feeling for, what was normal and what was not. For me it was an exercise in futility, but though my dad said nothing, the glint in his eyes told me he liked what he saw and, more important, what it would surely mean for the dogs in his future.

Whiskey had been with us for less than two weeks when the woman formerly known as my mother struck again.

"I'm going to take Whiskey to school with me. The kids are dying to see him and so is Mrs. Peacock."

Mrs. Peacock was the school's headmistress and if Mrs. Peacock and the kids knew about Whiskey, Mum must have been bragging about how impossibly cute and chubby and cuddly he was. The aliens had done a fine job.

Dad looked worried.

"I'm not so sure that's a good idea. He's not finished with his shots. I spoke to Mr. James and he suggests keeping them both away from other dogs and people who have dogs until he's fully vaccinated."

"Oh, Duncan, don't be so silly, he'll be fine."

And with that she headed off to her car with a golden fur ball tucked under her arm.

We thought no more of it. Later Mum came home from her day at work sporting something akin to a golden retriever bounce in her stride, working hard not to gloat over all the admiration her choice of dog had reaped. Whiskey, on the other hand, seemed beat, content but exhausted after, what for him, must have been a big day, handling his fans, working crowds, and delivering pleasantries.

Two days later I was about to head out to school when we saw the first sign of trouble.

"Careful," I said, reaching for a paper towel. "Which one of them has thrown up?"

Someone had deposited a silver-dollar-sized dollop of frothy, yellow-green vomit on the kitchen linoleum.

"I'm pretty sure it's Whiskey," said Dad and I noticed how he had instinctively turned down the decibels.

"Really," I said. "Do you think it has something to do with his trip to . . . ?"

Mum walked into the kitchen.

"What?" she said.

Dad and I were clearly busted, so I came clean.

"Dad thinks Whiskey is throwing up because you took him with you to your school."

I grinned. Dad grimaced.

"Oh, it's probably nothing," replied Mum. "You used to throw up at the drop of a hat. I'm sure Whiskey will be fine."

If Mum was worried about being even remotely responsible for Whiskey's first brush with sickness, she hid it well and to be fair, the fat little fellow seemed relatively chirpy. It wasn't until I came home from school that I saw reality take a bite out of her apparent indifference.

"Mum, what's wrong?"

I'd walked through the front door to find Mum speaking into the phone, tears drying on her cheek. Her mouth moved, emitting a slow series of yeses and noes, but the words weren't connected to the panic dancing in her eyes.

"Thank you," she said, and hung up. Mechanically she turned to face me.

"Whiskey is at the vet's. That was Mr. James. He says Whiskey needs emergency surgery. Right now!"

5.
THE WEIGHT OF HEALING

The news went from bad to worse.

It turned out Dad had checked in on Whiskey at lunchtime, found him listless and unresponsive, and rushed him straight over to see Ryan James. In different circumstances, office manager Arthur Stone might have quipped over the novelty of my father failing to create chaos in the waiting room with one of his pets, but any temptation to say something impish vanished as soon as he saw the pathetic creature Dad carried in his arms.

"He's dehydrated, Duncan," said James. "He's got a fever and his belly's very tender to the touch. Any chance he got into anything he shouldn't?"

Dad thought about the house, the ever-present possibility that an inquisitive puppy could get into trouble if he or she tried hard enough. And then he thought about the trip to the school. Who knew what Whiskey might have gotten into in a kindergarten classroom?

"Don't know," he said. "Don't think so."

Ryan James must have noticed the hesitation, the uncertainty. He backed up from the examination table on which Whiskey lay wrapped in a towel, unresponsive to his touch.

"Leave him with me. He needs some intravenous fluids and I'm going to want to take an X-ray of his abdomen. See if there's anything amiss inside."

A couple of hours later, Mum received a phone call telling her Whiskey's X-rays appeared to confirm that he had swallowed a ball.

"You can see it in his stomach," said James. "I'm pretty sure that's why he keeps being sick. The only way to get it out is surgery. And it's not going to be easy putting him under anesthesia. He's very weak and he's very young but I don't think we have much choice."

Mum had given her consent. James promised to call back when it was over. There was nothing left to do but wait, and — though Mum, Dad, Fiona, and I never said it out loud — pray.

There is no end to nightmare scenarios that

147

will leave a surgeon breathless: operating on the wrong patient; operating on the wrong leg; operating only to find there is nothing to find.

They call this last one the "negative exploratory," as if, by giving it a label, we can put some kind of a positive spin on an event that might otherwise be perceived as a disaster.

Invariably, it is nobody's fault. You take an X-ray and see something is clearly wrong with the intestines — a corn cob or a peach pit blocking a loop of small intestine. You take the dog to surgery and by the time you open your patient up, the obstruction has moved on, disappeared into the large intestine, the colon, from which it will be dispatched by the patient without a hitch. Time to call the owner and try to explain how the surgery turned out to be unnecessary.

Even in this era of fiber-optic endoscopy, our ability to insert a camera into the body and have a *Fantastic Voyage*–style look-see is restricted to only a small fraction of the very upper or lower portions of the gut. Sometimes veterinarians are forced to make a judgment call based on the limited available information, essentially what they see and feel, and faced with a deteriorating situation, they need to act, even if they risk being wrong.

I never saw the actual X-ray that sent Whiskey under the knife but I have a pretty good idea of what it looked like. Angle the X-ray beam just so, place the patient in a certain position, get the correct amount of fluid or solid in the outflow portion of the stomach (the area called the pylorus), and in cross-section a tube becomes a round, opaque structure identical to a solid ball. If this was what Ryan James saw when he held up his black-and-white image to the light, he was not the first to get it wrong, and not the last. In fact, he was probably one of hundreds, if not thousands, of veterinarians who, during this era, were seeing puppies succumbing to a mysterious, aggressive, and debilitating malady that frequently began with vomiting. These dogs were undergoing exploratory surgery and the veterinarians were finding distended, gassy loops of bowel and generalized intestinal inflammation, but nothing specific to account for the sickness. In many cases, if they had only waited a few more hours as the clinical signs progressed, they would have had their answer and a needless surgery would have been avoided.

Sometimes it feels like new diseases are a godsend for today's media, an opportunity to generate fear and redeem a slow or silly news day. SARS, chicken flu, swine flu, whatever the next pandemic scare, you can guarantee the twenty-four-hour news networks will be busy working on ways to make you panic and believe the apocalypse is happening now. On the whole, veterinary medicine doesn't pack the same media punch as its human counterpart, so back in 1978 the discovery of a new virus called canine parvovirus gained little attention. It took several years before this highly contagious virus got busy with Britain's canine population, but when it did, it had a field day, spreading easily by direct contact and indirectly via dog poop. At the time there was no vaccine, no herd immunity against an aggressive virus ready to attack a virginal unprotected canine population. Our Whiskey was destined to be one of Ryan James's first cases.

It is not the fever or the vomiting that clues the clinician in to a case of parvovirus, it is the bloody diarrhea. Sometimes it can take a while for the virus to have its way with the lining of the guts but once it does, what comes out of these wretched creatures is unique. Veterinarians, nurses, and kennel staff the world over will tell you nothing, and I mean nothing, smells quite like the stench of a dog with parvovirus diarrhea.

"It's not a ball in his stomach after all," said James, speaking to my father via telephone. "It's a new disease called parvovirus. I'm pretty sure of it. He broke with a horrible case of diarrhea."

"Can you treat it?"

"Not really. There's nothing we can actually do to stop the virus. The disease has to run its course. All we can do is provide intravenous fluids, stop him from getting dehydrated, and give him antibiotics to offset the possibility of infection."

Dad looked up, saw Mum and I hanging on every word of this one-sided conversation. He deliberated for a moment before asking, "Where would he have got it from?"

I felt Mum bristle next to me.

"Other dogs. The environment. From what I understand, the virus is tough and resilient, able to hang out in contaminated fecal material for a year, maybe more. Get it on your shoe and who knows how far it will spread. We're only just starting to see cases in the UK. This is the tip of the iceberg."

Dad had to sense Mum straining to overhear the answer. He closed his eyes and shook his head as if to let her know this had nothing to do with her. If he wondered about the day trip to school or the recent acquisition of Bess, a dog of unknown provenance, he never mentioned it out loud.

"What are his chances?"

Ryan James came straight back at him.

"I'll be honest, Duncan, they're not great. Untreated it is almost always fatal. I'm hoping we got to him soon enough to give the little man a fair shot. The next few days will be critical."

This was the line my father delivered — uncertainty, an uphill battle, but there was still a chance. The cost of all this care was never mentioned. Why would it be? Whiskey had been with us for little more than a week but he was already family.

For the next few days my father was our conduit to a drama playing out in a small cage, in a small veterinary hospital a couple of miles away. An innocent creature had been taken down by an invisible killer, attacking him from the inside out, sucking the life from a dog who wanted nothing more than to play and engage and be happy. Dad spoke to Ryan James at least twice a day, sometimes more, getting an update, riding the emotional seesaw of a disease that kept you bracing for the worst and hoping for the best. The hospital was not a twenty-four-hour facility, but Ryan James would check on Whiskey in the middle of the night, make sure his fluids were running on time, change the bloody and soiled bedding, dropper some fresh water into his dry and parched mouth. Dad even had James's unlisted home phone number and was invited to call for a final update every night before bed.

That week all of us were on tenterhooks every time the phone rang and then one morning a call came in before I left for school. We were all gathered in the kitchen when Fiona picked it up.

"Just one minute please," she said. And then, "Dad, it's for you. It's Ryan James."

Ryan had never called at this early hour. In fact it was always the other way round, Dad calling him.

Reluctantly Dad picked up the handset and, as if he already knew what he was going to be told, he braced for the worst, his words softening, decelerating before they fell out of his mouth.

"Yes. Yes. Yes. I understand. This afternoon. Yes. Thank you for everything."

It must have been the state of shock overwhelming his speech, because he looked up and was taken aback when he saw the angst and disappointment written all over our faces. Only then did he smile and realize his mistake.

"It's okay. He's rallied. Whiskey's going to be fine. Mr. James says we can pick him up this afternoon."

The news of Whiskey's recovery instantly erased the pall that had hung over all of us. I'm not suggesting there was fist-pumping or high fives or that Duncan cracked open the champagne. But it was definitely more than relief. It felt as though we could finally allow ourselves to let this dog into our hearts and imagine a future with him.

Dad and I drove over to Ryan's practice, thrilled to be reclaiming our golden retriever, having not seen him for over a week.

Nothing could have prepared us for what we found when we got there. We hadn't known Whiskey for very long, but the Whiskey we had first met, the chubby, love-handled, boisterous, fresh, golden ball of terror, was gone. He was no more. In his place was a gangly, leggy, dazed, and tentative creature that bore him no resemblance whatsoever. In the moment he wobbled into the waiting room to greet us I saw how close we had come to losing him, how beating parvovirus had sapped every ounce of energy and fight this ballsy little puppy possessed. All that was left was a golden husk still in need of significant nursing to get him back to full strength.

"I didn't think he was going to make it, Duncan," said James. "But one thing's for sure about this new dog of yours, he's a lion-hearted little fellow. No two ways about it."

And as Dad pumped Ryan's hand, I witnessed a mixture of gratitude and pride welling up in my father's eyes, triggered by the shock of what his dog had become, and by the fitting label "lion-hearted little fellow."

Here, for the first time, in this moment, it seemed all so personal, this business of healing pets, the way veterinary medicine can have such a profound effect on both humans and animals. Naturally, hanging out with James, I had observed the response of countless grateful owners, but here, with everything so close, with my dad and Ryan James, it was as if I could straddle both sides of the doctor–patient relationship, breathe in the sense of accomplishment, the power of what James had done, completely tangible and within reach. It was awesome. I just stood there speechless and ate it up.

Lion-hearted little fellow!

It wasn't long, though, before remnants of the old Whiskey began to resurface — trying to steal Bess's food, barreling her out of the way in order to be first through an open door, and, as testosterone began to kick in, a tentative experiment in meaningful mounting.

Unfortunately Whiskey's resurgence coincided with the appearance of some objectionable traits related to male dominance and what worried me most was the way his early brush with death was being used as some sort of a defense for his most unsavory misogynistic behavior. In short, my mum and dad were acting like the ineffective parents of a kid trapped in the terrible twos, crying out for a *Supernanny* makeover. While I was lost in the nuances of quadratic equations, organic isomers, and Faraday's law of electromagnetic induction, they were enabling their new "golden" boy to get away with murder. Whiskey may not have possessed the same protective streak as Patch, but his manners were already on a slippery slope, and he was likely to wind up with similar social foibles if we weren't more careful.

"I'm taking Bess in to see Ryan James on Monday," announced my father. "It's time to get her fixed."

"Why Bess," I said, "why not get Whiskey neutered instead, or even, as well as?"

Dad practically chuckled at my naiveté.

"Now, son," he said, bending down to tickle his prodigal son's belly, "remember what Mr. James said, parvovirus can cause damage to his heart. It's not worth the risk of a general anesthetic unless absolutely necessary. He may be a lion-hearted little fellow, but we still need to handle him with kid gloves."

By now both Fiona and I had moved well beyond rolling our eyes in response to what had quickly shifted from an endearing to an irritating line. We had heard it so many times, essentially whenever Dad gushed over his golden, which was often. Please, I wouldn't want you to think he played favorites. He doted equally on Bess. It was just that Whiskey always seemed to earn an excuse for his shenanigans. Stealing dirty socks from the laundry basket was simply a retrieval exercise. When he chewed the corner of one of my textbooks it was my fault for leaving it accessible on the bedroom floor. To me, it always seemed as though Bess got a hasty trial and a stern sentence, and she was a smart dog, quick to learn a valuable lesson. Whiskey, meanwhile, appeared to be blessed with the canine equivalent of diplomatic immunity, untouchable, as if his behavioral blunders were justified as merely rascally or acceptably rakish.

And so, despite my protestations, it was poor Bess who sacrificed her uterus and ovaries in order to avoid procreation, while frisky Whiskey got to retain his gonads. The "Labra-triever" threat had gone away, but, as Mum and Dad were about to discover, there can be other consequences to preserving a dog's virility.

The old and familiar habit of early morning walks had started up again. There was more to it than ritual and dusting off the obligatory flat cap, walking stick, and Wellington boots. To Dad it simply felt right, no better way to begin each day. This time, however, with Whiskey and Bess, his justification for getting up at four in the morning was quite different from the transparent excuses he had made with Patch. From his humble beginnings as a TV repairman he had ultimately attained his goal of becoming a lecturer in electrical engineering, but on those bottom rungs of the academic ladder, this meant working unsociable hours and included teaching night classes. He was determined to give "the pups" (a label all his dogs kept even into their dotage) at least a two-hour walk in the morning, knowing there wouldn't be much time (or inclination) when he finally came home from work.

To my surprise Dad began straying far from those nearby open fields of my childhood, choosing a lengthy, somewhat convoluted route around town that included playing fields and public gardens. Why change a formula that worked so well with Patch? The only possible explanation I could come up with was his pride in the better-socialized behavior of these new pups. Dad might have been hanging on to their leashes like the reins of a runaway stage coach when Bess and Whiskey insisted on saying hello, but embarrassing vocal standoffs, wrinkled lips, and displays of dental prowess were rarely a problem with this duo.

To her credit, even when off leash, Bess was a dog who preferred to stay close. She might meander a little, succumb to an olfactory distraction, but on the whole she preferred to maintain an even pace, slightly ahead, wanting to be companionable, to make every walk a walk shared. Whiskey, however, liked to roam, a golden ghost disappearing into the wall of darkness, trotting back into formation when he felt like it. Only on this particular occasion, he didn't feel like it.

Given the early hour and the close proximity to a housing development, my father dared no more than name-calling through clenched teeth, a worthless theatrical whisper. A couple of extra turns around the field were also unsuccessful in retrieving his retriever.

"Bess, go get your brother. Go get Whiskey. Go on. Go get him."

Bess did not move, did not reply, but with her eyes and the slight cant of her head I like to imagine she said, "Now you wish you'd got him neutered, don't you!"

"Bark, Bess. Bark for your brother."

Again, Bess did not reply. She had been cursed with an exceptionally shrill bark and was probably confused by the mixed signal of actually being encouraged to let it rip. Like I said, Bess was a quick study.

And so, with only one dog in hand, my father walked the three miles back home, wondering how on earth he was going to break the news to his wife.

"Morning, dear."

"What time is it? Why are you waking me up so early?"

"Here you go, here's a nice cup of tea for you."

"It's five-thirty in the morning. It's still dark outside. What's going on?"

"Glad you asked, dear. Glad you asked. See, here's the thing. Oh, don't let your tea go cold."

"Duncan! What in God's name have you done?"

Knowing my parents, I'll bet this is how things played out before my father finally fessed up to "misplacing" my mother's beloved golden retriever. I'll leave the choice rejoinders to your imagination as Mum grabbed some clothes and together they set off in the car to retrace the walk.

Two and a half hours later there was still no sign of him. Dawn had come and gone, commuters hitting the streets on foot and in cars. Mum and Dad had split up, accosted and interviewed every passerby, hollered Whiskey's name with abandon and all without success.

"We have to go to the police," said Mum, "and report him missing. See if anyone has found him. Tell me he was wearing his collar with the name tag."

Remember, this was long before microchips or collars with GPS. Whiskey was a pure-bred golden retriever, ridiculously friendly, irresistibly attractive. Name tag or not, the possibility of "finders keepers" had already crossed my mother's mind.

"Description?" said the police constable manning the front desk, just a kid but surprisingly tuned in, sensing the seriousness of my parents' loss. "Male, you said.

And has he been fixed?"

My father dropped his eyes and shook his head. How could this have happened? It was so unnecessary, so stupid. What if Whiskey was hit by a car? How could the dog have survived a bout of parvovirus only to be lost on his watch, after, of all things, going for a walk? Mum was still sensitive about the whys and wherefores of the acquisition of Patch. He couldn't imagine the fallout for his negligence over the loss of Whiskey.

"Very good, sir. I think we have everything we need. I'll be sure to call if anything comes up."

Dad heard the *if* and thanked the officer, and he and Mum headed home.

"Where are you going?"

Dad had veered off the direct route back to the house and was once more headed to the playing field where Whiskey had vanished.

"Duncan, we've done this three times already. Let's face it, he's gone."

"But what if we missed something?"

"What sort of something? A trail of paw prints? A discarded dog collar?"

Dad said nothing but he thought about a different type of clue, a far more sinister indication of what might have happened — a trail of blood.

162

Once more they pulled into the parking lot, got out of the car, and set off in opposite directions around the field. On the far side of the field, clockwise met counterclockwise, Dad saying nothing, Mum offering a futile shake of her head. They both called Whiskey's name, but by the time they were back at the car, the desperation in their voices had given way to resignation.

"Okay," said Dad, turning the key in the ignition. "Let's go home."

He found reverse and checked the rearview mirror, and then something bright caught his eye.

At first my father thought nothing of it, a glint of sunlight perhaps, until the golden streak drifted in from the periphery, shapeshifting in the reflected image and finally bounding toward them as a golden retriever.

"If a dog can smile," said Dad when he relayed the story, "and I believe they can, then Whiskey had a huge smile on his face."

Watching their reunion, great big golden bear paws forgiven for trying to jump into Mother's lap, tail thumping back and forth, Whiskey whinnying in delight like a horse, you might have been forgiven for thinking the three of them had been apart for a decade, not the last four hours.

"Of course you know why he wandered?"

I said to my father.

Dad dropped down on one knee to give Whiskey a hug around his neck followed by a conspiratorial wink.

"Now then, son, boys will be boys. It's quite possible a 'lady friend' was involved but then again he's never done anything like this before, have you, fella?"

And with this Dad roughed up Whiskey's head, loose skin falling over his eyes, just the way he liked it.

My attempt to challenge this antiquated, irrational absolution was waved away, and sadly, at the time, I lacked the academic tools to argue my point, to caution about the increased incidence of intact male dogs who get hit by cars and who sustain and deliver bite wounds interacting with other like-minded Casanovas as they desperately sniff out a receptive conquest.

"I still think it would be best to get him neutered," I said, and hurried off before he could even utter the word *lion-hearted.*

Though Whiskey would never succumb to castration, when another elective but necessary surgical procedure became unavoidable, the dark side of his personality began to emerge.

Where Bess was prone to embarrassing

and immodest disorders of her anal sacs, Whiskey was a victim of tenacious and pesky ear infections. While Bess would scoot, Whiskey would shake, scratch, and rub, and this led us to a rendezvous with Ryan James.

Unfortunately, my father had made the mistake of reveling in the improved social propriety of his new dogs with office manager Arthur Stone. After all, both dogs had become quite well mannered in the public domain. However, after only a few visits for nothing more than the occasional shot and general health examination, Whiskey began to object to any interaction in which he sensed the possibility of a veterinarian's touch.

"I'm sorry, Mr. James. I don't know what's come over him."

Ryan James looked down at where he hoped his hand would still be.

"No harm done," said James. "I think Whiskey might be starting to associate a visit to his veterinarian with unpleasant memories from his past."

To be honest, I'm not sure I bought into this excuse. I think Whiskey was used to being the top dog, to getting his way, and he disliked any situation in which he had to relinquish his power. Whatever the reason, my father had once again lost face, another dog in the Trout file about to be given the damning label of "difficult."

So, veterinary visits began to take on a format surprisingly similar to that followed in the days of Patch. The car was preferable to the waiting room. Arthur Stone would wave to Duncan from afar when the time was right and the dogs would be seen separately. Bess, bless her heart, was nervous (according to my father, tuned in to Whiskey's fears), but quietly accepted her fate. Whiskey, however, quickly advanced from anxious to deranged, inconsolable, and unmanageable to an extent that made Patch look as if he graduated top of his class from obedience school.

"Give him one of these and we'll see how he's doing in twenty minutes."

Dad recognized the little orange pills, the ones he had occasionally used to sedate Patch, worked one into the back of Whiskey's throat, and returned to the car, waiting for the drug to kick in.

"How're we doing?" said James, walking over to Dad's car.

Dad came round to the passenger door, and Whiskey bounded out of the backseat. He didn't appear to be the least bit sleepy.

"Might need one more of those tablets,

Duncan. Let's see if that does the trick in another half hour."

In the end Whiskey required three little orange tablets to send him to a place where his struggle to avoid veterinary contact was damped down enough for Ryan James to define the problem.

"No wonder the poor dog's upset to be touched. His ears are infected, rubbed raw, and he's got an aural hematoma in his right one."

Ryan read the puzzled expression on Dad's face.

"It's like a big blood blister between the layers of cartilage in the pinna, the floppy part of his ear. He's been shaking his head hard enough to burst some of the blood vessels in there. I'm afraid he's going to need a quick anesthesia to drain it. And I know what you're thinking, Duncan, worrying about the risk of putting him under general anesthesia, but I don't think we have much choice. He needs some relief from the pain and I promise you, I'll be quick."

When Whiskey came home, he was wiped, lying flat out on the living room floor like a trophy from some Kenyan safari. He looked as though those sedative pills he had been fighting had finally kicked in. I noticed that his eyes appeared to be completely red, as if he were wearing opaque pink contacts, making him look eerie, even demonic.

"What's with his eyes?" asked Fiona.

"It's his third eyelids," said Dad.

Fiona's wrinkled nose told him he needed to explain.

"Apparently dogs and cats have this pink, skinlike thing that can flick across the surface of the eye and help keep it clean. Mr. James warned me that anesthetic drugs can make the third eyelid more prominent but they should be back to normal in the morning."

"Ah . . ." said Fiona, getting down on her hands and knees, about to plant a kiss on Whiskey's nose. ". . . I still think you're . . ."

And that was as far as she got before Whiskey snapped at her face, canines and incisors missing her cheek by millimeters, the sound of enamel on enamel lingering in the shocked silence before Fiona's scream.

The combination of Fiona's hasty desire to attend to her sick retriever and my father's tardiness in mentioning that Ryan James had insisted nobody get too close to Whiskey's face could have proved disastrous. Protruding third eyelids can seriously impede a dog's ability to focus on an object, especially an object rushing into his personal space. Fight or flight kicks in and when your legs feel unresponsive, there's not much left but to stand your ground and offer up your teeth.

In time, Fiona would come to understand this explanation, but I sensed her fragile appreciation for dogs had been crushed. Her face may have been spared a permanent and disfiguring scar but deep down a different kind of mark had been made.

It was years before I discovered the real reason why my father was avoiding the convenience of our magnificent nearby countryside and choosing instead to take the dogs on tortuous treks around town. It all came down to the one set of circumstances in which trusty Bess came undone while Whiskey maintained a sense of decorum.

The open fields, hedgerows, and copses that defined my childhood memories of walking Patch were largely the property of one farmer, a Mr. Jack Shepherd, and most of his land was given up to grazing for about eighty head of cattle. The edges of the fields were well trodden, indicative of plenty of traffic taking advantage of the public right-of-way. The route was clearly labeled and posted, and it was our legal right to "pass and repass," to have a picnic, to take a rest

169

and cherish the view, but, and this is important, you had to "stay on the path."

By and large, my father obeyed the rambling rules, keeping both dogs on a leash, but one day Bess decided to slip her restraint, toss aside her goody-two-shoes image, and look for some premium mischief.

The cows, all big black-and-white Friesians, were over on the other side of the field, drifting toward a gate that would lead them down a path to the milking parlor and the promise of early-morning relief. Most of them had their heads down, still working on great clumps of grass or chewing the cud until this little black demon appeared, darting among them, whooping it up with her piercing and interminable bark. She made no attempt to bite them and her efforts to round them up were pretty pathetic but she clearly found them irresistible. Despite the disparity in size, Bess's speed and fly-by barking were making all the cows extremely nervous.

Dad acted quickly, tethering Whiskey to the trunk of a tree, taking no note of the retriever's expression, which surely said, "See, it's not just me!" By the time he had run into the center of the field, with at least a hundred yards between him and Bess, an old forest green Land Rover was pulling up to the gate and from the driver's seat emerged the farmer, Jack Shepherd. Dad saw him reach into the passenger seat of his vehicle and grab something long and metallic that glinted in the morning light. Even from where Dad stood, he knew exactly what it was. It was written in the way the man carried the object folded across his chest, in the precise expression contorting his ruddy face as he fought down the anger, savoring his power and the certainty that he could make all this fuss instantly disappear. By the time the gate began to swing back on its hinges, farmer Jack Shepherd had two cartridges slipped into each barrel of his shotgun.

"Wait!"

The cows were charging back and forth, bellowing, spraying up mud, fear in their huge brown eyes, and Bess was lapping it up, coursing from one to the next, buzzing and completely unreachable.

"Wait!"

Dad was screaming, breathless, closing in as the man in the distance squared his stance, pulling the stock of the gun tight into his shoulder as the barrel came level, eyes narrowing down the sights.

Bess saw the man, or maybe she felt his presence, the aura of someone who would stand his ground, and this stopped her in her tracks. Dad watched as the man pivoted ever so slightly, focusing on Bess's chest, ready to fire both barrels, the kill certain to be quick and clean, so long as she stood still.

"You know as well as I do," said the farmer, his words slightly distorted by his brawny fingers as they slipped inside the trigger guard next to his right cheek. "I'm well within my rights to shoot. Dog off a leash, frightenin' my cows. No questions asked."

Maybe it was the exhaustion of the run across the field, or maybe it was fear and the absolute certainty that Jack Shepherd would pull the trigger and walk away, taking his cows off to milking without a second thought. Whatever the reason, my father crumpled at the knees, collapsing to the ground, ready to plead and beg for his dog's life.

"I know," said Dad, sounding as though the round had already been fired, as though Bess were already dead. "I know it's your legal right to do it. But it was an accident. Somehow she slipped her leash. Look. There's my other dog, tied up to a tree."

The barrel never moved and neither did Bess, but Dad noticed how a squinting eye relaxed, looked away, followed the direction in which my father was pointing and found a golden retriever tethered in place.

Later Dad told me that in that moment, waiting to hear the blast, he thought he understood the man with his finger on the trigger. He sensed that any attempt to argue would have been a mistake.

The moment stretched, lingered, reached its silent crescendo, and came to an end, the barrel slowly lowered.

Neither man spoke, but the farmer cracked open the breech of the shotgun, pulled out the shells, and walked back to his truck. Leaving the weapon behind, Mr. Shepherd began herding the cows, compressing them into one corner of the field. This forced Bess to tighten her circles, eventually giving Dad a chance to hurl himself in her direction and grab her.

He didn't tell her off. He didn't curse her out. Dad held on tight to her scruff, reattached her leash and turned to Jack Shepherd, giving him the kind of resolute stare that transmits gratitude and a tacit appreciation of a stranger's gift, a second chance he thought he might not get.

"Sometimes," said Dad when he arrived home and relayed the story, " 'a still tongue makes a wise head.' "

I considered him with furrowed brow.

"Did you just steal a line from James Herriot?"

Dad affected outrage that gave way to a smile.

Not that it really mattered. Diplomacy may have saved the day, but this kind of incident could never happen again. This was, after all, farming country, where tolerance of and respect for livestock were mandatory. Bess's bovine obsession would be a difficult flaw to work around. Once again my father had been made acutely aware of his failings when it came to the appropriate socialization of one of his dogs.

By now, you will have noticed that my connection with Bess and Whiskey was quite different from my connection to Patch. Please appreciate that I did cherish their place in our family, loved the notion of having dogs (plural) jostling for leashes and open doors, padding around and bookending me on a sofa, faking toothy snarls and throaty growls, hamming it up as they acted out their pretend dogfights. Their presence reestablished the natural order of things and best of all, these two disparate creatures had slipped in effortlessly, eased our family gracefully back into the world of

174

dogs. At that time of my life, hoping to head off to college, there was a certain solace in knowing a familiar domestic harmony would fill my absence. It was like slipping on a pair of jeans, a wallet in my left-hand pocket, a set of keys in my right, the comforting awareness of a precise personal balance. Whiskey and Bess had become this kind of combination — they felt just right.

In order to study and properly prepare for my final high school examinations I decided to become a total recluse. Though this meant abandoning my friends and our preliminary forays into underage drinking on a Saturday night, in truth I missed out on very little. For the record, in England the legal age for purchasing and/or consuming alcohol is eighteen, and back then no one carried a photo ID. In other words, one's ability to walk into a pub and order "a pint of your best bitter, my good man" came down to whether or not you *looked* old enough. Rightly or wrongly (obviously wrongly when discussing the dangers of alcohol with my own kids) this "talent" set in when I was just fifteen years old. So, for some time, and long before we could drive (in Britain you cannot begin to learn to drive until you are seventeen), Nigel, myself, and two other "mates," Simon and Phil, would stroll downtown in order to familiarize ourselves with the effects of hops- and yeast-based beverages. Simon and Phil were friends from our days together as Boy Scouts, an organization we all abandoned pretty much as soon as we discovered girls. And please, I am at pains to point out that by *discovered* I mean "became aware of" rather than "achieved any measure of familiarity with." We were all horrendously inept around the opposite sex. Pimples, fashion faux pas, and a slew of dreadful one-liners guaranteed every evening concluded in much the same manner: wandering back to Nigel's house in order to raid his mother's refrigerator, watch old horror movies starring Christopher Lee and Vincent Price, and explain away the inadequacies of our earliest attempts at "chasing the birds."

Now, I think you can appreciate that I wasn't really giving up all that much to study for my final examinations — the ones that would determine whether I would be accepted to veterinary school or not; the ones that would determine whether my future and my dreams converged. In the midst of my cramming Dad came to me with a proposition.

"We were thinking of taking a short vacation, son. A family vacation, before you go away to college."

A self-absorbed teenager, fearful of being parted from friends or missing out on some momentous social event, I viewed the offer as an invitation to vacation at a maximum-security prison, with Mum, Dad, and Fiona my chatty cell mates.

"What about the dogs?" I offered, playing to a weakness, rummaging for an excuse.

"I know," said Dad, "we won't all fit in our little car but Grandma says she'd be chuffed to look after them."

"What! Marty will think it's Christmas — devour Bess, realize he has room for seconds, polish off Whiskey. You know he will."

"Now, son. Marty's not the dog he used to be, and besides, you know as well as me, Whiskey and Bess are usually fine around other dogs."

"But Marty isn't just another dog. You might as well suggest a sleepover with a canine version of Jack the Ripper. He'll be munching on Whiskey's throat like it's corn on the cob as fast as you can say 'jugular'!"

Dad pursed his lips.

"If I didn't know better I'd think you didn't want to go."

I thought about this. We never went on family vacations. If my father wanted to go somewhere requiring more than one tank of gas, if he was prepared to be separated from his dogs, this trip had to be important.

"Where are we going?"

Dad smiled his crooked smile.

"Surprise," he said. "Just you focus on your studies."

And I did, drowning in factoids and formulas, devouring textbooks, finally getting my chance to prove I had learned something as I embarked on a series of written examinations testing everything I had studied for the past two years in the subjects of math, chemistry, biology, and physics. And when the proctor said, "Ladies and gentlemen, please put your pens down" for the last time, I walked home and took off my uniform, and my high school career had officially come to an end. These days I have noticed that Nobel Prize and Academy Award winners have more understated celebrations than most high school graduates, and I don't mean to sound all "bah, humbug" and crotchety, but back in England, in my day, there was no prom, no formal graduation ceremony, no yearbook, no certificate, no gown, no "Pomp and Circumstance," no hail of mortarboards, no nothing. All that remained was time. We wouldn't find out our examination results for two months. A full eight weeks stretched before me with little else to do but stew about my final grades. Veterinary school had offered me a place so long as I made the grades. Any combination of three A's and one B and I was golden. Anything less and I was screwed. Not a lot of margin for error and room for an eternity of doubt. Suddenly a family vacation seemed like a welcome distraction from this inexorable countdown.

As soon as we began to head north up the M1 motorway, I had a pretty good idea where we were going.

"The town of Bedale," said my mother, quoting from a tourist guidebook, "is like walking up 'the garden path' to the Yorkshire Dales. From there it's a short drive to the market town of Leyburn, and now, you are at 'the front door.' Step beyond this threshold and Herriot Country lies ahead."

Obviously I was tempted to challenge the pushy realtor analogies, curious to discover "the kitchen" and, more important, "the lavatory," but I kept my mouth shut. Both my parents appeared to be captivated by the surroundings, overcome, and I sensed this journey had become the veterinary equivalent of a trip to Mecca. They had finally made it to their Holy Land, and to be fair, as our little car dropped down into the winding roads of Wensleydale, space expanded and stretched, my eyes filled with hills and valleys, all blanketed by an immense, verdant, patchwork quilt subdivided by dry stone walls, and it was hard not to be impressed. I managed stunned silence and Mum and Dad seemed pleased.

There followed several days of sightseeing and it didn't take long before Fiona and I realized what was happening.

"Do I recognize that house?" I asked.

We were standing on a cobblestone street in the village of Askrigg, staring at what appeared to be a large three-story brick building guarded by black wrought-iron railings.

"That's Skeldale House, son. Remember?"

"Skeldale House," I thought. "First official residence of one James Herriot."

Now I saw it. As I sidled into position for a photo op, I realized we were crisscrossing a trail blazed by the original production assistants from the TV series *All Creatures Great and Small* as they scouted the perfect locations for each scene. We moved on to the Drover's Arms, the ford through which Herriot's Austin 7 splashed in the opening sequence, Mrs. Pumphrey's Manor, Bolton Castle, and many more. My parents weren't just trying to visit Herriot country, they were trying to put me inside it, as though I might understudy James Herriot in every conceivable and memorable still from the show.

For a while I played along, unruffled by any fanatical undercurrent to our tour, genuinely enjoying the beauty of the countryside and the distraction from my exam results. Then on the Wednesday afternoon, my father asked me to join him on a trip to the nearby town of Thirsk.

"Someone I want you to meet," he said.

This time there was no attempt at surprise — the dozen or so American tourists burdened with newly purchased books and the brass plaque on the outside of the building were too much of a giveaway. And suddenly, there he was, shaking my hand, a surprisingly small, unassuming, even shy man, scratching his name on the page of a book with an arthritic hand — James Alfred Wight. Here was the real James Herriot, a man who had brought joy to countless millions of people all over the world, and what struck me more than anything else was how uncomfortable he appeared to be as the center of attention. He seemed to be astounded, almost embarrassed, as though it were completely new to him, as though his book had only just been published, and this obvious yet restrained humility was palpable. In my eyes, this common touch, this ability to be ordinary only made him all the more extraordinary.

It must have been my proximity to greatness that did it because on the drive back to meet up with Mum and Fiona, the fear of failing to make the grade got the better of me.

"What if I don't get in, Dad? What else am I going to do? Of course I can go and study genetics or animal husbandry but it's not as though I really want to. And you know, every time I was waiting to go and sit another examination there'd be some smart arse reminding me, 'Don't worry, Nick, you only have to get another A on this one.'"

My tone had shifted from one of reasonable concern to panic.

Now it should be said that my father tends to be cautiously optimistic, and by this I mean any predictions for some future outcome come prefaced with the phrase "touch wood" or "God willing." I half expected some watery platitude to tide me over.

"No matter what happens, son, I saw how hard you worked for those exams and there was nothing more to be done. That's all any parent can ask."

He was right. I had given it everything. There really was nothing more I could have done. Good answer, Dad, I thought.

"Besides," he said, "things always work out for the best."

And there it was, the trusty cliché I had anticipated.

Fortunately Dad didn't leave things hanging any longer.

"Your mother and I have some news."

Oh, God, I thought, after all those lectures on safe sex I was about to get a little brother or sister.

"We've decided to buy a house up here in the Dales. Actually it's more of a cottage — small, two bedrooms, one bathroom — but perfect for our needs. It will be a place for us in our retirement."

He waited a beat, took his eyes off the road, and glanced at me, trying to gauge my response.

To my left there was a field full of sheep. To my right there was a field full of cows. My mind flashed to an image of Bess and wondered where on earth this dog who had an unhealthy obsession with livestock would get some exercise. Then another thought struck me, one with far greater reach, with ramifications that could last a lifetime. What if this was all a ploy? This vacation, the sites we visited, the trip to see the real James Herriot, the purchase of a property in the middle of the Yorkshire Dales. Mum and Dad would retire in another decade or so and this would be where they would live. If I was lucky I would go to veterinary school, and in another decade or so I might be looking to settle down, to buy a practice of my own. I wondered which geographical location they might suggest. I wondered who might get to play the part of Arthur Stone, the venerated office manager, the man who made it happen, who made sure the "veterinary" fixed your animal up. In that instant I took a disjointed collection of stars and made a constellation. I had been groomed for this opportunity — inspired by James Herriot, with a chance to live the life of James Herriot. As far as my dad was concerned, the stars were beginning to align.

"That sounds great, Dad," I said, looking back at him, keeping the uncertainty out of my smile.

6.
TRYING TO LEARN AND LEARNING TO TRY

Six years in six minutes. That's pretty much what it felt like, thanks to time's knack of flying when you're having fun. One day I was a boy, rudely awakened by a man smiling into his tears, yanking me upright in my pajamas, hugging me to his chest as he whispered, "You did it, son. You did it." The next I was a man in a long black gown clutching a piece of paper proclaiming my membership in the Royal College of Veterinary Surgeons.

Whiskey and Bess had been co-conspirators on that early-morning reconnaissance mission, visiting the front doors of my high school, where the examination results had been posted. Like most teenage boys, even on this particular morning, I was unlikely to get out of bed much before noon, so, in fairness to my hyperventilating father, I have to admit that his impatience to wake his bleary-eyed son with the good

185

news was perfectly reasonable. Besides, how angry could I possibly be?

The remaining few weeks before I headed off to college marked the end of an era for me with regard to the dogs. Whiskey and Bess were, according to my father, about to transition from mere pets to VIP patients with their own personal physician. I played along as we bought my first stethoscope, veterinary textbook, and rectal thermometer, excited by this prospect and convinced that by the end of my first term my hands would progress from performing meaningless patting to meaningful palpation through which I would divine life-saving information.

The University of Cambridge was less than a three-hour drive from where I lived, but given my upbringing, it may as well have been another planet. Ask the average English person their thoughts on Cambridge and responses will range from an eight-hundred-year-old bastion of learning that produced such great minds as Darwin, Newton, Wordsworth, and Hugh Laurie to a retreat for overprivileged toffs spending their days punting down the River Cam drinking champagne and reciting Keats. Imagine the backdrop to an episode of *Inspector Morse,* only prettier (sorry, Oxford) and dotted with far fewer fatalities. Then throw in lots of clever people on bicycles wearing Batman capes. You're taking every big fish from every high school in the country and depositing them all in the same pond — apex predators reduced to chum. It's an adjustment, but what struck me most was the way my classmates seemed so much more worldly than me. They had passports. They had taken gap years. Boarding school educations made them appear assured, their transition to life away from home painless. They were instantly natives of college life while I was a tourist. And living in a room overlooking a pristine grassy quad and a Georgian Gothic chapel didn't help matters. Raiding the refrigerator or taking a gamble on my mother's haute cuisine was replaced with formal dining, too much cutlery, and grace in Latin. I had no gift for small talk, my vocabulary was too provincial. I lacked political inspiration. I was tentative and self-conscious.

After a first week of failed friendships, we started to find kindred spirits. We freshmen began to click. We no longer felt as though everyone else was having a better time than we were. We relaxed into who we were and not who we thought we should be. After a month, I could confidently say to my professors if they offered a glass of sherry during our afternoon tutorials, "Dry, or sweet, Professor?"

Dessert and fish forks started to look different. Friends came over for coffee. Those blank spaces on my calendar began to disappear and by the end of that first term I left for winter break reluctantly and already eager to return.

"How 'bout giving the dogs a once-over?" asked Dad, almost as soon as my suitcase hit the floor.

Though I returned home for the holidays with little more than some basic physiology, some esoteric biochemistry, and some rudimentary anatomy, I gave it a shot, Bess as generous and tolerant as I would have expected, happy to lie on her side as I slowly worked my way through the muscles of the forelimb. I had discovered something soothing and wonderfully finite about anatomy, the way it was laid out before you, the answer in plain sight. You either knew it or you didn't, the ultimate proof of knowledge equating to power.

"This is the region of the omotransversarius muscle, which acts to bring the leg forward, arising from the distal portion of the scapular spine and extending all the way to the wing of the atlas."

Dad tried to be impressed, but it was obvious he was hoping for something more practical.

"You know," I said, "cats have a clavicle, a collar bone, but dogs don't. Whereas dogs have a bone in their penis and cats don't."

"Really?" said Dad, his face a parody of edification. "But are you finding anything amiss?"

Though Bess may have resembled our formalin-infused greyhound cadavers in terms of her temperament — she was completely malleable, savoring this newfangled Reiki spa treatment — her layer of seal-like insulation made it difficult to define the details in her structure.

"Not really," I said. "But it's going to be a few years before I get to all the relevant clinical stuff."

"Of course it is. Of course it is. Need to get the basics down first." And then, as if unable to help himself, "But what about our Whiskey?"

He was watching me, maybe testing me, waiting to see if I would try to excuse myself. I didn't hesitate. Crouching down, I beckoned to the big golden to come. Whiskey bounced over, incredulous that he had had to wait for his moment in the spotlight, loving to be roughed up, to shake and tousle his lion's mane before I spun him around and started scratching around his back and butt. Then, as he settled in, helpfully backing toward me, my hands began to change, fingers flexing, flat palms drifting away from his fur. My playful stroke became a clinical touch, probing, defining, and interpreting. I got a little more than five seconds before the smile vanished from his face and he shot around, snapping and growling in my direction.

"Hey, hey, we'll have none of that," I said, bouncing to my feet, taking Whiskey's head in my hands, and angling his skull to align our eyes and to let him see my disapproval. It was my turn to growl — a stern "no." But he was already back — Whiskey the pet, no longer Whiskey the patient — staring up at me with a "Lighten up, I'm just kidding. I save the serious stuff for the real vet, and let me tell you, you ain't no real vet."

Over the next six years I would continue to attempt a "once-over" with Whiskey, seeing how far I might get before he lost it, learning to sense that moment of hesitation when pleasure morphed into suspicion for a few seconds, and then he finally realized he was being played. To be fair to him, I was getting to listen to a few heartbeats, caressing a little spleen before he called time-out, and he never progressed to anything more than a growl or a bristle and quick about-face. I began to liken my once-over sessions with Whiskey to the pebble test performed by the late David Carradine on the TV show *Kung Fu.* Studying to be a vet might be a little different from studying to be a Shaolin monk, but "Grasshopper" would only have completed his mental and spiritual training when he could snatch the pebble from Master Po's hand. Maybe Whiskey was my Master Po, the pebble my full physical examination. Either I would get it done without his objection or he would try mauling me in the manner of a starving wolf. This would be my crowning achievement, my ultimate recognition as a professional and, clearly, "time for me to leave."

Inadvertently, visits home were honing my education. The dogs were proving to be an immutable reminder of the family life I used to know — and an era that had passed. Returning home can be awkward for any college-age kid. We spend our teenage years learning to be obnoxious and short with our parents. We prefer to confide in friends. We connive, we become reclusive, we strive to become remote. We may still have a little voice somewhere deep inside pleading, "Just keep loving me, I'll come back," but for the most part, coming home from college is like reaching for the end of an umbilical cord we worked so hard to cut. We enjoy the security, the lazy familiarity, but we have left the nest, proven our capacity for independence, and now demand the respect afforded adults. Whiskey and Bess had no interest in this petty convention and all its theatrics. One minute you were gone and the next you were back. They didn't mourn my departure, miss me, or anticipate my return. Enthusiastic or indifferent, they were a wonderfully reassuring constant, the perfect reminder that I was home, particularly as I clawed my way back from detached offspring and reprised the role of son. Besides, Dad made sure the dogs were never far from my thoughts. He refused to stop acting like a father, knowing that if you hold your hand out long enough, eventually your kids will try to grab it again. While I was at college he wrote to me every week, prattling on about the monotony of his life, about Mum's schoolwork and Fiona's desire to become a nurse, but there was always something about the dogs. It might be a minor health issue for me to research, but more often than not it was something trivial they had done, something they had encountered on their walks. Without fail, he always signed off on these letters with love and he always included Whiskey and Bess in the list of individuals sending this love my way. At the time it made me laugh, it made me embarrassed, but as soon as I softened, as soon I matured back into his son, I came to appreciate what he was saying — an endearing and magnanimous reminder of how family will always be the sum of its individual members, be they human or animal.

For me, becoming a veterinarian would take six years — three years of basic medical sciences with a hint of clinical relevance, two years of clinically relevant material with a hint of hands-on experience, and a final year of masquerading as a real doctor. Through all those hours of study, the necessary mistakes, repetition, and academic information soaking into my brain, the process of veterinary education successfully transfers essential skills and core knowledge to a receptive audience of animal lovers. However, when you think about it, all academic osmosis really does is create the possibility for higher learning, for experiences that resonate in a distinct voice rather than get lost in the murmur of background noise. During vacations, not only was I required to gain skills in all manner of animal handling — grooming horses, feeding pigs, herding sheep, and milking cows — but more important, I had to spend twenty-six weeks visiting veterinary practices around the country and trying to apply my book smarts to practical matters.

This didn't leave me much time to mooch off my parents or catch up on my *All Creatures Great and Small* trivia. Naturally I would check in with Ryan James from time to time, savoring my new status whenever he introduced me — "veterinary student," a title that sounded to my ears very prestigious and accomplished — but I also traveled all over the country, trying to gain exposure to as wide a variety of techniques, opinions, and styles of working with animals as possible.

In those early days (except when I was with Ryan) I was pretty much a wallflower, keeping my mouth shut, hesitant to ask the redundant question. I was all about observation — itchy Westie gets a shot of the milky liquid; lethargic Siamese gets a shot of the pink liquid; worms mean big brown tablets; shampoo and little white pills for fleas. I didn't know what anything was, I didn't know how anything worked or why it had been chosen, but before long, with about a 50 percent success rate, from a distance of six feet, without even touching the animal, I could prescribe likely cures with the best of them.

Of course this approach was a wholly unsatisfying guessing game, so I began edging away from the wall, mingling with pets and owners, helping to restrain fractious animals, offering to clip, shave, and prep animals for surgery, timing my questions, weighing their merit, and, most important of all, learning when to keep my mouth shut.

During this early period in my training, the veterinarian was always right. I never questioned a course of treatment or a diagnosis. I never witnessed a single encounter with an owner who challenged a medical decision, demanded a second opinion, or appeared bullied into a course of action they did not want to take. For all of us nonveterinarians standing in an examination room it was understood that every action was grounded in fact and experience, every action made in good and absolute faith. The same was true in the operating room. From time to time a cat or a dog would be diagnosed with an abdominal mass or a growth, something the vet picked up on palpation but could not isolate to a specific organ. Some owners would pursue surgery, an exploratory laparotomy, where the doctor would look around the abdomen, inspecting the organs hidden and lurking inside. I was introduced to the phrase "peek and shriek," a facetious colloquialism meant to reflect the surgeon's awe at what he or she might see, and to serve as a reminder that disease can be formidable, inoperable, and more than capable of besting their intentions to cut and cure. In the quest to separate benign from malignant, the surgeon will fall back on a number of simple guidelines: Is the tumor well encapsulated or does it invade surrounding tissue? Are the local lymph nodes swollen? Is there evidence of spread to other nearby organs? There are no absolutes in medicine: these questions can be helpful but objectivity can be over-whelmed by our instinctive reflex to reel and gawk at something that by its sheer size or ugliness has to be bad. Taking an intra-operative biopsy and waiting on the word of an in-house pathologist are luxuries few veterinary institutions have to this day and therefore, in many instances, the man or woman in the latex surgical gloves is forced to play God. I witnessed many cases in which an animal was simply woken back up, the mass deemed malignant and inoper-able, or in some cases, at the owner's request, the animal was put to sleep on the operating room table.

I have no reason to suspect that any of these decisions were wrong or inappropriate; however, I was struck by our inherent tendency toward pessimism and resignation based on how disease looked to the naked eye and how it made us feel. It got me to thinking, and about a decade or so later (okay, so I think slowly) I published a scientific article about a particular liver tumor that affects cats. Pull back the muscular curtains of the kitty's abdominal wall for your peek and this particularly unsightly growth will certainly get your attention. It's big, covered in cysts, invasive, butt ugly, and yet surprisingly benign. Catch your breath, cut it out, and most cats will return to leading a normal, healthy life. Believe me, it's not a scientifically earth-shattering publication, but I like to think a few veterinarians might have read it and, when next faced with something attached to a cat's liver that looks like an alien parasite, hesitated and decided to give the animal the benefit of their doubt.

Veterinarians the world over, far better ones than I, develop this uncanny knack for being able to root around in their long-term memory and dig out pertinent recollections for the benefit of future patients. Though it might feel like these cases play emotional hide-and-seek, details blurring until they get lost and eventually disappear, certain characteristics and minutiae somehow endure, all the more precious for having been found. As a fourth-year veterinary student, while I was doing the work experience thing in an unfamiliar small animal practice in East Anglia, Delilah, a black and tan smooth-coated dachshund made such a mark, though for the longest time I failed to appreciate her significance.

"I came home from work and found her like this at the bottom of the stairs."

Delilah's owner, a young woman in her late teens or early twenties, put her down on the floor, and after a moment's hesitation, Delilah began scampering around the room, racing over to say hello to me.

Though it pains me to admit it, I was still learning to get comfortable around small breeds of dog. Life with Patch, Whiskey, and Bess had predisposed me to a certain type of dog. Give me something big, intimidating, and boisterous and I was fine, but any dog that could be carried in the manner of a running back holding an American football gave me pause. It must have been a throwback to my experiences around Marty. I had trust issues — I found them difficult to read, flighty, likely to bite first and ask questions later. Delilah, however, belied my harsh generalizations. She was delightful, racing over, all smiles, eager to lick my outstretched hand, seemingly ignorant of the disastrous blow to her mobility. She wasn't walking so much as dragging herself across the tile floor, both back legs lifeless.

"And she was fine when you left her this morning?" asked the vet.

"Perfectly."

"And what time did you leave the house?"

The young woman looked a little thrown by the question

"Sevenish."

"What time did you get home?"

Kneeling down, the vet joined Delilah and me on the floor.

"I don't know, usual time, five thirty. As soon as I saw she couldn't walk we came straight over. Are her legs broken?"

The vet placed his hand under Delilah's tummy, offering support, trying to place her back legs into a normal position, then extending them like the legs of a folding card table only to discover that they had the consistency of palm-warm gummy bears, bendy and weak, incapable of supporting weight. And weight was something Delilah had in spades. She wasn't just a "sausage dog"; she was a "stuffed like a sausage" dog.

"Just distract her," the vet said to me, and I did, letting Delilah shatter my stupid myth about small dogs, as she charmed me with her perfectly timed lilting head movements, offering a look of disbelief if I stopped scratching under her chin for more than a second.

I watched as the vet pinched the toes of her back legs between his fingers before pulling a mean-looking surgical clamp from his pocket. He must have noticed how my eyes had become a little too wide.

"I'm just trying to work out how much sensation is left in her toes," he said by way of a justification as he crushed pads and black nails between the serrated metal tips.

In a split second I realized what most dogs would do in response to this stimulus — cry out, turn, and bite — and that if Delilah could not reach her target she might have to make do with a little collateral damage, someone with his fingers closer to her mouth. But nothing happened; Delilah remained completely focused on me and my attention to her chin. The clamps were reapplied, more forcibly this time, and still nothing registered.

"At least she moved her leg," said the owner, noticing that Delilah did pull her leg away, even though the movement seemed slow and mechanical.

The vet got to his feet.

"I'm afraid that was just a spinal reflex. I was more interested in seeing if her brain could register a painful sensation in her toes. And as you can see, she doesn't appear to feel a thing. The information from her toes telling her brain to make it stop isn't getting through."

"So, she hasn't broken her legs?"

"No. Her legs are physically fine, they're just not working properly. I'm guessing she's slipped a disk in her back."

He gave us both a brief synopsis of the purpose of intervertebral disks, those clever little shock absorbers that lie between the bones of the spine. Dachshunds, like Lhasa apsos and Pekingese, are designed with short legs and long spines, focusing a great deal of stress and strain across the middle of their backs. Add a few extra pounds of lipid love and you have a recipe for disaster — a significant risk of a ruptured disk causing sudden and severe paralysis to the back legs.

"I was asking about the time because I was trying to work out how long Delilah might have been this way. Course we'll never know for sure, but from what you told me, it could be getting on twelve hours. What we do know is that she has no deep pain sensation in her back legs and that is as bad as it gets."

Hearing this, Delilah's owner bent down and picked her dog up, extending her chin and tears into Delilah's kisses. How scary, I thought. You leave your dog in the safety of your own home and return to a natural disaster. I could see a little shoelace tail poking out between the fingers of the owner's splayed hand and from the look of satisfaction on the dog's face I suspected Delilah *thought* it was wagging, even though nothing moved.

The vet offered to take an X-ray of Delilah's back to see if there was any evidence of narrowing between the bones of her spine where a disk space might have collapsed, but her owner declined. Money was a big problem and she would have to trust a conservative approach — oral steroids to reduce inflammation, muscle relaxants, and, most important of all, strict cage rest. Surgical options were never discussed. Maybe the vet had a better feel for the owner's fiscal situation than I realized or maybe he wasn't convinced that surgery could save poor Delilah. Back then, in the minds of some old-school general practitioners, spinal surgery was impractical, expensive, limited to academic institutions, and, to their way of thinking, yielded inconsistent results.

I wish I could tell you what became of Delilah, but I don't know. That said, as a curious veterinary student with complete access to pertinent and current data on all manner of disease, I did try to discover what her future might hold. I tracked down several scientific articles that suggested this conservative approach was destined for failure in a dog with such severe neurological deficits. Not what I wanted to read. In my mind I clipped this depressing pearl of wisdom to a mental picture of Delilah scuttling across the floor and simply kept going. I never thought about her again until decades later while visiting a practice in Bermuda, when the recollection of Delilah's sad case paid me an unexpected visit.

Perhaps I should clarify that for the last thirteen years I've been working at the Angell Animal Medical Center in Boston, one of the premier state-of-the-art facilities in this country. However, from time to time, I hop on a Delta flight out of Logan and in less than two hours I'm driving on the left-hand side of the road in a former British colony famous for pink sand and a style of shorts. I consult and perform surgery at a general practice run by a couple of friends of mine and I know what you're thinking — nice excuse to go sipping Dark and Stormys and work on my tan — but the truth is I've pretty much got a scalpel in my hand from the moment I arrive until the moment I depart. The fundamentals of this particular Bermuda case were practically the same: another charming dachshund (this one far more slender and fawn-colored, and named Peanut) presenting to the primary veterinarian acutely paralyzed, no deep pain sensation in either of her rubbery back legs. Ordinarily, at Angell, a "down dog" would undergo a CT scan or an MRI to precisely define the location of diseased disk, immediately followed by a surgery aimed at meticulously cutting a tiny window into the delicate bone of the spinal canal with the aid of a high-speed drill and a steady hand. But I was in the real world, in a general practice that had no such drill. When we scrambled around for alternative spinal surgery equipment, the closest thing I could find to what I needed lived in a pack labeled "dental." With luck, I could still access the ruptured disk by nibbling and chipping away at the bone with a variety of handheld instruments, but this would be the surgical equivalent of mowing a lawn with a scythe.

Finding the correct disk space was even more problematic. Advanced imaging wasn't available and the practice's X-ray equipment was broken, leaving them dependent on a portable unit meant for equine use. As you can imagine a machine designed to discover bony disorders in a horse's limbs struggles when it comes to the subtleties of a dachshund spine. At best, if I removed my glasses and tilted the grainy image just so while implementing a lemony squint, my vivid imagination could only suggest a faint narrowing between two bones of the lumbar spine.

It was decision time. Should I take this dog to surgery trusting an X-ray that was barely readable, let alone diagnostic, only to tackle one of the most delicate, sensitive, and unforgiving areas of the canine anatomy with equipment as subtle as pruning shears? And suddenly, while I was trying to decide, there she was, little Delilah — her face, her winning attitude, and her awful dilemma — front and center in my mind.

I was as restricted in my ability to operate on Peanut as if Michael J. Fox had bundled me into his DeLorean and taken me back in time to my encounter with Delilah. Sure, I may have been carrying an invisible bag of surgical skills acquired in the intervening years, but my current predicament in terms of limited facilities and equipment was virtually identical. Back then, Delilah's owner hadn't even entertained the possibility of surgery. Given the suboptimal service I could offer, was backing down the honorable, most professional way to go?

Then I remembered that unpleasant little addendum based on my additional research into Delilah's case, the one that said a conservative approach in a severely paralyzed dog was virtually guaranteed to result in paraplegia. Of course I had seen hundreds of similar cases over the intervening decades, cases where I didn't hesitate to reach for a scalpel, but not when my hands were cuffed to equipment meant for teeth and horses.

"Let's give it a shot," I told Peanut's vet and in under an hour I was pulling wads of fibrous and calcified disk material away from a grateful spinal cord.

I want you to know I ached over this decision, worked in a state of regret, certain I would be operating in the wrong space, certain my ill-suited instrumentation would let me down. But I kept coming back to Delilah. Deep down, I knew she never walked again. Why should Peanut be destined to suffer a similar fate? And what was my alternative? By the time we organized the necessary paperwork, boarded a flight, and made it to a veterinary hospital in the United States, even surgery would be unlikely to keep her out of a paraplegic cart.

When back surgery goes well, the certainty of knowing a physical act has relieved pain and pressure on the spinal cord, giving a dog a chance to regain something as fundamental as walking, is intoxicating. That was certainly the case with little Peanut, who was cured by the surgery. I'm not talking about whooping it up and celebrating this surgical war story with stiff drinks. I'm talking about taking yourself off to a place where you can be alone, breathe the biggest sigh of relief you ever breathed, and take a moment to remember a different dachshund from a different era who wasn't quite so lucky.

Not every practice I visited as part of my required work experience provided a positive lesson. Mr. Malcolm Snide, as I will call him, was a new veterinary graduate who took every opportunity to crush my line of questioning in front of his clients. In the absence of an audience, he preferred a look of silent contempt over a witty put-down, as though I wasn't worth the effort when I challenged his educational advantage. To be fair to Malcolm, his facial expressions were difficult to read since he was cursed with a deep furrow cut into the fleshy skin between his bushy eyebrows, like an ax chop on a log, that rendered him permanently vexed, perplexed, or dismayed, depending on what he said.

I, like all the other visiting veterinary students, felt as if I was a burden when I joined him for evening appointments, so the first time Snide actually invited me to help him, to draw up a vaccine from a glass ampoule in front of an owner, I was caught off guard, dangerously clumsy and unsure. Yes, I could flick the glass a couple of times with my fingernail like we've all seen on TV, but when it came to cracking it open, I cut my index finger, which forced me to curl it into my palm to avoid contaminating the vaccine with my own blood. When I inserted the needle into the clear liquid and pulled back on the plunger of the syringe nothing happened. Snide noticed I was struggling.

"You have to tilt the ampoule a little," he suggested, trying hard not to sound testy, but when I did, the vaccine trickled out over my hand, leaving me with less than half the necessary dose.

"I've lost it," I said, referring to the liquid running down my wrists, though from the way the pet owner rolled his eyes, he and Snide obviously thought I was alluding to my overall composure.

I felt humiliated. Vaccines are expensive, and here I was pouring the remains of one down the sink while the owner looked on, a new vial cracked open as if they had only nominal value.

"Sorry about that," I said as soon as the doctor and I were alone.

Snide turned to me and it was clear there was way too much pleasure contorting the muscles of his face.

"Get it right next time. Or don't even bother trying, yeah?"

He fixed me with a stare that showed how quickly, how completely, he had forgotten where he had come from, where we all start, as though he had always been incapable of making such a trivial mistake. He kept his cold eyes and the ax chop on me as he picked up the next file, stuck his head out of the door, and cried, "Next please." Only then did he reapply his mask, his best approximation of the conscientious doctor, showing too many teeth in his wolf smile. I never had a problem loading a vaccine from a glass ampoule again, and came to realize how so much of veterinary medicine depends upon performance under constant public scrutiny.

To my way of thinking, there were far better ways to evolve as a doctor and, in a different practice, I found myself gravitating toward a much older mentor with a very different attitude. Mr. Vaughn was a senior partner and a man permanently on the brink of retirement due to his inability to abandon the pets of a loyal fan base and his love of teaching veterinary students the kind of lessons ignored or overlooked by university lecturers and textbooks. He was irresistible — round and cheerful — the kind of old man who could have made a decent living during the holiday season as a Santa Claus if you ignored his affinity for the Ronald Reagan school of hair dye.

"Come help me anesthetize this dog," he said to me. "It's just a neuter, but you may as well knock him down."

"Fantastic," I thought, and Vaughn coached as I placed my first intravenous catheter and taped it in place. Before handing me a syringe loaded with a pale transparent yellow liquid, he said, "You got your tube?"

I nodded, and held up a selection of

different-sized endotracheal tubes, just in case.

"Laryngoscope?"

I reached out to the side of the dog and produced a metallic speculum fitted with a handle and light source for illuminating and visualizing the back of the patient's throat.

"Then here's your induction agent." He passed the twelve-cubic-centimeter syringe, loaded to the ten-milliliter mark. "Go ahead and knock him down."

So I did, inserting the needle into the rubber stopper at the end of the catheter and driving home the plunger, all the way, the entire dose.

The dog was lying on a table, but he flopped over on his side, instantly lifeless.

"Did you just kill your patient?" asked Vaughn and, to be honest, I missed the calm unruffled tone of his question. I was too busy inserting the tube into the dog's airway, fumbling for a pulse that was nowhere to be found.

"Do you know how much drug you used? Did you calculate the dose?"

Of course I didn't have a clue. I was acting the part, pretending to be a vet, mimicking a performance I had witnessed dozens of times before. I had been so drawn to the action, so focused on the fun stuff, I had overlooked everything that really mattered, the choice of drug, appropriate dosage, speed of delivery, and the vital baseline parameters of the patient. I had never stopped to consider what doctors were doing with a calculator, what they were reading in the patient's record, why they were listening to the heart for the umpteenth time.

Vaughn quickly found the dog's femoral pulse, took my hand, and guided it into position.

"Got it?" he asked, as the dog huffed an enormous breath as if he were blowing out birthday candles.

I nodded, speechless.

"Don't look so worried. I had a feeling you might do that. I gave you the low end of the dog's appropriate dose. But have we learned something today?"

There are few more effective ways to learn than thinking you have killed your first patient before you even graduate from veterinary school. From here on out I would pay closer attention to the sleight of hand and not just the trick itself.

A week or so later, I was seeing appointments with Mr. Vaughn when we were confronted with a seven-year-old black Labrador called Shadow. His owners, the

Stoddarts, were one of those couples who could have been siblings, sharing short, mousy hair, gold-rimmed glasses, pallor, and height. Shadow sported the English Labrador genes — short legs, meaty black rudder, and broad head that cried out for firm pats.

"He's been acting off for the past fortnight," said Mr. Stoddart. "Not that interested in going for walks. That's not like him at all. Sometimes he even backs off when I try to put his leash over his head."

Vaughn called his name, but Shadow sat there, looking off into space.

"Shadow!" This time Vaughn shouted and clapped his hands and for a moment Shadow came back, the tail offering a couple of brisk wags but fading fast, as he quickly lost all interest.

We took him outside the building and Mrs. Stoddart walked him up and down while we watched, and I was struck by the poor dog's utter lack of enthusiasm. It seemed like such an effort for him to just move his legs forward. No spring, no bounce, paws barely getting off the ground, and a tail that belonged to gravity, no beat, no swish, no joy. If I didn't know better I would have said Shadow was clinically depressed.

"I'd like to run some blood tests," said Vaughn, "to make sure there's no metabolic abnormalities going on inside of him. There's no chance he's got into some kind of poison?"

Husband and wife shook their heads in unison.

"Not a chance," said Mr. Stoddart. "We . . ."

". . . never have anything like that around the house," said Mrs. Stoddart, as though she were used to finishing her husband's sentences for him.

"And there's no chance he's been in an accident, fallen down stairs, or been hit by a car?"

Husband and wife turned to one another, silently conferred, came back in the negative.

"Can you leave him with us?" asked Vaughn. "I want us both," and he gestured to me, "to keep an eye on him through the day. We might want to take some blood, run some tests, get some X-rays of his head. Nick's going to do some research into what's going on and he'll give you a call later this afternoon. Sound okay?"

Taking Shadow behind closed doors, Vaughn joined me and asked, "What d'you reckon?"

I looked down at the pathetic creature slumped at my feet. We were in a large work area with dogs barking, cats taunting from a bank of cages, doctors and nurses rushing back and forth. At the very least Shadow should have been nervous, excited, or engaged. This indifference to his surroundings seemed all wrong.

"If his blood work is okay, especially his glucose, I guess I might think he's acting neurological. He doesn't seem to be all there," I said, squatting down to pat the dog's head, noting how he pulled back a little before my palm made contact with his cheek, the action of a dog that was suddenly head shy.

"I think you're right," said Vaughn. "And I'm going to leave this one with you, if that's all right. We'll go through his cranial nerve reflexes together, get his blood work started, and then I want you to hit the books. See what you can dig up. If you don't do it, I'll have to do it myself because after forty years of practice there's no way I can keep all that neuroanatomy straight."

And so, to my surprise and delight, Shadow became *my* case, the first case whose investigation, whose clinical course, would be driven by and ultimately dependent upon me.

Naturally I was all in, making detailed notes about blink reflexes, pupil size, gag reflex, facial twitch, head position, tilt or aversion, ticking off boxes, rifling through textbook pages, trying to make Shadow fit, to give him a label that held up, to assign a diagnosis that matched his clinical signs. By the time I had finished I thought he was clumsy, his responses to external stimuli, including hearing, seemed depressed, and I suspected his ability to balance was impaired. I didn't think there was a problem with his brainstem, where the facial nerves originated, but other than that I was stumped.

"Could be a lesion in the temporal lobe of his cerebrum or maybe his balance is off because of disease in his cerebellum or vestibular centers," I said.

Vaughn offered a frown and shrug combo.

"Sounds reasonable. Our in-house blood work is all normal. So now what?"

I suspected he knew the answer and this question meant so should I.

"Maybe I'll call someone at the vet school. Run Shadow's history and clinical signs by one of the experts in medicine. See what they think."

I got a brief smile, but better still an "Off you go then" that told me I was on the right track. After all, a little second opinion never does any harm.

When I reported back, later that afternoon, I had a new appreciation for the complexities of veterinary neurology. Yes, a detailed history and a systematic examination can help you to pinpoint a problem in a certain area of the brain (in Shadow's case, a possible lesion of the temporal lobe), but it couldn't tell you exactly what it was and, more important, what could be done about it.

"They think we should X-ray Shadow's skull, for the sake of completeness, just to make sure there are no bony abnormalities, but what we really need is either a CT scan or better still an MRI."

Bear in mind this was England in the eighties and as far as I remember only a few university veterinarians had ever sneaked into human hospitals in the middle of the night to get a shot at cross-sectional images through canine gray matter. On-site advanced imaging specific to animals remained a pipe dream.

"The only other thing to do is a cerebrospinal fluid tap. They said there's a remote chance Shadow's clinical signs could be due to an infection or inflammation affecting the brain, and if the fluid is abnormal, maybe we could offer some kind of treatment."

Vaughn looked at me, looked at Shadow, and came back to me.

"Poor bugger," he said. "I think we've got to try. I've never done one before. You think you can talk us through it?"

"Of course," I said, because I was thinking to myself, "Isn't this what a huge part of school is all about, learning to have faith, learning to trust the written and pictorial descriptions of a technique without actually having had the opportunity to put it into practice under a watchful eye?"

"Good," said Vaughn into my reverie. "I'm going to call the Stoddarts, let them know what you've discovered, and see if they are okay with your plan."

And as he went off to do so, I began to wonder where the blame might fall if any of this went wrong. Once again I could be about to lose my veterinary license before I even got it.

Vaughn came back, saying, "They want us to give it a shot," and I remember thinking how this, of all the various diagnostic procedures out there, is not something a clinician can afford to be hit or miss about. Obtaining a sample of cerebrospinal fluid (a tiny quantity of the precious, transparent liquid located around the brain and spinal cord) necessitates the insertion of a long needle into the base of the skull of an anesthetized patient. The risk of accidentally penetrating Shadow's central nervous system meant there was no margin for error.

Books open to the appropriate pages, I shaved a neat square into the base of Shadow's skull, performed a surgical prep, and carefully flexed his neck to optimize access to the target.

"Two fingers on the wings of the Atlas," I read out loud, "one on the occiput of the skull. Imagine a line drawn between the two points and insert the needle at the intersection."

For an older man, Vaughn had great hands, rock steady in sterile latex gloves, incrementally advancing the needle through fat and muscle, withdrawing the central stylet with every tentative millimeter it poked forward, just in case he had already entered the spinal canal. He was, however, a top-lip licker during moments of intense concentration.

"Apparently you should feel a distinct tactile popping sensation when the needle tip goes through the ligament," I said, as though nothing could be simpler, as though by saying it out loud I could will it to happen, as opposed to the alternative of Shadow suddenly twitching as the end of a steel spike slid inside his sleeping brain.

The top-lip licking stopped, Vaughn removed the stylet, and stood back as we watched a bead of clear, colorless liquid roll out of the hub of the needle and onto the floor. I swooped in to catch our sample inside a purple-topped sterile tube. Neither of us spoke. We let our eyes share the satisfaction of the moment.

Shadow woke up none the worse for wear and went home to await the results of the fluid analysis. Sadly I had to be going myself — my two-week externship coming to an end, a new term at college about to begin — but Vaughn promised to give me an update regarding my first patient.

It was several weeks later when a card arrived, along with a note on which was scrawled a single sentence:

See, it's not about the winning. Vaughn.

It was a thank-you card from Mr. and Mrs. Stoddart and directed primarily at Mr. Vaughn. It turned out the fluid analysis had come back as normal, or rather, no underlying cause of Shadow's disease was detected. A course of steroids had been tried, with modest success for a few weeks, but when Shadow began to have seizures, the Stoddarts could not stand by and see him suffer any longer and they had him put to sleep. There was a paragraph dedicated to "Nick, the veterinary student," for trying his hardest to get to the bottom of the problem, for going "above and beyond." It was just a sentence or two but it hit me hard, gratitude and recognition in spite of failure. It was the first veterinary thank-you I ever received, and with it came the understanding and wisdom of a veteran — what matters most is how hard you try.

Invariably, while I gallivanted around the country, my father would continue to suggest I make use of our cottage in the Yorkshire Dales and avail myself of some *real* veterinary practice.

"It's all well and good you broadening your horizons, son, but there's only one place on God's green earth where you can experience the real thrill of becoming a veterinarian, isn't that right, Whiskey?"

My father would crank up the northern edge to his fake Yorkshire accent and offer his golden the appropriate visual cue (normally, mouthing a bark), and Whiskey dutifully bestowed his verbal agreement.

"There you have it. Straight from the dog's mouth."

There was an element of ritual to this, our playful banter, but at the same time, I sensed a genuine undercurrent of concern. I was approaching the end of my fifth year of vet school and naturally my father was beginning to brood over the future. Wasn't it prudent to plan ahead, to be putting some feelers out for a potential job when all this training was over? But as yet, his son had failed to visit a practice anywhere near the Yorkshire Dales. Time was running out for me, and perhaps for him too. It wasn't that I didn't want to work in the Yorkshire Dales, it was, after all, intoxicating, beautiful country, but at the same time, it wasn't an obsession in the same way it seemed to be for my father. I was getting to the crux of my education — all those seemingly point-less hours in a lecture theater finally start-ing to have practical meaning. You could feel it falling into place. That "stuff" the teachers had thrown at me from so many different angles had percolated into some-thing meaningful. Suddenly I was no longer that wallflower student playing his guessing game, and I didn't want to discount any facet of veterinary life or be pinned down or committed to becoming a country vet in one specific part of the country. I wanted to keep my options open, and one day Dad caught me in the wrong mood for our passive-aggressive game.

"You really want me to?" I asked him.

My tone was all wrong, the question coming out like an ultimatum or a concession — if I do this now, you'll stop bugging me and we can move on. It was as though I put it out there like I might be surprised by the answer, even though my falling in love with the Dales was something Dad had clearly been craving for years, a desire akin to his old nicotine habit, a yearning that could still stop him in his tracks and cozy up when he least expected it.

"It's entirely up to you, son," he said, and I knew he had sensed the change in me, his phony accent abandoned.

I dropped my head, ashamed, realized I was merely pushing against his pull. I had resisted for as long as possible, like a shrewd politician dodging sanctions by evading talks, but eventually, as I had known all along, I would have to give his plan a chance. Maybe it would feel just right and if not, he could never say I didn't try. Now seemed as good a time as ever for my obligatory James Herriot rehearsal.

I chose the first couple of weeks in the New Year, trying to give myself an unfair advantage, knowing a Yorkshire winter would make it hard to win me over.

I found a practice only a short drive down the dale from our cottage, and on a perfect cloudless morning that brought the bitterest cold I had ever known, I set out down a narrow winding road cut through a valley of frosty white fields. The veterinarian I would be working with was Brian Hastings, a man who hailed from the south of England and spent many years doing volunteer work in South America before finding his niche in Herriot country.

"How are the farmers and the pet owners to work with?" I asked at the earliest opportunity. "I mean, is it still like it was during Herriot's day?"

Brian hoped I would be able to answer my own question at the end of my two-week stint and promised to remind me of it before I headed back to college. I liked this laid-back approach, his wanting me to find out for myself, not wanting to influence my opinion, but I particularly liked the fact that Brian didn't fit the *All Creatures* caricature I had expected, what with his hippy hair and unruly beard. He had more than a hint of Grizzly Adams about him and I couldn't wait to get out and about and see how he fit in with the locals.

At least 80 percent of his practice involved

farm animals and I quickly discovered three features particular to this line of work — endless driving, professional frustration, and physical exhaustion. It seemed as though we spent more time on the road getting from practice to practice than we did actually working on the creatures in need of our services. Farms were spread far and wide, and if we ever got stuck behind a milk tanker or a tractor, we were virtually guaranteed our Land Rover would obtain a geological sample from an adjacent drystone wall when we had an opportunity to pass. Thank goodness Brian knew the unmarked shortcuts, the high roads above the snow line that took us over the top rather than through the valleys. I couldn't imagine how long it would have taken a stranger like me to navigate my way from farm to farm. By the time I arrived, the farmer would have given up all hope, the sick livestock shipped off to the slaughterhouse. And this proved to be another troubling discovery — the ruthless economics of farming. This was the era of Chernobyl, when British farmers feared a radioactive mushroom cloud might kill their livestock. And there was this little-known disease of cows that appeared to be making them "mad." The diagnosis and treatment of diseases in sheep and cows and pigs was no less fascinating than caring for cats and dogs, the only problem being that all the doctoring in these cases — the workup, the medicines and the thrill of the cure — was, for the most part, theoretical. If a case of mastitis in a ewe did not respond to the first course of treatment, the animal found itself in the wrong column on a balance sheet — a financial loss, destined to be culled, denied a second chance. I knew this was how it had to be, with the emphasis on herd health, prevention over cure, but it was so frustrating, the feeling that I could have turned an animal around, but I was denied the opportunity because it didn't make good business sense. Standing in the back of a dark, wind-whipped barn watching Brian shake his head after examining the blackened udders of an accommodating sheep, I understood this harsh reality of rural practice would always be a major stumbling point.

The final realization came one afternoon after helping Brian remove the budding horns of eighty steers. No matter which way you cut it, farm practice can be grueling and potentially dangerous work. On the plus side, I got a taste for the camaraderie and playful banter that exists between vet and farmer, the way these kinds of physical endeavors and the sense of accomplishment that comes with them bring you together. It had an irresistible appeal and moreover, you never had to worry about getting to sleep at night.

When it came to my initial question, about whether much had changed in this part of the world since Herriot's day, one particular farm visit provided the perfect answer.

Brian and I pulled into a farmyard of frozen mud, like brown concrete set in front of an isolated stone farmhouse with a sagging slate roof, and when we stepped out of the Land Rover we were greeted by a snapping border collie with a piercing, unrelenting bark.

"Easy, Shep," said a hefty bald-headed man whose crown and cheeks were seared red and raw by the cold. He walked toward us and offered me an explanation for the dog's hysteria. "Every time veterinary turns out our Shep thinks he's gonna lose his knackers I reckon."

The bald man laughed to himself as we shook hands and Shep went quiet.

"What you got for me, Trevor?" asked Brian as I trailed the two of them toward a distant barn.

"Three of me best ewes started coughing. Reckon we'd best nip it in t' bud."

"How long has this been going on?"

Trevor made to reply but was cut off by another round of incessant barking behind us in the yard. I turned, half expecting to see another vehicle pulling up but looked back to see Shep standing on the roof of the Land Rover, legs akimbo, savoring a moment of copious urination.

Brian ran back, cursing and waving his arms, as Trevor and I laughed from the doorway of the barn. Shep ignored all of Brian's protestations until his bladder was completely empty and the front and sides of the vehicle were stained by a series of irregular yellow stripes.

Brian headed back our way, his face betraying his irritation.

"What's wrong with that bloody dog of yours, Trevor?"

Trevor stifled a smile.

"Nah then, Veterinary. There's nowt wrong with our Shep. He just wants to make sure you'll be knockin' summat off t' bill. After all, he just gave you a free car wash."

The reckoning with my dad came on my last day, as I was shutting down the electricity, draining the water from the pipes, and otherwise readying the cottage for a few weeks of wintry isolation before my parents'

228

next visit. Dad phoned, clearly prompted by my mother, to offer an unnecessary reminder to make sure everything was switched off. Somehow or another he caught me completely off guard when he managed to slip in the question "So, is this the kind of vetting you see yourself doing when you qualify?"

"No," I said, and I was shocked by how quickly I had answered, how the silence on the other end of the line stretched between us. It was more than the negativity and the way I managed to sound lackadaisical and heartless, so capable of crushing a dream years in the making, it was the fact that I never hesitated, didn't need to deliberate, as though I had never even entertained the option in the first place. This was my father, the man who had kept me on task for all the right reasons, to whom I owed so much for having this chance, and here I was, cutting him down, consigning his hopes to the garbage with one word.

"I mean, I don't know. It's still too early to decide," I said, but I'm sure he saw my offering for what it was, an attempt to backpedal, like someone who windmills his arms after he has lost his balance and moved beyond the point of no return, the long fall inevitable.

What made it all the worse was the way he managed to carry on, changing topic, as though my answer had never really mattered. By the time I said goodbye and hung up he seemed perfectly fine, but I was pretty sure he was about to mull over the same scenarios starting to run through my mind. We were both thinking about his role as Arthur Stone, practice manager, the man with the connections, the liaison between the pet-owning and farming public and his son. He was leaning into a fence, wearing his beloved flat cap and Wellington boots, sharing a joke with a farmer at my expense as they looked on, enjoying my attempts to extricate a calf from its mother. He was sticking his head around an examination room door asking if I could just have a quick look at the cat of an elderly widow, pro bono. It was the life I knew he had imagined the two of us would savor and share. I wished it were different, but before I closed the cottage door behind me, he and I both knew this dream of a veterinary life had vanished, the stuff of fantasy and nothing more. As much as my honesty hurt him, fooling myself, trying to be someone I wasn't, was destined to fail. I had to trust my subconscious, the way it had spoken faster than my brain could think. The bigger question, the one my father had dared not ask, still remained.

"If you're not interested in the Yorkshire Dales, son, then where?"

7.
IN DEFENSE OF HAPPINESS

It was to be our last walk together across those familiar fields, though, of course, I didn't realize it at the time. Autumn was just getting started; gray, thumb-smudged sky, swirling wind, the satisfaction of a golden crunch under every footfall. I had joined the trio — Dad, Whiskey, and Bess — striding out along the same public footpath, passing through the same farmland across which Bess had strayed all those years before when she had been eager to meet some cows and nearly met her maker instead.

"Even though I rarely see 'the girls' out and about this time of day I always keep Whiskey and Bess on a leash for the next three fields," said Dad. "Then they can run loose a bit until the way back."

"Is it okay, I mean, for Whiskey, what with his tendency to go after a . . . what did you call her . . . a 'lady friend'?"

Dad frowned, as if it were an effort to answer such a ridiculous question.

"He's fine. He can't go too far out this way. There are no other houses for miles."

I noticed he was setting quite the pace, or maybe it was the dogs eager to get to freedom beyond the third field. With one leash in each hand, he looked like Ben-Hur sans chariot. He had blown off my offer to take one of them as if it might upset the natural order of things, the routine all three of them savored, and so I focused on keeping up. The wind was really gusting at times, though it still held some leftover summer warmth and I found myself working to keep the hair out of my face and eyes, noticing that my bald father had the advantage of unimpeded vision. Over the years his receding hairline had fused with a monk's tonsure, leaving a neat corona of gray hair over the back of his head and ears. Enjoy the windblown sensation, I thought, seeing into my future.

The footpath was well worn, the bare earth tacky but not slippery, so no problems with traction for canine footpads or a sturdy pair of Wellington boots. I was sporting a "hunter green" pair (and matching Barbour jacket), the classic attire of a British equine veterinarian and the closest I would come to fooling the world into thinking I knew what I was doing around horses. Dad was in an industrial charcoal pair, and though he had forsaken the flat cap (since it would have been a challenge to keep it in place given the windy conditions), he was striding out in the same raincoat, and armed with the same infamous walking stick of my childhood.

For a while the four of us were content to keep our rhythm, juggling our thoughts, letting the brisk air and the countryside in.

I was about to go back to college for my final year at veterinary school and I had just returned home after a three-month visit to the Unites States. There was a great deal for my father and I to discuss, not least my plans for what I might do after graduation, a subject he and I had purposely avoided after my apparent dismissal of a future in the Yorkshire Dales.

"It's funny," I said as we crossed over a wooden stile, "it's always been Whiskey and Bess, not Bess and Whiskey, even though, technically, thanks to Mum, Bess got there first."

Dad considered me and kept walking.

"Nobody ever says, 'The Sundance Kid and Butch Cassidy' now do they?"

I smiled, kept the pace, and said nothing.

These three really were a trio.

I had come to accept that they were happy for me to join them but, as with Patch, I felt like an outsider, never really felt part of a quartet. If ever I was asked, "Do you have dogs of your own?" I wouldn't hesitate to talk about Whiskey and Bess, to proudly recount their virtues, their foibles, and their individuality. But how much could I really claim to know about them, having not been around them for the greater part of their lives? In this context, my sentiments about Whiskey and Bess seemed so broad and sweeping, lacking the nuance and fine detail I remembered from my life with Patch. I watched them, these two dogs, constantly monitoring my father, connected, visually checking in, trotting forward and dropping back, another glance, eye contact, connection made, trot forward and drop back. They were all around him, moving in and out of formation, canine wingmen, covering him from all sides. I found myself thinking that they had come to feel more like cousins, still family, but, to me, slightly more distant relatives.

"So how was the trip?" said Dad, now that both dogs were loose, as though he could finally relax, all bovine danger behind him. Whiskey was off, last seen disappearing into a copse whereas Bess stayed within a fifty-yard radius, checking in every fifteen seconds or so.

"It was good," I said, choosing my words carefully. In truth, I wanted to gush, I wanted to share my excitement, but I sensed the need for diplomacy.

"I hope you can do better than that," he said.

I paused, deliberated, found the mental notes I had previously prepared when I suggested joining him for this walk, and started in.

"You know this was all very spontaneous. I was lucky to get a place, it was so last-minute." Solid opening gambit, I thought, pointing out the fact that none of this was premeditated or part of a cunning plan I had been working on for years. What I didn't tell him was how I had been eavesdropping on a conversation in the school cafeteria between two of my classmates regarding their upcoming summer visit to the Veterinary Hospital of the University of Pennsylvania. They were part of a small number of English students who were about to blend in with our colonial cousins across the pond for specialized final-year rotations. Most veterinary schools have a lecture-free, purely clinical final year and theirs had already started, whereas ours did not begin until after the summer break. Here was an opportunity to get a sneak preview, to discover a fresh, American perspective on veterinary medicine and visit a country I had always wanted to visit, all at the same time. Even though it had felt as though they were discussing a party to which I had not been invited, in that instant, I became Cinderella, determined to get to the ball at all costs.

"I had so much more responsibility, meeting with the client one on one, taking the history, doing the examination of the pet myself rather than just watching the real vet do it."

"I can appreciate that," said Dad, "but was it so different from what we do over here?"

I noticed how he picked up the pace a little. Perhaps this was his defensive prelude to an uncomfortable turn in the conversation.

"I doubt it," I said. "I guess I'll find out during this next year. But, I did have a few . . . let's call them, communication difficulties."

"What do you mean?"

"Oh, nothing major." I smiled at the recollection. "Everybody was great, really friendly, it's just that we happen to say a few things differently. For example, I had a rottweiler with dirty ears and I wanted to clean them up, so I asked the nurse for some 'baby buds' and she looked at me like I had two heads."

Dad glanced my way, visibly confused, trying to fathom the nurse's problem.

"She didn't know what a baby bud was?"

"No," I said. "Apparently they call them 'Q-tips.' "

My father played with "Q-tips" in his mouth, didn't like it, spat it out, and shook his head in disgust.

"What else?"

"I don't know, silly stuff, like that. One time I cut my hand and asked for a plaster and everyone thought I wanted to put a cast on the cut instead of wanting what they call a 'Band-Aid.' In surgery they use 'sponges' and not 'swabs,' and when I told another female student I would see her in theater rather than the 'operating room,' she practically fluttered her eyelashes and asked which show we were going to see."

Dad laughed and Bess padded toward him, as if to make sure all was well.

"Go find your brother," he said, waving her away. "Go on. Go find him."

Bess seemed to understand and trotted

off, but still she refused to stray too far.

Whiskey and Bess, I thought, brother and sister, and now son and daughter, the replacements for me and Fiona. Maybe it is inevitable, the transition of pets into surrogate children for empty nesters, the kids who always want to stay home. Perhaps this was what I had noticed most about my sporadic visits over the years, the increase in direct verbal communication between my father and the dogs, as though he wanted to share his thoughts with them and even sought their input, their approval. Was this part of a natural evolution in the relationship between a man and his dogs or was it a sign of isolation and loneliness?

"You think she's overweight?"

Safe territory, I thought, pulling me away from what I wanted to really discuss about America. Lie, use tact, or use honesty. This was Dad. I knew which he would prefer, for this question and for the bigger one both of us knew we still needed to address.

"Definitely. She needs to lose five pounds, maybe a little more."

"Oh, dear," he said on a lengthy exhalation. "I'll have to have words with your mother."

I huffed a fake laugh because we both knew who was to blame for too many treats and secret handouts under the kitchen table.

"But what about her coat? Just look at the shine. Now you can't complain about that. That's a teaspoon of cod-liver oil added to her food every —"

"Dad, I want to talk to you about something that really hit me during the summer."

I'd stopped him in his tracks even though we kept marching at the same pace, his hazel eyes telling me to go on.

"I think I might want to become a surgeon."

"Surgeon," he said, shocked, sounding almost affronted, as though I might have told him I was quitting veterinary medicine to become, oh, I don't know, a puppeteer or perhaps a mime artist. "But I thought that was what you were: a veterinary surgeon — MRCVS — a member of the Royal College of Veterinary *Surgeons.*"

"Yeah, of course," I said, "but I'm talking about trying to become an actual specialist in surgery, someone who focuses solely on surgical problems in cats and dogs and fixes them with surgery."

My father pursed the blood out of his lips, looking troubled by what he was about to say.

"Not being funny, son . . ."

This phrase, "not being funny," a rejoinder

frequently employed as a preamble to a polite snub, instantly had me on the defensive.

"Not being funny, son, and remember, I love you dearly, but, in fairness, you've never been exactly . . . well . . . dare I say . . . practical or particularly good with your hands."

I wasn't affronted because he was right. I may have put together a few plastic airplane kits as a kid, but they never turned out anything like the picture on the box they came in. At school, my pottery class bowls always wobbled precariously on level surfaces and my dovetail joints in woodwork wept with obligatory sticky white glue. In short, I was not handy and we both knew it.

"I know. And I'm not offended. But I hope I can learn because, for some reason, surgery just seems to feel right."

"In what way?"

This was a question I knew he would ask though I had never tried to put an answer into words before.

"Well," I started, caught myself, laughed. "Um . . . I don't know, so many different ways. For example, I like the idea of being someone to turn to when you're out of options, or when you need a definitive fix, or when you are an animal's last hope. I like this responsibility, I like the weight of it because the heavier it gets, the greater the reward to the pet, the owner, and finally, to you. It seems so . . . what's the word . . . dynamic, scary, exciting, difficult, and demanding. That was part of the reason for going to the States, the chance to try out lots of different specialties and of all the ones I tried, surgery felt like the best fit. I'm not sure why, but I felt most at home in scrubs and a paper mask."

Dad nodded, as if he wanted to let me know he was listening.

"I felt like I had found a key I didn't even realize I had been looking for. I have no idea if I'm going to be able to use it. I don't know whether it will unlock any doors. All I *do* know is having found it, I should probably pick it up, try it out, and see what opens up."

Dad stopped nodding, made to speak but hesitated, and I sensed he was racing ahead, pausing as he took this information to its logical conclusion.

"So, if I'm not mistaken, this means you're not really interested in general veterinary work, period?"

I knew he was already way ahead, but I said, "That's right. I'm just not sure it's right for me."

I could almost see my father's brain joining the dots.

"So, no interest in working with farm animals? Or horses for that matter?"

What he really meant was, this is my last appeal for rural veterinary practice in the Yorkshire Dales.

"It's not that I don't have any interest. I do. But I think I would be happier and, hopefully, do better focusing on a small, single, specific area of veterinary medicine and for me, that area would be surgery."

"Does this mean you'll be leaving us for America, *permanently?*"

"No," I said, "I don't see why it should. We've got exactly the same kinds of specialized equipment as they do across the pond. And besides, we're supposed to be the 'nation of animal lovers' and not them and that should mean plenty of call for a vet with good surgical skills on this side of the Atlantic."

My father came to an abrupt halt, paused, and called the dogs.

"Time to turn around," he said, already heading back.

Bess was on it, quickly turning fifty yards back into fifty yards ahead. Whiskey, on the other hand, required several calls before he emerged from a hedgerow, blowing by us, treating us to the sight of a brown stain along the fur of his back and the fleeting aroma of something feral and decomposed.

"Looks like the 'lion-hearted fellow' is going to need a bath when he gets home," I said, hoping to get a rise, but Dad didn't seem to hear me and we walked in silence for a while. I imagined he was probably letting what I had shared sink in, and at the same time, I worried that he was thinking I saw myself as too good for general practice. Nothing could have been further from the truth. Humility had been high on his list of priorities to instill in his children. "Always hide your light under a bushel," he would say, but this was different. Ambition is not the same as conceit.

We reached the point where we needed to put Whiskey and Bess back on their leashes, but before my father called for them, he turned squarely to face me, reached out, and squeezed my upper arms.

"I want you to know that if you're happy, then your mother and I are happy. Whatever that is. Wherever that takes you." I saw the familiar intensity in his eyes, fiery, trapped somewhere between anger and tears, and he gave me an extra squeeze with his hands, as if to underscore the sentiment. "You understand."

"Yes," I said, lasting as long as I could without crying myself.

We set off and this time when I offered to take Bess's leash he gave it up. She let me walk her for a while, but I could tell she was restless, the balance seemed off for her, and within a hundred yards my father had taken her back, her stride instantly happier, her demeanor less confused.

"You know this doesn't mean I don't like the Dales."

"Of course," he said. "What's not to like? What's not to love? It was just that . . . having you up here, working, while I was in my retirement, well, it was only ever a pipe dream. No harm in dreaming, eh?"

"No, of course not. And who knows how things will turn out."

At this my father refused to meet my eye, perhaps because he knew better.

"But part of me feels as though I've let you down."

"Don't. Please," said Dad. "Not on my account." He paused, and then added, "So long as the pups always get to the front of the queue if they need a veterinary consult from yours truly."

"Sure," I said. "If Whiskey will ever let me."

It was his turn to smile, and I remember

feeling good, pleased to have broached the subject and cleared the air about my imagined role in that whole Herriot fantasy. I had sought and obtained his approval for the direction I wanted my career to take, a path at odds with his own dreams. It would be decades before I came to appreciate how selfless my father, like so many good parents, had been that day. He knew there was nothing he could do or say, that argument and condemnation would surely lead to isolation. So he chose the tough option — the sacrifice of unconditional support.

"So," I said, "when are you thinking of moving up to the Dales permanently?"

"Couple more years," said Dad. "I'm going to have to be careful though. These two will probably have to be on leash walks for the rest of their days."

I considered this aspect of Herriot country, spectacular walks and hikes, and all of it through potentially hostile farmland. There were cows everywhere and they were sparse by comparison to the number of sheep. Bess would lose it if she ever got off her leash. And then Dad would lose her. How frustrating, I thought, to be tethered, in all that wonderful open space, because you've never learned how to ignore livestock. Or rather, never been taught.

"Did Nigel enjoy the trip?"

By this time we were back in the first field, our last field of the walk, Bess's cow field, though once again there were no cows in sight.

"Yeah, he had a great time."

My friend Nigel and I had taken many trips together during our summer vacations when I wasn't immersed in matters veterinary. Most of Europe, Pakistan, China, Hong Kong, and Thailand had been checked off and therefore it seemed only natural to fly west. Nigel had joined me after my formal training program was complete, and the two of us had been up and down the East Coast, driven across the Midwest, and up and down the West Coast, all in a hectic three-week tour.

"But he doesn't think I'm much cop as a vet."

I couldn't hide my smile.

"Why's that?"

This was my cue to narrate a story from our road trip, when we drove a dilapidated Ford Tempo (a vehicle now extinct) from Washington, D.C., to Phoenix, Arizona. Late in the day we had crossed the mighty Mississippi in St. Louis, taken a peek at the Arch, and were looking for a place to sleep somewhere on the border between Missouri and Kansas. We were both exhausted, our concentration and nerves shot from driving on the wrong side of the road, constantly buffeted by the biggest trucks we had ever seen, and so we pulled over at some kind of campsite just off Highway 70.

"You sure about this?"

"Not really," said Nigel, sharing my trepidation as we stopped outside a single-story wooden building that looked remarkably similar to the Bates Motel in *Psycho*.

"I don't see anywhere to pitch a tent."

"Maybe it's out back," said Nigel as the two of us headed toward a porch lit by hanging lanterns. It was a ridiculously hot and sticky night and as we rang the bell, moths the size of crows flew kamikaze missions all around.

"You lookin' for somewhere to camp?"

The question came from a compact, wizened old woman with thick braided gray hair coursing down her back.

"Help yourself," she said, looking the two of us up and down in the manner of someone inspecting a cut of beef for Sunday dinner. Then she smiled a cruel yellow smile that stayed in place for an unnaturally long period of time. She didn't ask us to register. She didn't ask for any money. She just thumbed over her shoulder and added, "Go wherever y'like," which we took to mean "I'm gonna kill you anyway, but I likes me a challenge!"

We thanked her and backed off, trying to match her smile as we did, and drove around the back of the building, the old Tempo's headlights playing across a totally deserted campground. Save for the occasional tumbleweed blowing around there appeared to be no one else but us. There were, however, rows of empty campsites demarcated by small trees as far as we could see.

"You want to stay?" I asked.

"Not really," said Nigel. "But in spite of Norman Bates's mum I think it's too late to find something better."

I agreed and so we pitched our tent, trying to laugh off our paranoia.

Nigel was already cocooned inside in his sleeping bag and I was zipping up the tent when I thought I saw something moving between the trees.

"D'you see that?"

"No," said Nigel, working his apathy into the single syllable.

I watched and waited but nothing moved.

"What?" asked Nigel, clearly unable to put the element of unease to rest.

"I don't know. I thought I saw something

249

moving, a shadow of something."

"What kind of something?"

"Something big."

"You mean grizzly-bear big, mountain-lion big, or gray-haired-lady-deranged-killer-who-doesn't-ask-for-money-because-she-knows-she's-going-to-get-it-anyway big?"

"Could have been any or all of the above."

"Perfect," he said. "How are we ever going to sleep out here?"

I didn't bother answering, I was too busy listening.

This time we both heard the unmistakable snap of a twig.

"Seriously," I whispered, "they have all kinds of dangerous stuff out here. And I'm talking a whole lot bigger than badgers and foxes. Rabid too!"

"Seriously," said Nigel, "why are you whispering?"

And with that something feral, focused, and determined lunged at the bottom of the tent, the weight of the creature pressing on the canvas walls.

What followed was not the response of experienced mountain men, or men, period, for that matter. There was much kicking and inappropriately high-pitched screaming, as our sleeping-bag-encased feet beat back hungry teeth and raking claws. Soon we were both sitting up, catching our breath.

"I'm pretty sure I made some sort of contact," said Nigel.

"With what?"

"How should I know? You're the animal doctor."

We waited, fighting to control the noise of our own breathing so we could hear what was going on outside.

"You think it's gone?" said Nigel.

"Oh yeah," I said, "I'm sure it's completely satiated by its encounter!"

"Well I'm not lying here waiting to be devoured," said Nigel. "I vote we sleep in the car."

He would get no argument from me and so, after a period of lengthy surveillance for the creature of the night or the crazy lady from reception, we both made a mad dash back to the security of the Tempo.

Needless to say, the following morning, the two of us emerged from our cramped sanctuary as cranky, stiff, red-eyed monsters.

In the light of day I recognized our attacker, moving slowly toward us, a subtle limp in her front leg from where my best friend's big toe had landed a cushioned blow.

"I think this might be our rabid mountain lion," I said, bending down to pet a small gray-haired kitten.

She was incredibly friendly and obviously hungry, and after I checked her over to make sure there was nothing swollen or broken in her front leg, we offered her some food.

"Some vet you are," said Nigel. "For all the dogs you've had, it might be time to get a cat."

I couldn't argue the point as I squatted down to have my picture taken stroking this delightful, yet abominable creature. Little did I know that I would first see this photograph on my wedding day, in a poster-sized version. The accompanying story was presented as part of Nigel's best man's speech, evidence of my fear of cats (though this humiliation was nothing compared to the photograph of me sporting a perm — to this day I swear the hairdresser promised me her product would simply provide my flat hair with a little bit more body)!

"Ah, son, not to worry," said my father when I finished the story. "Easy mistake, especially for someone who's grown up around dogs and not cats."

Of course I wasn't worried, just a little embarrassed, but what struck me was the

252

way my father jumped to my defense, eager to provide a valid excuse. Amazing, I thought, how that parental "papa bear" or "mama bear" instinct to protect never goes away.

"Why haven't we ever had a cat?" I asked, as Dad and I left the footpath behind and headed down a gravel trail, over a brook, and back to the world of asphalt and concrete that led to our house.

Dad looked at me as though I had come up with a novel idea.

"We had cats when I was a kid," he said, adding, "lots of them." Then he took a moment to sift through these memories until he found the answer. "For me, it always comes back to not being able to know what they're thinking. You look into a dog's eyes and they let you know what's on their minds by their expression. With cats, there's not much written on their face."

"Maybe not," I said, "but there's usually a great deal written in their body. Besides, I think the element of mystery and independence is part of their appeal."

Dad's shrug told me he couldn't argue the point, but at the same time, he didn't necessarily agree.

There was more to my story, but I like to think he and I just ran out of time, our final walk across those memorable fields at an end, our cue for the conversation to conclude. Looking back, though, I think it was more that I chose not to let him in on the last part of my story, because it was, after all, more of a feeling than an actual event.

Nigel and I had only a few days left before we returned to England. We were driving down Santa Monica Boulevard in Los Angeles on the way to the beach to "catch a few rays" and "play a little Frisbee" (by the end of the trip we were trying a little too hard to be hip to the local jargon and it never felt right coming from us). We had ditched the Ford Tempo and suitably upgraded to a friend's Jeep convertible, so, as you can imagine, we were feeling pretty good.

"Why is it," said Nigel, "when you watch a movie, and it's filmed somewhere on the East Coast, the ocean is always on the right of the screen, but in California, the ocean is always on the left. Why is that?"

I thought about it, tried to summon up an appropriate waterfront scene in *Jagged Edge* or *Fatal Attraction,* and couldn't, but reckoned he was probably right.

"Very astute," I said, adding, "I don't care what they say, you're not as stupid as you look," not knowing then that Nigel was about to lose the Jeep's keys in the sand and we would spend four hours hunting for them.

But that was for the future, because at precisely that moment I turned on the radio and out of the speakers popped Sheryl Crow's "All I Want to Do Is Have Some Fun," and suddenly I was caught up in the song and the lyrics and my precise location in the world and at that very moment I vividly remember thinking, Wow, this really is great — this country, these people, this land of opportunity.

Nigel tuned in to my reverie as we pulled up at a red light.

"Please, don't do that again."

"What?"

"Sing along in a convertible. If you feel you have no choice I recommend being alone in confined spaces where no one else has to suffer."

I smiled, pretended to start up again as Michael Hutchence and INXS let rip with "Need You Tonight."

"You think you'll be back?" he asked, as if he could intuit where my mind had been wandering.

"I don't know," I said. "It's been a great three months." And then felt the need to add "So, maybe."

Nigel studied my expression, hesitated, and smiled as the light turned green.

"Huh," he said, the Jeep accelerating as he shifted from first to second.

"What?" I said, and getting no reply, tried again, even louder. "What?"

"Nothing," said Nigel, still smiling, "only I've seen that look before and I think you meant to say 'definitely'!"

■ ■ ■ ■

PART TWO
STARS AND STRIPES

■ ■ ■ ■

8.
C Is for Cat

I thought his name was Reggie, but apparently I was wrong.

"His full name is Reginald C. Cat."

And with this, the floppy feline was deposited in my lap though he chose not to settle. Within seconds he hopped down and strolled out of the room in the manner of someone who knows his exit is being watched. I had to ask the obvious question.

"What does the *C* stand for?"

The little girl with the freckles, neatly trimmed bangs, and the gummy gaps in her smile considered me as though I might not be all there.

This was our first encounter, our memorable first conversation, and back then I had no idea that this girl and her peculiarly named cat were about to become an integral part of my life.

Three years earlier, I had been walking the dogs with my father in the English countryside, professing my indifference to a future in America. I returned to my final year of college and thanks to a series of unfortunate events, there was a chance that I might fail to qualify. In my soft-tissue surgery rotation, one of my mentors, Dr. White, requested my assistance on a thoracic surgery. For many students, scrubbing into surgery can be a nerve-racking endeavor, teeming with opportunities to contaminate the sterile field and ruin any chance of success. Masked, gloved, and gowned, about to make the opening incision, Dr. White asked me to pass him the foot pedal for the electrocautery unit, meaning to kick it his way underneath the operating table. Determined to be helpful, I reached down to the floor, picked up the pedal with my latex-gloved hand, reached over the prepped surgical site, and cheerily said, "Here you go!" All I heard was a communal gasp at my heinous breach of sterile technique before being ejected from the OR. And then, during a rotation in equine medicine, I was in charge of overnight treatments for the horses. In a daze, I stumbled into a stall with what I believed to be an appropriately prepared meal, walked away, and thought no more about it until the following morning when an irate clinician screamed at me for trying to kill his patient.

"Do you know what happens to horses that eat beet pulp that's not been soaked properly?"

Clearly I did not, so he barely paused.

"They get something called 'choke.' Ever heard of it? Think it might be called choke for a reason? If it wads up and gets stuck up in their esophagus they can die. Fortunately for you this particular horse was smart enough not to touch it."

In spite of another good reason *not* to become an equine veterinarian, I managed to get by, to pass the rotation and my final examinations, and graduate — a proud, newly minted member of the Royal College of Veterinary Surgeons. I took a position as an intern at the University of Liverpool, what they called a "house officer," and it was during this time that the addiction to surgery took hold and had me dreaming of opportunities in America.

I could argue that programs offering both didactic and practical training in small-animal surgery were few and far between in Britain, forcing me to look further afield. Still, I didn't need to put an ocean between myself and the Yorkshire Dales, but ambition and the insight gained from my previous visit to the United States had given me the necessary nudge to apply for a three-year residency position at Tufts University and the Angell Memorial Animal Hospital of Boston. Why not, I had thought, it wasn't as though I stood any chance of getting in. And before I knew what hit me, I was standing with Mum, Dad, and the dogs, saying my goodbyes, burdened with a one-way ticket that felt like a mistake — that smacked of finality and, worst of all, of running away.

I hate goodbyes. I tend to blank them out and with this one all that remains is an overwhelming memory of reassuring my parents, letting them know that this was temporary, a vacation from which I was certain to return. Funny how a little patch of bumpy air at thirty-five thousand feet cleared my mind, helping me focus on a new and flagrant truth — there were now three thousand miles separating a son infatuated by a dream at odds with a father's harmless aspiration. I was abandoning the only people who had been, and always would be, there for me.

When I started my residency, the designation of "Doctor" took some getting used to. This sounds silly, but in Britain veterinarians graduate with no title. This custom hails from the hierarchy applied to our counterparts in human medicine. British med school graduates are called doctors, but if they are fortunate enough to become surgeons, paradoxically, they revert back to the more highly esteemed title of "Mr." or "Ms." Because veterinarians are licensed to practice animal surgery, they too are afforded the professional honor of being Mr. or Ms. To be honest, after all those years of college, I quite liked the idea of getting a title that packed a punch of academic respect understood by all, and not only the enlightened few.

From the get-go, my experience of being an actual doctor was quite different from my earlier stint in Philadelphia as a veterinary student. Somehow I had failed to appreciate certain characteristics of the American pet-owning public. Perhaps I had been indoctrinated by my own country, with its system of socialized medicine, and was overexposed to amenable, accommodating owners who demonstrated an unquestioning trust in their animal's veterinarian. Perhaps those folks from Philly had taken pity on an enthusiastic if ineffectual apprentice. Here in New England, however, I was blindsided by an attitude I would eventually grow to love — edgy, persistent, dedicated, and educated. Complacency met a new reality and I found myself on the defensive.

"What d'ya mean you're going to put my dog on antibiotics just in case! Which antibiotic? For how long? Is your choice based on a culture and sensitivity test and if not, why not?"

For the first time in my short career I had to articulate my veterinary thought processes and offer up what had previously been an inner monologue. I had to learn to appreciate the art of clinical justification and honest communication. Cards on the table and hold nothing back. If you don't know, say so. Make time to shut up and listen. If your clients are uncomfortable or unhappy, give them a chance to let you know. It wasn't long before I came to the realization that animal health care is at its best when it becomes this kind of focused, collaborative effort rather than a product to be dispensed and accepted without question.

Those first few months of the residency program were all about adjustment. No matter how much I enjoyed my previous visit, I was still a stranger in a strange land. And how different a land it was. When Nigel and I drove across the country, our vehicle served a specific purpose, allowing us to traverse thousands of miles from A to B.

How had I failed to notice the American car culture? Why did everything necessitate a vehicle? Why did it feel as though so much of my day was spent inside a vehicle? Why does every quaint town in central Massachusetts look virtually identical, every major intersection marked by another indistinguishable white wooden church and the absence of meaningful signposts? No wonder I felt as if I was living in my car. I was permanently lost, ensnared by the stubborn New Englander's philosophy that "If you don't know where you are, you don't belong here"!

Making matters worse was my ignorance of American pop culture and my indifference to American sports. What was *Saturday Night Live?* Who was Walter Cronkite? What's a Ding Dong? What happened at Kent State? So much uncommon ground; so little familiar about the fabric of our lives. Invited to "shoot some hoops" with a few of my colleagues after work, I truly believed all I had to do was show up and the necessary dribbling and dunking skills would come naturally. Not for one moment did I consider my basketball skills to be at the level of a seven-year-old. If the cricket bat and ball were in the other hand I imagine most Americans would fare just as poorly playing "silly midwicket" or trying to bowl "a googly," but I wasn't thinking straight because I was in such a hurry to fit in.

Probably because I was so busy trying to assimilate all things Americana, I never had time for loneliness. I was too excited, too engaged to feel isolated and unhappy. I wasn't looking for companionship. I wasn't looking to fall in love. And maybe that's precisely why I did — hopelessly and irrevocably with a woman named Kathy.

Ours was not the kind of romance that might entice the likes of Sandra Bullock or Kate Hudson when they read the movie script. You know the one, the *Pride and Prejudice* plot — boy meets girl, there's a show of early indifference, a thaw, an admission of mutual love, and everyone lives happily ever after. No; to my way of thinking, ours was much better.

Kathy and I met while I was at Tufts University. We were wearing paper mask and bouffant cap disguises, trading baby-blue stares across sterile space in the OR. There could be no love at first sight based on physical appearance (though I was not to be disappointed). However, there could be total focus on what so many of us crave in a good relationship — the discovery of a big personality and a wicked sense of humor.

Kathy was working in the large-animal hospital, primarily anesthetizing horses, but if she swung by the small-animal side, we would find each other and end up sharing a story and a laugh. I recall one particular exchange from early on.

"How was your weekend?" I asked.

"Not so good," she said. "I was up in Maine, out sailing with my daughter and my niece."

I tried to remain nonchalant, to "be cool." Maybe everyone sails in America, just like everyone has a swimming pool and goes out to dinner at least once a week. But we both knew that wasn't what gave me pause. This was the first time I had chatted up (or, to use the lingo of my new surroundings, "hit on") a woman who was letting me know she had a child.

"You have a yacht?"

"No," she said, "I was with a friend, a boyfriend . . . this was the final straw and now he's an ex-boyfriend. He ran us aground. Coast guard had to come and rescue us. Scared us all to death."

I nodded, sagely, as though affairs of nautical consequence run through the veins of all the men of Her Majesty's empire.

"That's too bad," I said, stifling a grin.

"Why's that," she said, bowling me over

with a big smile that lit up her eyes. "Because now you can ask me out?"

"No," I said, enjoying my advantage, "because I was hoping you might take me on a boat ride!"

Ask anyone who's been there — when it feels right, you just know it. An instantaneous connection between us made something shift inside me. In less than two weeks of dating, I knew this was the woman I wanted to marry.

When I first met Kathy's daughter, Whitney, I was standing in the living room of their farmhouse. And it was here that Whitney was introducing me to their cat, Reggie.

"So what does the *C* stand for?"

"*C* is for cat."

I nodded like the simpleton I obviously was, delighting her with my show of slow understanding.

"Got it," I said, "Reginald Cat Cat. But is it okay with you if I call him Reggie, for short?"

The little girl worried, deliberated, rocking her head and shoulders in unison from side to side and finally came back to me with a carefully considered nod.

"I suppose so," she said.

It wasn't long before I had moved in with these two relatively unfamiliar and intimidating creatures — a five-year-old girl and a New England barn cat. Whitney would become my step-daughter, though we abandoned the unnecessary "step" part of the designation long ago. The cat would become *the* cat in my life, finally, my first cat, the cat who filled my feline void, the cat against which all other cats would be measured — Reginald C. Cat.

The Renaissance man's guide to familial integration suggests one should be prepared for hostility, standoffs, icy stares, tantrums, and the line all men fear hearing from a child who is part of the package deal in a relationship — "You can't tell me what to do because you're not my *real* dad." Fortunately Whitney demonstrated none of these traits. On the contrary, I could not have wished for a more welcoming, cheerful, and affectionate soul. Instead, my anticipated confrontation, and battle against indifference, centered on the prickly feline in my new arrangement.

Unlike Whitney, Reggie could not be won over by bedtime renditions of "The Very Quiet Cricket" or hours of playing dollhouse. From across the room he would regard me with a look I interpreted as "You're pathetic," occasionally training his green eyes on Whitney as if to say, "Quit selling out on me." Every time I would go up to him, clucking, cooing, calling his name, my voice ridiculously singsong and high-pitched, he would freeze, wait until I closed in, and then leap away at the last minute. It was similar to one of those cheesy horror movies where the audience knows Damien is really the son of Satan while his parents misinterpret all his demonic antics as the spirited high jinks of an angel. Reggie was sweetness and light around Kathy and Whitney, affectionate, malleable, and calm. Alone with me he would practically whisper, "I don't have to pretend around you" as he hissed or flashed me the middle claw before dancing off to the barn, with just enough of a flourish in his tail to let me know he was actually enjoying himself.

Some of Reggie's standoffish personality may have stemmed from unknown traumas in his early life. Kathy had gotten him as a stray about five years earlier, picked up by a Good Samaritan who found an emaciated but handsome male short-haired tabby cat wandering the streets in search of food. Nobody knew his age, except to say he was an adult with a mouth full of permanent teeth in fine working order. His head was broad and his skin felt thick and durable, suggestive of an animal neutered later in life, his body lapping up all the available testosterone before it was stolen, and he had all his claws. Judging by the healed rips and holes in his ears, he had been in some fights and knew how to defend himself. In short, he was a "slumcat." But it was precisely the bad boy in him, this cheeky, indifferent 'tude that made him all the more irresistible. He was simply too cool and I realized I was trying too hard.

I decided to go with a different approach, a little subterfuge. I forced myself to act indifferent, hoping this tactic might spark his curiosity. If Reggie was ever going to warm to me it would be on his terms and so, for a while, I stepped back and simply observed how he lived his life.

Kathy owned a small horse farm in the middle of nowhere, truly the perfect feline environment. With no busy roads nearby, acres of woodlands, and a barn to call his own, Reggie had the best of both worlds — the perfect indoor/outdoor combo. He would sleep in the main house, oftentimes with Whitney, happy to utilize her head as a convenient pillow. He would rise early and stroll down to the kitchen, where he would expect breakfast to be ready and waiting — dry cat food, not wet. From here he would amble over to the front door and did not like to be kept waiting too long. Having to cry out in order to be let out might necessitate significant retribution, but more of that later. Once he was outside, the day's work would begin, starting with a clearly defined excursion around the property. He always took the same route, adopting the same even pace before dropping off my radar. What happened during the rest of the day I might catch in glimpses. He was a natural and talented predator, patient and methodical, rarely unsuccessful. He had no problem with trees. Whatever happened in his former life, whether he stayed close to his mother and learned some valuable tricks or was simply smart enough to work it out, Reggie knew how to back down from high up in a tree. This was not a cat afraid of heights or in need of a fireman's ladder.

Reggie regularly frequented the horse barn, creating his own haven, a venue akin to a gentlemen-only bar in an exclusive country club. Here he could hang out, high up on his favorite shelf among the fleece leg wraps, surveying his domain and ridiculing the horses imprisoned in their cold stalls. If and when he felt like it, he might engage in a little sport, catch a mouse or two, happy to leave the kill out for everyone to see, preferably close to a bag of feed, ensuring praise and treats on his return to the house.

Toward the end of the day he would stroll home, choosing to enter the house through a sliding door in the back, as though only by using this entrance had he completed the official duties of his security detail. Once inside he would take his supper and then relax — sofa, fireplace, or linen closet, whichever took his fancy. When the lights went out and everyone went off to bed he might pad around a bit, but for the most part he would slip in with Whitney, there after she fell asleep, gone before she woke up.

"What's with that meowing, crotch-licking thing I've caught him doing?" I asked Kathy one day.

I was referring to this weird posture Reggie would adopt from time to time, hitching one of his back legs over his shoulder like the opening move in some disturbing contortionist routine, followed by a rant as he appeared to inspect his manhood.

"Didn't I mention he had a PU? The little man's keeping his surgical site clean."

PU stands for perineal urethrostomy, a urinary diversion surgery employed in male cats who suffer from recurrent urinary tract blockage due to the accumulation of crystalline grit and sand. To my surprise, tough guy Reggie did not have a penis!

"Is that why he's cranky with me? Still mad somebody stole his unit? Wants me to be next?"

It was Kathy's turn to give me a withering stare, as if Reggie put her up to it.

"And what was with the precious gift I received this morning when I stepped out of the shower?" I asked.

Since I was first up in the morning, I took it upon myself to feed Reggie, hoping to work my way into his good graces by being identified as the purveyor of his breakfast. After delivering coffee to Kathy I would shower. No one ever thinks twice about stepping out and onto a cotton bathroom rug to towel off. However, on this occasion, the rug had been pulled back and folded inward from its corners in the manner of an oversized crab Rangoon, only there wasn't a heap of succulent crab meat lumped into its center. Instead, when I made to unfold the rug, my big toe brushed up against a sizable feline turd.

"He must have been mad at you," said Kathy.

"Why?" I asked. "I'm the one serving him breakfast. I had hoped he was starting to thaw out, finally getting used to me. Instead he's leaving a crap in my path."

"He's telling you to let him out before you go veg out in the shower for twenty minutes." And with that she swept him up and into her arms in a way I could never imagine doing without losing a cornea or contracting cat scratch fever. Was it me? Was I destined to be hopeless around cats because I had been denied their company as a kid? Did they sense, in a way I was sure the horses sensed, that I didn't get them, didn't understand them, didn't speak their language?

I took some comfort from knowing I wasn't the only one who found Reggie to be intimidating. Like I said, Reggie always chose to return home at the end of another exhausting day torturing wildlife and berating horses by following the exact same route — around the deck in the back of the house, up the stairs, patiently waiting to be let in through the sliding door at the rear. Only on one particular occasion an enormous female harlequin Great Dane belonging to a friend of Kathy's was chained up outside this door, blocking his path. The Dane spotted Reggie on approach and lunged at him, caught up in a relentless barking frenzy, stretching his metal chain to the point of breaking, desperate for a piece of cat chow.

Most animals, undergunned and undersized by comparison to this canine leviathan, would have backed off and avoided the confrontation, opting for common sense over deluded valor. Reggie saw things differently. He saw a mouthy lug of a dog blocking his route home, messing with tradition, stomping on his turf, compromising the civilized routine he savored. So Reggie kept coming, his rhythm steady, limbs loose and fluid, eyes focused on the growling beast towering way up and over his head. He drifted closer to the danger zone with no hesitation, no second thoughts, picking up the pace, moving in and up, and suddenly Reggie was on him, a big polydactyl paw swiping across the Dane's cheek, the ultimate bitch-slap. The Dane was dumbstruck, speechless as he backed off. And what did Reggie do? What else would he do? He sauntered past, problem solved, one hundred and fifty pounds of dog turned into Jell-O, and, without a second look, he stood politely in his usual spot at the back door, waiting to be let in.

The first hint that Reggie was starting to thaw toward me came shortly after a hard frost in late fall. The house had cathedral ceilings and was a devil to heat, dependent on a wood-burning stove in the living room.

For the first time since my days as a Boy Scout, I found myself trekking outside in the morning darkness, chipping away at a frozen cord of wood, and gathering fuel for a fire.

After finding that chocolate fortune cookie in the bath rug I was timely about letting Reggie outside for his morning constitutional, but on this occasion, as I pried the cut logs apart and loaded them into my carrier bag, Reggie appeared, rubbing up against my legs, sliding in with a firm body slam as he nudged me with his right flank and then his left.

"What's up, little man?"

He stared up for a second and trotted back to the house, breaking his routine to wait at the closed front door.

I imagined he must have been surprised at how cold it was that morning and preferred to let the day warm up before heading out on patrol, encouraging me to get a move on in building a decent fire while he waited.

I thought no more about it, but that evening, for the first time, he jumped up on the sofa next to me, something he normally avoided, walking over my legs as though they didn't exist before settling down within stroking distance. I dared to lay a hand on his head and began to work backward down his neck. Kathy and Whitney were watching, holding their collective breath, waiting to see his response, and to their delight and mine, Reggie closed his eyes and offered up a deep, soulful purr.

Of course I blew it by being lazy. My arm tired of reaching to pet him so I decided to pick him up and place him on my lap. Reggie was having none of it and leapt off the couch and out of the room.

"He's getting there," said Kathy. "You just have to work on his timetable."

And I knew she was right. Reggie was simply a cat you had to get to know over time. You couldn't force the relationship. It had to unfold naturally. He didn't do speed dating and he wasn't easily won over by grand gestures or excessive familiarity. Reggie understood how to do new relationships right — to have meaning, depth, and longevity, they will either naturally evolve on their own, or they won't.

"Of course," said Kathy, "you've still got two more tests to pass before you get his complete stamp of approval."

"And what are they?" I asked.

She turned to Whitney.

"What does Reggie do when he loves you?"

Whitney beamed, knowing the answer to this one.

"He falls asleep in your lap and drools on you."

"And?"

"He licks your hand clean."

Slowly, over the next month, I ticked them off, one by one. Reggie waking up on my lap, acting all surprised, like a passenger on an airplane with a saliva string stuck to his chin. And then, from nowhere, a bizarre rasping sensation from a barbed pink muscle attending to the back of my hand, working methodically, unhurried and seemingly happy to oblige. It felt as though it had taken forever, but looking down at the tabby street urchin busy and content to make me presentable, I had an overwhelming sensation of finally feeling accepted as part of his family.

For my first Christmas in the States, Mum and Dad came to visit — first passports, first time on an airplane — ostensibly for an opportunity to meet Kathy.

"Ah, she's a grand lass," said Dad with his best Yorkshire inflection as he and I stood outside on a smoky, snow-swept wooden deck, beers in hand, working the grill.

I smiled appreciatively, but I sensed there was more to come.

"You're sure this is what you want?" he asked.

When I registered the question, I was about to take another pull on the bottle, but it stopped me mid-sip. I had already discussed my intention of getting married and both my parents seemed to be thrilled by the idea. Had I been wrong? Then I zeroed in on another interpretation of what he was really asking. This wasn't about planting a seed of matrimonial doubt or quietly venting unspoken disapproval, this was about my commitment to a life in America. By choosing this new life did he think I was betraying the old, ensuring I would stay far from home, far from my parents?

There was no plea in his eyes, in fact, he seemed to light up, relieved, when I answered with an unequivocal "definitely," but with hindsight and the wisdom of too many intervening years, I imagine he must have felt as though a door had been shut tight between us, a door he had tried to leave unlocked and slightly ajar, in the hopes that someday I might find my way back through, back home.

"Well, I'm sure our Fiona will not be far

behind. I reckon she'll be heading down under once she's finished her course."

My sister had gone on to become a registered nurse and was training to be a midwife when she met an Australian pediatrician. It was quite possible my parents were about to see both their children disappearing to opposite ends of the world. Suddenly it seemed as though we were all destined to live our lives along different lines of latitude and longitude — remote, parallel, and entirely independent.

"Good for her," I said, but felt better adding, "so long as she's happy."

"She is," said Dad. "Just like you, and that's all that matters, isn't it?"

I supposed it did matter, but it certainly wasn't everything. I couldn't hear regret or sadness in his voice; then again, at this stage in my life, I probably wasn't listening as well as I should have been. Dad simply believed in any future in which his children were happy, no matter what the sacrifice. As we stood there, downing our beers, neither he nor I truly appreciated what this sacrifice would mean, how three thousand miles changes everything. I had destroyed any chance for us to share an impulsive, casual encounter: "I was in the area so I thought I'd stop by. See what you're up to. Hang around for a while."

Instead, at this distance, everything would have to be planned, time allotted, all the thrill and possibilities of spontaneity abandoned. My parents had every right to feel sad and betrayed. It's one thing to leave the nest, it's another to leave the country.

"How's Whiskey and Bess?" I asked.

"Grand. Staying with your grandma. Funny how quickly I miss them."

"Well, now that Marty has passed on, at least there's a good chance that they'll be waiting for you when you get back."

I should point out that for a while there, it looked like Marty might live forever. In the end he was nearly eighteen when he died peacefully in his sleep, a few years before I graduated veterinary school. Naturally Grandma was devastated. Naturally my sadness for her was tainted with the relief of knowing Marty and I were to be deprived of a professional relationship.

Dad chuckled but his mind was elsewhere, working on logistics regarding the dogs.

"Now if anything were to happen to them, I could call you, right?"

"Of course. Don't be silly."

" 'Cause sometimes with the time difference it can be awkward."

"Call whenever. Day or night. I'm not sure

what good I can do over the phone but I'm happy to try. Besides, when it comes to Whiskey, I might not be able to do much even if I was in the same room."

"Well, if they ever need surgery, keep your passport ready. We'll have you on the first flight back home."

I agreed, feeling good to be able to promise this much — the best, the only, concession I could offer.

"Anyway, I'm sure I'll be back soon. We'll all come visit you in the cottage. You can show off the Yorkshire Dales."

What do they say about the best-laid plans of mice and men? How does the cloying childish taunt go? "First comes love, then comes marriage . . ." Well, my plan to go back to Britain soon went awry because, before I knew it, a baby carriage was just one of many essential prenatal purchases being made in a new life that seemed to have shifted beyond my control.

Like most doting fathers I could wax lyrical about the pregnancy, the labor, and the precise moment my life changed forever, but instead let me focus on a few specifics.

Firstly, Kathy's obstetrician, Dr. Mendel (a man who, during the legitimately ferocious phase of labor, she mistakenly referred to as Dr. Mengele), strongly suggested an amniocentesis in order to better assess the health of our baby girl (working in a veterinary facility affords access to ultrasound machines operated by curious and persistent ultrasound technicians and before long I had discovered the sex of my firstborn via water cooler gossip!). This Kathy did, the procedure painful and disturbing but ultimately indicating a normal healthy pregnancy.

Secondly, despite my medical background, it was not until Kathy's water had broken and we were riding the elevator up to delivery, that it finally struck me how, one way or another, this child *would* be born, naturally or via cesarean section, and the need to evacuate the mother ship guaranteed things were about to get . . . well . . . *intense.* If I had been thinking clearly, I might have appreciated the stupidity of having an impacted wisdom tooth extracted that very morning, wafting the aroma of decay and clotted blood out with every soothing word of support, into the vicinity of a woman harboring a superior sense of smell and a desire to see me dead. But, when Emily Sydney emerged, I crawled out of the doghouse, cut the cord, and did my fatherly duty, reporting back, "Ten fingers, ten toes, perfect."

When we brought Emily home from the hospital, I felt a twinge of trepidation about introducing Reggie to our new arrival given the challenge of my own initiation into his posse. And it didn't help that I had become a Howard Hughes germaphobe overnight. The prospect of gaining his approval through an endearing lick from his tongue seemed more like an opportunity to contract disease via oral bacteria. If nothing else I wanted to spare her baby-soft skin a feline sandpaper abrasion. But to my surprise, Reggie proved to be intuitively cautious. He would curl up nearby and fall asleep in a manner that took months with me and he avoided direct contact. I interpreted his distance as indifference, maybe even respect, and I concluded that he had accepted our noisy pink interloper.

During the three years of my surgical residency I managed to get back to England only once, a memorable visit by virtue of my awareness of change.

Whiskey and Bess had aged, especially Bess, her muzzle more gray than black, and both dogs had been packing on the pounds. Descriptions over the phone had been verbally airbrushed compared to what I saw in the flesh and it was obvious that my absence had been an opportunity to let the rules slide. I was seeing too many overweight dogs suffering from arthritis, heart disease, kidney disease, and type 2 diabetes not to have an opinion regarding unnecessary overindulgence in the food department. So what if I had started to sound nagging and repetitive? With the disciplinarian away, the unruly kids had taken over, and at dinner one night it almost felt as though my parents were totally unfazed by expectant, hungry snouts resting on the table. Ordinarily, I would have been an outspoken critic but I sensed I had to be careful. If their son visited more often perhaps he would play a bigger part in the dogs' welfare. If their son visited more often the dinner table would be full of grandchildren and not dogs.

My obligatory "once-over" session found Bess to be in good health, aside from a number of small, smooth, encapsulated lumps just below her skin.

"Almost certainly lipomas — benign fatty growths. But best to have them checked out with your regular vet and then keep an eye on them."

This discovery of a health issue, albeit minor, and my dependence on a veterinarian other than myself appeared to hit me more than it hit my father. He gushed over their new vet in the Dales and I confess to having felt a pang of jealousy.

"Does he know about me?"

"No, not really," said Dad.

"Well, he either does or he doesn't."

Dad looked uncomfortable, as though I had caught him in a lie.

"I suppose it's never come up."

I didn't press the issue. How could I? My father needed to develop a connection with a veterinarian of his own. Never given to bragging, what would he stand to gain by telling this man his son was training to be a veterinary surgical specialist? And there was no dig, no reprisal in his comment. It was simply fact.

To be honest, when I tried to examine Whiskey I was thankful there was an independent doctor in the picture. Prior to going to America, I could fake my way through a cursory examination, integrating enough pats and scratches with genuine palpation to get a reasonable sense of his physical well-being. A few years later and Whiskey's fear memory was much sharper, his growl a warning of serious intent.

"Whoa, I think my work here is done."

Dad apologized for the outburst, even though Whiskey and I were already buddies again, a golden muzzle rooting for my hand

and forgiveness.

"You think you'll ever get a dog of your own?" Dad asked as he watched us rough-house. Whiskey loved these games, puffing up, all frisky if I tickled his nose with his own feather duster tail, or if tried to encourage him to take a bite.

Earlier, I had changed Emily's diaper, laying her down on the duvet in my parents' bedroom. She had been wearing a wool cardigan, and when I picked her up my daughter had transformed into a retriever puppy, she was so covered in golden hairs. Was this observation a sign of my new appreciation for the tidiness of cats over the shedding of hairy dogs?

"I don't know. I think so. At some point in time, maybe when life is a little less hectic."

Dad looked troubled, as though my answer was too vague, as though getting a dog sounded too much like a chore to be put off, perhaps abandoned altogether.

"Does Kathy not like dogs?"

I worked my brain around the question and shook my head.

"She's had dogs her whole life. She had a husky who lived to be sixteen and then a standard poodle. Right now, neither of us has enough time to devote to a dog. That's why independent Reggie is perfect."

Dad winced on a sharp intake of breath, as though I had uttered words of blasphemy, or at least infidelity.

"It's true. He's such a great cat. He's tough but affectionate. He's autonomous but loves to be with you. He's our little man. I've even found myself missing him since we've been away, wondering if he's all right."

This declaration of feline love did little to assuage my father's fear of never seeing me with a dog of my own. Fiona, he knew, was a lost cause. No point in even trying to persuade her to get a dog. But now his son, the veterinarian, was sleeping with the enemy, preferring the company of a cat. James Herriot would turn in his grave.

Nearly twenty years had passed since an anxious little boy fretted over uprooting his beloved German shepherd when his family decided to move to another town. Now it was my turn to be the father, to uproot my family and do right by an altogether different but no less important animal, Reginald C. Cat.

With the completion of my residency and a limited number of job opportunities, I decided to take a chance on a job as a surgeon at a small specialty practice in Arizona. Kathy was up for something different — happy to help run the business in her spare time as a stay-at-home mom — but her biggest concern was Reggie.

"He'll be fine," I said. "How different can it possibly be?"

And all of a sudden I realized I was taking a barn cat and basically dropping him in the middle of Mars. The Sonoran Desert has a unique beauty, spectacular space, saguaro forests, and light like nowhere else on earth, but it is rife with fauna and flora designed to pierce, maim, or kill an unsuspecting indoor/outdoor cat.

I can't imagine poor Reggie's astonishment when he first stepped foot in his new home. Here was a cat rooted in routine, and without his approval I had canceled his membership in the barn he thought of as a country club and traded woodlands and green grass for cacti and barren caliche soil. He was a creature of four seasons, adept at finding a warm nest in the winter, cool shadows on a humid July afternoon. Suddenly it was practically summer all year round, and by now I knew enough about Reggie to believe the stock phrase "but it's a dry heat" would be met with the response "so is the inside of a blast furnace!"

For the longest time Kathy and I debated about converting Reggie to a life indoors. There seemed to be so much unprecedented danger out there. If a jumping cholla didn't get him, there was always a scorpion, a Gila monster, a tarantula, or a pack of coyotes. How could a street-smart New England kitty survive in a desert? But, as it turned out, we couldn't wean the independent streak out of him. He clawed and pawed, demanding to be outside. At first we watched him from a distance, monitoring his route, as though we might be able to intervene the first time he got into a fight with a rattlesnake. But after a while, when he returned home with nothing more than the occasional cactus spine caught up in his fur, we began to worry less.

By the time the gifts started to arrive, I knew Reggie was becoming acclimatized to his new surroundings. By gifts I mean dead, eviscerated small birds and rodents, deposited on the welcome mat at our front door. Every morning I would get up, step outside to retrieve the newspaper from the driveway, and my bare foot would be hovering over another sacrificial offering.

"This is getting out of control," I told Kathy. "It's disgusting. Do you think he's trying to punish us?"

"Maybe or maybe he's trying to let us know he's having a good time, enjoying life as a desert predator. He probably thinks we can't take care of ourselves so he feels obliged to provide for us."

"All I know is I'm cleaning entrails off the doormat far more often than I want to."

Truth is you can't take the hunting instinct out of a creature perfectly designed to hunt. Imprisonment seemed too cruel for Reggie. It's like first class and coach. Get the taste for the good life and there's no going back. We briefly tried the collar fitted with a small bell but he was having none of it.

The problem was brought to a head, however, when Sally, a new neighborhood friend, dropped by for late-morning coffee and was forced to step across a threshold on which lay another of Reggie's anatomical experiments on wildlife. Apologies were made and Sally seemed to find the display more curious than repulsive, but the damage appeared to be done. Reggie was labeled as a feline serial killer with a penchant for displaying his victims in public.

Some weeks later I found myself joining a veterinary colleague as co-host of a local talk-radio pet show. We were taking live phone calls and after all my years of surgical specialization it wasn't long before I realized how useless I was when it came to answering the kinds of questions most pet owners really want to ask — all that important stuff regarding vaccines, nutrition, and behavior that I had managed to forget. For the most part I found myself either deferring to the other doctor or mumbling a vague answer. The hour crawled along until a woman called in and said, "I have a cat that brings me dead birds and mice and deposits them on my doormat every morning. What can I do to stop this behavior because it's driving me nuts!"

"Me too," I said, leaning forward into the microphone, suddenly all animated. "My cat Reggie does exactly the same thing. And you're right, it's so annoying."

I related the story of Sally's recent visit, and how embarrassed I'd been over Reggie's inappropriate offering, and talked briefly about the feline predatory instinct, about how there wasn't much you could do unless you enforced an indoor lifestyle.

I finished up genuinely pleased to have taken her call, telling the audience, if there really was anyone out there listening, "Wow. What were the chances! I'm glad to know I'm not the only cat lover out there suffering at the hands of a skilled hunter."

When I returned home I received a phone

call from Sally, letting me know how much she enjoyed the show. How nice of her, I thought, hanging up, but at the same time, I was struck by something that felt a little off. Sally seemed, I don't know, almost giddy, as though her sincerity was teetering on the brink of snickering. And then it hit me . . . her voice . . . I recognized her voice. Sally had been the woman calling in about a cat who insisted on delivering daily hunting gifts. Sally had been seeking advice from me about my Reggie!

Ironically, as it turned out, the biggest danger to Reggie's health would be me.

I had long grown accustomed to finding him in unusual locations — in linen closets and wardrobes, under cars. He might hear you coming, or look straight at you, eye to eye, when you opened a door, but either way he would disappear, his speed suggesting he couldn't believe his privacy had been interrupted.

On this occasion he must have been hanging out in the garage. I pulled my car inside, pressed the button for the door to descend and headed into the house. There was no one else home and it was a good ten minutes before I registered the sound of a meowing cat and at least another sixty seconds before

I tracked it down to the garage.

There, trapped beneath the heavy retractable door, were the back legs and lower body I recognized as belonging to Reggie. This was a time before mandatory childproof automated garage doors, and somehow Reggie must have gone all Indiana Jones on me as the gap into daylight began to narrow, misjudged his window of opportunity, and ended up with the weight of the door crushing his little body into two halves, pinning him to the concrete below.

How he managed to move his rib cage and vocalize with all that dead weight on top of him I'll never know, but in that instant I felt what I had seen in the eyes of so many owners who feel directly responsible for their pet's demise.

"He slipped his leash. I never even got to call his name before the car hit him."

"I just put the car in reverse. How was I to know she was sleeping on the driveway? I never saw a thing. The first thing I knew was when she started screaming."

My heart ricocheted inside my chest, panic mingled with guilt as I hit the button and the garage door began to rise. Reggie just lay there, unable to move, responsive to my touch but almost in a state of shock.

I examined him where he lay. By the looks

of things the door had pressed down on him along his spine, behind his chest, crushing his abdomen. His color was good, he was breathing fine, and I could feel his heart racing to catch up with mine. Carefully I palpated his belly. He could easily have ruptured his spleen, lacerated a liver lobe, burst a loop of bowel, but everything felt pretty good, relaxed and nonpainful. Then I discovered a major problem. Reggie's back legs refused to move, in fact, when I pinched his toes he made no response, no recognition whatsoever of discomfort. Given the location of the direct trauma, there was a good chance that when the door came slamming down, poor Reggie had broken his back.

Carefully, I got him onto a plywood board and drove in to work, united with all those owners I had known, the ones shaken and devoured by remorse. We are desperate to act, to do something, anything, no matter what the cost, to make the animal's pain and our own pain go away. My mind was way ahead, thinking about spinal surgery, planning which technique I would use to stabilize the fractured bones. What would I say to Kathy and Whitney? Their indestructible Reggie had come undone on my watch. And now there was a new and ugly truth waving to get my attention — what if, despite your best efforts, this cat never walks again?

By the time I was taking the X-rays of Reggie's spine, he was beginning to get upset, releasing a stream of feline obscenities as though he was in significant discomfort.

"Hang in there, little man," I said as the film rolled out of the processor.

Secretly, I often hold my breath when I am viewing an X-ray after a surgical repair, forced to face the black-and-white reality of my work, making sure a fracture is adequately and appropriately secured. This time, I threw in a prayer, hoping, at the very least, it would be something I could attempt to fix.

As it turned out, it wasn't. I don't know how he did it, but you can't fix what's not broken. Miraculously, Reggie's spine remained intact. The meowing, however, continued unabated, and I began to wonder if he was beginning to feel the equivalent of pins and needles as blood started to rush back into numb and lifeless extremities. Could the weight of the wooden door on one side and the unforgiving concrete floor on the other have pinched off the blood supply to his back legs, temporarily causing his paralysis? I supposed it was possible, so I started massaging and bicycling his little feet, much to his displeasure, but over the next hour or so, sensation and movement began returning to his legs.

That night I was giddy with relief, weak and sentimental, pouring on the affection, offering a consolation supper of milk and a can of tuna by way of an apology. Next time I would be more attentive when closing the garage door. Better still, time to upgrade to some childproof sensors. By the following morning, he seemed completely back to his old self. And the day after that, I was actually pleased to discover a gift on the doormat.

Though Reggie taught me a valuable, if painful, lesson in sympathy for pet owners burdened with a direct responsibility for their animal's predicament, his enduring legacy will always be associated with Emily.

Emily had been a difficult baby — irritable, prone to coughs, colds, ear infections, and colic. Though I am subject to the bias of every proud parent, I would have to describe her as a stunning blue-eyed blonde with perfect rosebud lips and a smile that could make me cry from twenty yards. Yet something about her was clearly not right.

How similar are the frustrations and limitations of pediatric and veterinary medicine, the infant and animal trying to communicate in the only way they can — by expressing their suffering.

I kept coming back to the amniocentesis Kathy had endured during her pregnancy, proof positive that Emily was free and clear of all possible major congenital defects. With these diseases ruled out, what could it possibly be?

For a long time, asthma was believed to be the culprit. Emily was started on aerosolized medicine to open up her airways and make it easier for her to breathe, but placing a plastic mask over a baby's face induces a response similar to that of your average cat or dog — screaming, kicking, and fighting. We battled on but the treatment wasn't helping. All the tests kept coming back negative, but all of us, including the doctors, knew something serious had to be going on.

Just after Emily's second birthday she developed a severe, merciless cough. Obtaining a meaningful sputum sample from an infant can be tricky at best, especially in a pediatrician's office, so when she whooped up a prize specimen on the front of my shirt and I happened to have a sterile kit on hand for taking samples for bacterial culture and antibiotic sensitivity testing, I seized my opportunity. I took my sterile Q-tip, shoved it in the blob, inserted it into the special growth medium, and labeled the sample as belonging to the lungs of one "Reginald C. Cat." This I submitted to the veterinary laboratory I used for my patients.

When the results came back, Reggie had grown a weird organism, bacteria never found in the lungs of healthy cats let alone healthy humans, bacteria that could thrive only if a severe abnormality existed in the lungs' natural ability to clear the airways of mucus and junk.

"I know this is weird," I said to our pediatric pulmonologist, handing over a copy of Reggie's results. "But this is what I grew from Emily's lungs."

From a quagmire of contradictory signs and negative tests, Reggie's paperwork leapt out at the doctor and pointed her in a highly specific direction. Emily's lung, sinus, and bowel problems, so debilitating in such a little life, had to be caused by a congenital disorder genetically acquired through her parents' DNA, an incurable disease called cystic fibrosis.

"But she's been tested for CF," I said. "The test was negative. My wife even had an amniocentesis and cystic fibrosis was one of the things they were supposed to rule out."

I was reminded that no test is foolproof; there can be false negatives and only common genetic mutations are considered in a test.

"Have you ever noticed if Emily's skin tastes particularly salty?"

She went on to describe how the problem with CF kids lies in an inability to appropriately move salt in and out of the body's cells. It didn't sound like much but it was everything, the difference between normal functional airways and airways clogged with lethal, tenacious goop. Perversely, it also drives too much salt out and onto the skin with sweat.

"What does this all mean? Is she going to die?"

The pulmonologist did what all good doctors do, she answered directly, with clarity, compassion, and honesty.

"Currently the average life expectancy for a child with CF is about thirty years. That's average, which means sometimes more, sometimes less."

Kiss the forehead and woe to the child who tastes like salt for he is bewitched and soon must die.

Emily's skin was not excessively salty and believe me, I had performed this test from medieval folklore enough times to know. Then again, had Reggie? To my knowledge, Emily had never achieved the ultimate mark of his approval, the lick on the back of the hand that defined entry into his inner circle. Was this because he was tuned in, superior animal senses tasting the salt, an aberration, something not quite right and therefore something from which he should keep away?

We decided to subject Emily to one more test and waited for the results. In private, I already knew the answer. Though I had not and could not process this answer, why else would I insist the pulmonologist call me on my cell phone with the results? I needed to be the one to break the news to Kathy and when the call eventually came, I was driving home from work. Even before I flipped the phone open I pulled over to the side of the road. Like I said, subconsciously, I already knew. The doctor's words crawled inside me and as they did, the prospect of seeing my two-year-old daughter lead an average, ordinary life came to an end. Struck hollow and breathless, I felt like I had been told my child had gone missing, left to wonder whether she had simply wandered off or been abducted, never to return.

I should have been cruising home — smiling with relief, one hand on the wheel, windows down, feeling the bass from the stereo resonating in my bones. Instead, all I could do was envy the normal people walking the streets or driving home to their uncomplicated lives. Men who would get to see their daughter go to the prom. Women who would grow old enough to get married. Fathers who would get to walk their daughter down the aisle.

By the time I walked into the house and Kathy saw the look on my face, there was no need to speak, the test result written in the tears running down my cheeks. Her knees buckled and she fell to the floor before I could reach her. For the longest time we just held each other, trembling, fighting down the screams we so desperately wanted to scream for fear of waking Emily as she napped in the next room.

Kathy finally managed to string some words together.

"Now what do we do?"

Between gasps I managed to reply, "The doctor says she wants to meet with us next week to talk about the disease."

"But did she say . . . I mean, how long does she . . . ?"

And with this thought I lost her to another

303

round of grief and fear. No amount of crying has ever or will ever rid me of this fear, but on that day it was raw and fierce and just getting started.

"Will we lose her?" said Kathy.

Suddenly, dropped into this frightening new reality, all I could offer was one of the most painful yet honest statements any father will ever have to make.

"I don't know," I said.

Meanwhile our innocent little girl slept peacefully in her crib as a curious tomcat cruised by, a tomcat who never knew that the culture results for one Reginald C. Cat reside near the very top of Emily's permanent medical record to this day.

9.
THE END OF GOODBYE

Everyone knows that mothers and fathers the world over possess an innate unwavering desire to protect their offspring. Though this instinct remained strong and intact, Emily's diagnosis had effectively crushed my ability to stop all harm at any cost. Only now did I understand how I had been denied this parental right from the moment she took her first breath.

Pain can manifest itself in many forms, but our reaction is fundamentally the same — a desire to escape, to make it go away. As a veterinarian, I was familiar with a certain look, the one an animal gives to its owner when it has to be restrained for a shot or has to have a bandage changed or an intravenous catheter placed. This look is directed upward, eyes wet and sorrowful, a look that whispers, "Why are you letting them hurt me?" How many times did Emily floor me with the exact same look? When Emily was sick and in the hospital, getting stuck with needles and being restrained for X-rays, how many times did I scream inside my head when she added, "Please, Daddy, make them stop!"

I suppose there are plenty of parents out there who when told that their daughter has a terminal disease will try to carry on as normal, apply a smile, and force themselves to engage with the world. My hat goes off to them. They are better parents than I because all I could hear was a ticking clock, time passing by, a death closing in, until the only thing I knew for sure was that something quiet and peaceful had crawled inside of me, curled up, and lay down to die — hope.

I knew I was in trouble when I owned up to a shocking knee-jerk response to one of my more difficult cases.

His name was Buster, a big, brawny white American bulldog, capable of winning hearts with his goofy grin. He lived with his owner, I'll call her Doris, in a beat-up VW Beetle and together the two of them would cruise around town, panhandling, raiding trash cans for recyclable aluminum cans, and hopping from soup kitchens to food pantries as part of the daily grind of the abandoned, ignored, and homeless.

Doris may have had some mental health and personal hygiene issues, but when you saw her around Buster all that hit you was the unabashed love of a beleaguered, forgotten member of our society for the one genuine, nonjudgmental beacon in her life, the dog who always called shotgun.

It was the fire that caught the local media's attention — homeless woman falls asleep while smoking a cigarette — classic scenario in a peculiar domicile, glowing nicotine stick fueled by fast-food wrappers littering the car. Doris managed to wake up in time and escape the VW unscathed. Buster, asleep in his trash nest in the front passenger seat, wasn't so lucky, succumbing to second- and third-degree burns over about 30 percent of his body as his homestead turned into an inferno.

Buster was presented to me for burn wound management and reconstructive surgery, and I was happy to do the work given his situation and knowing full well that Doris, now completely homeless, would never be able to pay me back.

At the time, I was heavily involved in fund-raising for the CF Foundation, convinced that this was my best hope for my daughter, a way I could make a difference and help in the quest for a cure. There is nothing pleasant about begging for money. There are too many deserving causes, Doris and Buster in-your-face reminders of untold suffering, of people with far bigger problems, facing hurdles that would make them grateful for my daughter's situation. There I was busting my hump, trawling for a few dollars here and there, pleading with the intensity of a father who would do anything to help his sick child, and then just one day after the story of Doris and Buster's plight, money had poured into the fund set up by a local newspaper, to the tune of nearly ten thousand dollars.

Of course I should have realized that you cannot trump a sad injured-animal story. There's a reason why the final segment of the news is more often than not given over to a touchy-feely tale regarding a lost cat or the heroism of a dog. But I wasn't in a good place. However open-minded I tried to be my new reality pared Buster's story down to a simple choice — a sick dog or a sick child, and the world had voted unanimously for the animal. My sickened heart was convinced that if Emily had been the one pulled from that burning VW she would never have won over the public's sympathy in the same way as poor Buster.

The well-deserved slap across my face

came weeks later at Buster's discharge. Even if we have never experienced severe burns all of us seem to understand that they are synonymous with unremitting pain. The application of every dressing, attention to the wounds, daily bandage changes compounded this dog's agony, but throughout it all, Buster was tolerant and forgiving, his goofy grin letting me know the real Buster still resided somewhere below the black and seeping scabs and the thick shellac of creams. It took several surgeries to put him back together and, given his short white fur, Buster would always have to be cautious to avoid exposing his fleshy pink scars to the powerful desert sun, but seeing this patchwork quilt of a dog melting with delight in the arms of Doris after his last suture was removed brought the reality of my former resentment into focus in an uncomfortable way. Since when did helping sick animals and restoring happiness in the lives of their owners make me unfaithful to my daughter? What had I become now that I no longer recognized myself? Here was a woman with nothing to offer this dog other than herself. She had distilled their bond to its bare minimum and what was left was joy and a future that opened up all kinds of possibilities so long as they had each other. Wasn't this precisely what I owed my daughter? Strip away the negativity, forget about the grim reality of her medical statistics and the daily burdens of what she endured, and see a sick child who wants to be happy and make others happy. Who knows what the future will hold for any of us. What kind of happiness could she possibly achieve, what kind of memories could she build, burdened by a father selfishly consumed by his own fear and grief? Doris and Buster had nothing but the joy of living with each other and by the looks on their faces they were the wealthiest couple on the planet.

A clinical success like Buster's might lead me away from unfocused heartache for a time, but it felt like little more than a balm — calming, soothing, helping the pain abate but not go away altogether. I was consumed by the uncertainty of my daughter's future. I couldn't see a happy ending. How could I enjoy a story that ends when it has hardly begun?

I tried forcing my brain to appreciate how lucky I was simply to have this child in my life. I would think about Kathy's amniocentesis, wonder what might have happened if Emily's mutation had been detected. To this day the possibility of not having her, of aborting the pregnancy had we known, hits me like a sucker punch, leaving me light-headed and with a lingering dull ache in my gut. It took two more difficult cases to let me know that I was finally on the right track to finding a new equilibrium that I could live with.

Arizona is home to a variety of unusual wildlife, and where suburban sprawl meets unspoiled desert, animals such as jackrabbits, tortoises, packrats, and javelina can be forced into unnatural interactions with man, sometimes with disastrous consequences.

The call for help came from a wildlife rescue volunteer who had discovered a young female bobcat lying on the side of the road, alive but only just. She had obviously been hit by a car and was unable to stand, and her breathing was erratic.

"We think she's broken her left front leg and her right hind leg. Do you think there's any chance you might be able to fix her up?"

My mouth said, "Yes, bring her right over," but my mind said, "Are you nuts? This is a wild animal. There can be no 'nice kitty-kitty,' no assertive grabbing by the scruff of her neck to make her behave. She's got serious teeth and serious claws and as frightened as she is she's going to want to use them. If she's having problems breathing chances are she's sustained some serious chest trauma — broken ribs, lacerated lungs, who knows what might be going on in there. How do you propose getting a listen with that stethoscope of yours? And let's say you are able to repair the broken legs. How on earth are you going to convince a wildcat to take it easy, to go watch soap operas on TV and eat bonbons for a few weeks while everything heals up? As soon as this cat stands up it is going to have to use at least one of the broken legs you just put back together!"

When the cat arrived she was sedated, enough to take some X-rays of her chest. Though her ribs and her diaphragm were intact, normal lungs should be full of air, showing up black and empty on the image. The bobcat's lungs were more of a murky gray with patches of dense whiteness, the signs of severe bruising from the trauma, the kind of lungs you don't want to anesthetize.

"Taking her to surgery at this stage might be a disaster," I said. "But I'm not sure we have much choice. Most domestic cats won't tolerate a temporary cast or a bandage on one leg let alone two so I don't hold out much hope for a wild bobcat."

The volunteer was a woman in her forties, with kind eyes framed by the crow's feet of an outdoorsy desert dweller. She wore a T-shirt with a logo touting her wildlife rescue group, like a uniform, to make sure I realized she was legitimate.

"Just do your best," she said. "It's all you can do. If she makes it we can do the rest. If she doesn't . . . well, it's got to be better than dying on the side of the road."

Have you ever had that feeling you get when someone says something and their pitch and timing are so perfect that you can feel the words reaching inside your chest?

"Do you want to die, or do you want to die trying? Give up or give it a shot."

This was what I was hearing, in the most candid, honest, and unemotional terms possible.

And so I decided to try, working on this magnificent anesthetized creature with the biggest paws I have ever had the privilege of squeezing, attaching all manner of stainless steel plates to bony shards with a liberal sprinkling of screws in an attempt to shore up the fractured humerus and the fractured femur.

I was about three hours into the surgery and things were not going well. The bobcat's lung damage was catching up with her, the oxygen saturation of her blood on a steady decline, when an urgent phone call was

313

piped into the operating room.

"Hi, this is Ms. Saunders, I'm a fifth-grade elementary teacher and my class of students heard about the injured bobcat and wanted to help raise money for her rehabilitation."

In the background I could hear the shrill screams and laughter of marauding children high on the possibility of rooting for a cause, of doing good, and for an instant I flashed back to my memory of rescuing a bagful of abandoned kittens as a kid.

To their delight, and not least because I needed to focus on a patient who was trying to die on me, I hastily agreed, the teacher thanking me, wishing me luck, informing me that the class had already named the bobcat Lucy.

What was I thinking? If this cat died in the OR or the repair went on to fail, it would mean I had just broken the hearts of thirty impressionable fledgling philanthropists.

But Lucy didn't die. Call it the resiliency of the wild, a surplus of feline lives, or the power of positive thinking from a bunch of rowdy ten-year-olds. Whatever the reason, Lucy came through the surgery and the anesthesia and was safely transported to a rehabilitation center, where she remained for nearly three months.

The fifth-grade class painted pictures, sent her homemade cards, had bake sales and penny drives, rooting for Lucy to get well soon and, some six weeks after the surgery, I was invited to see how she was getting on. This was one of the few occasions in my professional life in which I was thrilled to receive a hostile reception. Though there was still some residual lameness in her front leg, she was strong on her back end, receiving me with the kind of wide-eyed animosity that makes you say, "My, what big teeth you have."

When the time came, Ms. Saunders's entire class went along to witness Lucy's release into the wild, feeling joy with a hint of sadness as the cage door opened and she bolted for freedom, sprinting into the scrub, fluid, powerful, and perfectly balanced. A year or so later, a client of mine claimed to have spotted Lucy through a pair of binoculars, disappearing behind a saguaro with a litter of kittens in tow.

There was nothing remarkable about what I did; I put my hands in the right place and surgical training did the rest. For me, what was remarkable about this case was the creature's uncanny determination to survive, which served as a reminder of something I was in danger of forgetting. My efforts with Lucy were never about my ability to guarantee a positive result, rather, they were about being open to the possibility of trying to achieve one. To be open to hope.

For a while, misguided vanity made me think I could go back to school, study to become an MD, enroll in an internship and residency and, in under a decade, know enough about my daughter's disease to start making a clinical impact on her life. Alternatively, I could try to rekindle my science background, get a master's, then a PhD and make my attack at the level of clinical research. What was wrong with me? Emily didn't need a dad who spent his time becoming a pediatrician or a mad scientist, she needed a dad who would spend his time being her dad.

Maybe it all comes back to them and us, veterinarians and "real" doctors, pets and humans, because on some level I could feel esteem for my vocation slipping away from me. I had begun to devalue my profession. Driven by the fear of losing a priceless and irreplaceable child I questioned the comparative merits and worth of an animal. Of course it's sad and painful to lose a loyal dog or a beloved cat, but come on, it's only a pet, it's not a child, not a genetic part of you. How could I get emotionally invested in my cases when they felt so inconsequential compared to my investment in my daughter?

Thankfully a golden retriever called Gracie decided to set me straight.

Gracie trotted into my examination room, working the retriever bounce, doing that trick of carrying her own leash, showing off as though she was quite capable of walking herself.

"What's with goldens in America," I said to her "lady in waiting," "taking themselves for a walk? I don't remember noticing it in England."

Ms. Carey laughed and introduced herself. It turned out she was the single mother of two high school students, a boy and a girl, working full time as a nurse to put food on the table and a roof over their heads. She wore colorful scrubs, presumably on her way to or from the hospital, had a tight frizzy perm, and exuded that upbeat no-nonsense attitude of so many health-care professionals who work in the trenches. But something told me she was toiling a little too hard to maintain her smile. Maybe, on some level, I sensed a kindred spirit, because I thought I recognized a familiar long shadow lurking behind eyes determined to remain bright and shiny.

"Gracie's not really my dog. She belongs to Danny, my son, my eldest. He wasn't able to be here today." She waited a beat before adding, "but he would have been if he could. The two of them are inseparable."

There are a hundred and one reasons why a teenage boy might not be able to attend a veterinary appointment for his dog, so I thought no more about it.

"Gracie got out of the house about two weeks ago, ran across the street, and got hit by a car. Oh, it wasn't a big deal," she said, as if she could make it better by hurrying her way through the details, "the car just clipped her. Gracie stumbled forward, hitting her chin on the pavement, and I'm no doctor but I know if a leg is broken or not and she seemed fine. I cleaned up the road rash on her chin and, okay, she seemed a little quieter than usual, but otherwise none the worse for wear. Then, a few days ago, I noticed she was having a hard time breathing, so I took her to my regular vet and he took an X-ray of her chest."

She handed over a film that showed a large distended loop of bowel where her lungs should have been. Poor Gracie had a hernia in her diaphragm. As a result of the trauma, the muscular wall separating her chest cavity from her abdominal cavity had torn, creating a sizable rent. With her guts in the wrong compartment her lungs were unable to fully expand, making it difficult to breathe.

I knelt down to introduce myself properly, hesitating for a split second, as my recollection of golden retrievers in England brought to mind a certain lion-hearted example of the breed. Fortunately, there was no chance of a Mr. Hyde transformation with Gracie. She had her flirty routine all ready to go — work the muzzle under the free hand, beat the veterinarian to death with the tail, roll over and flash the belly, defying him not to offer a scratch. Sometimes I wonder how I might feel as the owner of such a dog: proud of her trusting, friendly demeanor, troubled by the ease with which she betrayed me for anyone who showed her affection.

"Hope you have a decent alarm system at home. If someone broke into your house Gracie might love them to death."

Nurse Carey smiled, but it never connected with her eyes, her mind was elsewhere.

"They said she's got a diaphragmatic hernia, that she needs surgery."

"They're right," I said. "When the X-rays were taken some of her intestines were

319

trapped in her chest. Has she had any problems eating or drinking?"

"Not really. But she did throw up the other morning. Is that what made her sick?"

"It could be," I said. "Either way, I need to get everything back in its proper place and close up the opening in the diaphragm. She might be with us for a day or two but then she gets to go home and recuperate with Danny."

The willful effort to curl up the edges of her lips began to intensify, as though my reply had sliced through the invisible strings that were keeping the smile in place.

"Here's the thing," she said, "Danny's in the hospital himself. Has been for some time now." The smile had essentially vanished and I could feel the pain coming off her, shimmering like desert heat. "He's recovering from a serious head injury." She let the statement hang there for a second, not for effect but because saying it out loud to a stranger had been an effort, an uncomfortable acknowledgment of the severity of her son's situation. "He was . . ." and I lost her for a second. "God, you'd think I'd be over this by now, I'm sorry." She took a deep breath, extended her hand to pat me on the arm, confirming her apology, and set off again. "He was with his buddies, riding in the back of a pickup. Don't ask me what he was thinking. Well, he obviously wasn't thinking, was he? First sharp corner, out he goes, landing on his head."

A hint of anger flashed behind her eyes, fueled by her son's stupidity.

"But I swear, he's coming back, slowly, every day, a little bit at a time. Dr. Trout, what you have to understand is how important Gracie is to his recovery. Danny can't really speak, no more than a few words, but he can see and he can touch and every time this dog pays him a visit he lights up, as though he remembers, like I get a little glimpse of the boy who used to be my son."

And like that, she had me, tears welling up in my eyes with the empathy that comes from witnessing the pain of another vulnerable parent. Even for a child with perfect health, the future will always be fraught with uncertainty. The only thing we can control is the attitude with which we embrace this future.

"I wanted you to know what Gracie means to my son so you'll take extra special care of her. Promise me you will."

And I did, without hesitation, taking comfort in my previous surgical experience dealing with the problem at hand. Her confession prompted me to open up a little about Emily. Like her, I was awkward, my feelings new and difficult to articulate, but she got it in the same way I got her.

"Believe me," she said, "I'm not trying to put you under too much pressure. I just thought it might help, knowing where I'm coming from."

I assured her it was all good, that I completely understood and I was all in. Only later would I berate myself for forgetting one of the cardinal rules from my surgical training — the more emotionally invested you become in a case, the more problematic it is destined to become.

Gracie's hernia repair went well. The challenge lay with the lazy loop of bowel that had become pinched off. Its blood supply had been compromised, an extensive length of the intestinal tract left purple and lifeless. It needed to be cut out and the two fresh, healthy ends sewed back together to restore normal continuity. Not a problem until a few days after the surgery when Gracie spiked a fever.

I placed an urgent phone call to Nurse Carey.

"Her temperature's one hundred four point five Fahrenheit and she's got free bacteria in her abdominal cavity."

She didn't need an explanation. She

understood that Gracie's intestinal surgery had to be leaking, spilling bacteria-laden fecal contents into her abdomen. A raging peritonitis was a given. Getting her guts to heal in the face of overwhelming infection and contamination was going to be a major uphill battle.

"Do what you need to do," she said, her tone surprisingly calm, as though nothing could be simpler. Why wasn't she furious, cursing my incompetence? Why wasn't she reiterating the essence of my mission — save the dog to save the boy?

Humbled but determined, I took poor Gracie back to surgery, going with a simple plan — unzip the previous midline incision, find the leak, repair the leak, clean up, and get out. But when I looked around the abdominal cavity I discovered fine particles of partially digested food liberally sprinkled over every organ like seasoning. Imagine your dinner guest tells you she is highly allergic to pepper and you have to go back and remove every last grain from every steak waiting its turn on the barbecue. You might as well invite her to uncap the needle on her EpiPen syringe because the chances of you getting every ground and dusting of the condiment are slim to none. The same held true for Gracie. I could do a decent job, but even if I removed every obvious piece of contamination those invisible bacteria would still be lurking in their gazillions.

"The surgery went well and the leak's fixed but I had to leave Gracie's abdomen open."

Sometimes, working with a nurse can make life a whole lot easier. An "open abdomen" meant that I had not stitched up Gracie's belly, at least not to the extent of making a tight, permanent seal. I needed to let the "bad vapors" out because I couldn't risk locking all the residual bacteria inside, so I had loosely whipped the walls of her abdomen together. This afforded her some natural, gravitational drainage into a meticulously applied sterile bandage wrapping its way around her entire abdomen, a bandage that helped hold her guts and every other abdominal organ in place. It would have to be changed at least twice a day. There was a significant risk that more bacteria might get in than got out, but given the amount of homespun pollution I had witnessed I felt as though I had no choice.

Ms. Carey instantly grasped the gravity of Gracie's situation, the touch-and-go nature of her dilemma, but she also understood that I would not have gotten into this situation through carelessness or negligence or hasty judgment. She let me know that she lived the uncertainty of modern medicine every day. She made sure I felt her trust. In short, she was the one reaching out to me, doling out the reassurances. Relieved and grateful, I shared my unwavering commitment to do the only thing I could guarantee — my best.

It is nothing short of amazing what animals will tolerate in the name of veterinary health care, all the unnatural interventions we impose on them. Having had my appendix out I know what it's like to have your belly cut open, but if I were left with some halfhearted attempt at closure, stitches like loose shoelaces, wondering if I were going to spill my guts every time I coughed or sneezed, I'd be inviting my surgeon to get himself a good lawyer! But here was a dog who greeted me twice a day for her bandage change as though I were a long-lost relative flying across an ocean from afar, and she was there amid the smiling throngs, waiting for the moment I burst through the arrival doors after clearing customs. Ironically it was her desire to please that created one of the biggest challenges to her recovery, her feathery tail wagging into the sterile surgical site, her proclivity for rolling on her back in need of a belly rub when I needed her to stand still. We place so many strange demands on our patients, make them endure interventions that would be so much easier to deal with if we could communicate our intent. Remarkably, despite these drawbacks, our patients are largely cooperative. Gracie certainly was, and after one more minor surgery I am happy to report she healed like a champ.

In the end Ms. Carey and I never had a specific conversation in which she told me her secret for moving forward with her life. She didn't need to. It was written all over her, woven into her body language, her attitude, intrinsic to the way I perceived her. She made me understand that she had no choice in the matter, that drowning under the weight of grief and pain helped nobody, certainly not the person who needed her help the most. What was the point of believing her son would never get better at this stage of his recovery? What kind of future can you possibly offer your child if you are constantly saying goodbye?

Perhaps you are hoping I can report that Gracie resumed her responsibilities as Danny's dedicated therapy dog, that slowly but surely, his muse cast her golden spell, worked her feathery magic and helped him step back into a world of recognition, higher thought, and independence. In truth I don't know exactly what became of Danny. What I do know is that I played my small, indirect, complicated but ultimately successful part in helping a sick young man through the power of canine companionship. Here was my lesson in the reach of veterinary medicine, in how an animal doctor may not be the one standing up when disaster strikes and someone shouts, "Is there a doctor in the house?" but occasionally, if he or she is lucky, a vet can help heal a sick loved one.

Gracie was the perfect case at the perfect moment. Her story made me realize something so simple, yet something I had been unable to see. It doesn't matter who it is you love — a son, a daughter, a dog, a cat — just get busy with the loving of life. For the first time after Emily's diagnosis I realized it was finally time to stop saying goodbye.

10.
THE SECRET TO NORMALCY

Every now and then children wield their uncomplicated perception of the world like a scalpel cutting through all the fluff and social niceties, deconstructing a complex situation into its basic elements. Whitney was one such child and when she gave me the benefit of her keen understanding, the simplicity and painful honesty of her words reached deep inside me.

Emily had returned home after spending two weeks in the hospital undergoing all manner of torture in the name of modern medicine, and neighborhood friends kept dropping by to wish her well. Every time the doorbell rang the irresistibly cute kid in the footie pajamas knew she would be the recipient of another gift, and we were all so caught up in having her home, no one thought to ask about her older sister. Eventually, as the parade of visitors began to subside, I went looking for Whitney and found her hiding on the other side of a closet door, able to listen in on Emily's fanfare.

"Whit, what are you doing hiding round the corner? Why not come out and say hello?"

Nine-year-old Whitney looked up at me and in a conspiratorial whisper said, "But I don't want them to feel bad."

"Who's them and why would they feel bad?" I asked, taking her hand.

"The neighbors. Because they forgot to bring something for me."

I whisked her up and into my arms and gave her a hug. This moment summed up Whitney, sensitive and selfless, the sibling of a child with a chronic disease, grounded in values beyond her years — supportive, resilient, and secretly afraid for her little sister's future. We had been caught up in our shock, just trying to survive, and as a result, an innocent little girl had suffered. This wasn't neglect, there had never been a double standard, but I ached over the possibility that she felt forgotten. How best to put this right?

In the two years that we had lived in Arizona, Reginald C. Cat had flourished. With hindsight we must have been mad to let him outdoors — too many predators and not enough knowledge of the locality — but cats adapt and Reggie was smarter than most. So, convinced our cat was settled and content, we began to entertain the notion of a canine companion, and though the choice of dog would have the appearance of a unanimous family decision, secretly Whitney's input took precedence. And please, don't be thinking this was conceived as a bribe. Rather, our goal was to make Whitney feel grounded in a normal family, to offer her some companionship, fun, and distraction, to counter some of the difficulties of her situation. To her credit, Whitney never showed any hint of resentment, but I worried that with time and fear, she might try to build a defense against the uncertainty of her sister's future. Her parents would always be there, but here was a chance to confide, share, and vent with a creature guaranteed to become a sounding board and best friend, a family member for whom you were always the center of attention.

I had no preference either way, big or small, mutt or pedigree, though quite what possessed my wife to agree to a rough-coated Jack Russell terrier I will never know. One day I came home to find a white and tan Tasmanian devil sprinting around the house, intermittently attending to furniture that, in her opinion, could clearly benefit from a good gnawing to achieve a fashionably distressed look.

"Isn't she cute?" said Whitney, scooping her up. "Don't you love her?"

The tiny terrier was placed in my hands and, in all fairness, like virtually every puppy in existence, she was irresistible. In England, Jack Russells are a popular breed (often ranked around number four in popularity), with a reputation for being feisty and ornery in the hands of a veterinarian. Right now this little girl with symmetrically tanned ears and two large brown circles on her back remained amiable but squirmy, wanting no part of my embrace, way too much exploring to be done.

"What are we going to name her?" I asked.

"Wishbone," announced Whitney, with a triumphant tone of finality.

"Isn't Wishbone a boy?" I asked.

Wishbone was a children's TV show on public broadcasting featuring a talking Jack Russell terrier. Was the choice of dog Whitney's cry for help, her need to have someone to talk to, to share her secrets with when those around her weren't listening?

"The only Jack Russells I've ever seen have been short-haired but one thing's for certain, the breed originally comes from

England. So why not give this little girl an English-sounding name?"

Whitney wasn't convinced but she played along as I teased her with Ermintrude, Priscilla, and Clarissa before focusing on Olivia, Jessica, and Lily.

"What about Sophie?" said Whitney.

After a pause marked by raised eyebrows, sage nods, and good-natured approval, our little JRT was christened Sophie. So what if the name, though popular in England, originated in France!

It was always going to be an awkward conversation. My only advantage came from knowing with some certainty how my father would respond to the news.

He and I had gotten into a routine, alternately calling each other every weekend to discuss the minutiae of life in the Dales, my mother's health, the adjustment of being retired, and last but not least, "the pups."

"How's Bess enjoying life among the sheep? Have you dared to let her off leash?"

"No, son, and I'm quite certain I never will. I'm sure she pines for those days when she ran loose across the fields, but it's just not worth taking the chance. Besides, last thing we need as we settle into a new community is a reputation as irresponsible dog owners."

And with that, I took my cue.

"Talking of owning a dog, we've finally gone and got one."

"Well, by heck," said Dad, "that's music to my ears. I had begun to worry you were never going to get a lion-hearted fellow of your own. Isn't that right, Whisk? He says it is."

I could picture the scene, Mum working her knitting needles, Dad with the newspaper in his lap, both seated in front of a roaring coal fire, Whiskey perking up at hearing his name.

I hesitated, a part of me hoping the pause might serve as fair warning for what I was about to disclose, knowing full well that our choice of dog was very different from what he would have chosen.

"So what is he? Or she?" He added the phrase with an air of self-congratulation, as though pleased with himself for being politically correct.

"She is a Jack Russell terrier. Rough-coat, not short. And the girls want to name her Sophie."

I imagined him pulling the telephone receiver from the side of his head and inspecting it, as though a communications gaffe had occurred in the intervening thousands of miles, with some stranger jumping in on the conversation.

"Huh," was all he could muster, and then, "I never reckoned you for a small dog, son. Didn't you once tell me Jack Russells can be a little —"

"Snappy," I broke in.

"Exactly."

"But I was referring to my experiences in the examination room. It's hardly the same as the domestic situation."

"Aye, but it's still the kind of dog you need to be careful with around children."

Here was a classic passive-aggressive maneuver, a throwaway line with a "told-you-so" punch to be pulled out at a later date if necessary. To some extent Dad was right, but this held true for any dog, and with appropriate socialization, that is, something more effective than I had witnessed with poor Patch, I was confident a regrettable mauling was not in the girls' future.

"Don't say you've forgotten all about Marty."

"Of course not," I said.

"And how are you going to take her for a walk?"

For a second he lost me, until I realized what he really meant was "How are you going to *feel* taking her for a walk," a small furry creature dragging you down the street.

"Why don't you come right out and say it — in your opinion, a Jack Russell is not a real dog."

"Now, son, that's not what I'm saying. It's just . . . they seem so strong-willed, and as for their bark . . . well . . . talk about piercing."

In the phrase "strong-willed" I heard something else, something I had known for some time about his relationship with Whiskey, but until now kept to myself.

"To me it sounds like you worry about getting a dog who could dominate you, who could rule the roost."

As soon as my words sailed off into the empty static between us I wanted them back. I never wanted to be critical of my father's way with dogs. Who was I to say it was wrong? He was happy and they were happy. This conversation would have been so much easier at a brisk pace in Wellington boots.

"Maybe you're right," he said.

"No, I didn't mean that," I said.

Another pause, and then he said, "If anything, I think I have a problem with any dog that can be picked up and placed in my lap. If I wanted that kind of a relationship with a dog I'd get a cat. I love our dogs being next to me on the sofa, but I also love their size, the amount of space they fill. To me a dog is a dog, not something I need to cuddle like a baby. That's all I'm saying."

For a while we both backpedaled, settling with a neutral conviction that Sophie might be perfect for the girls.

"To each his own," I said, "but I think Sophie is destined to become a huge part of Whitney's life."

"I hear you, son," he said. "I'm sure she will. And not just Whitney's."

Anyone who acquired a Jack Russell having been seduced by Wishbone or by Eddie from the popular TV show *Frasier* would probably be pulling out their hair and looking for a full refund within days of bringing the dog home. Jack Russells make the Energizer bunny seem insipid and slovenly. Burrowing and geological exploration are inherent in the breed. This was where the hard caliche desert topsoil came in handy. Sophie could while away hours excavating in the backyard. She also demonstrated an incredible talent for catching tennis balls on the fly, her incessant Jordanesque vertical leaps making her look like she was attached to an invisible yo-yo. Her problem lay in the release phase of the game because of those implacable terrier jaws. Obsessed and refusing to drop or let go, Sophie loved to hang off the ball with her teeth, little tail flicking back and forth in ecstasy if I added some whirling dervish action to the mix.

One of her most disturbing tricks centered on Whitney's extensive collection of stuffed toys. Whitney's actual bed lay somewhere beneath mounds of beady-eyed creatures — Beanie Babies, rabbits, teddy bears, frogs, ducks, cats, and dogs — all facing in the same direction. Naturally this was familiar territory for Sophie, squeezing in between Elmo and a Velveteen Rabbit wannabe, but what freaked me out was the way Sophie would try to blend in, to be perfectly still, staring out into nothingness with the rest of her creepy menagerie. I might be at the other end of the house, call her name, get no response, and eventually track her down to Whitney's room. It was always when I wanted Sophie to go back into her crate, as though she knew what I was after. It was more than hiding. It was impersonating a stuffed animal because she had discovered that stuffed animals get to stay on the best bed in the house.

For all her craziness, perhaps Sophie's most appealing trait was the way she relished the diligent attention Whitney bestowed upon her. Our photo albums are full of pictures of Sophie wearing a pink and blue floral shower cap, utterly content to be driven around the house in a wicker baby carriage.

In Arizona, the swimming pool is often seen as a necessity, not a luxury, and pool-related pet deaths are a very real concern. I had heard of an obese Corgi who fell into a black gunnite pool and was unable to climb the stairs to get out. The thought of that poor animal paddling around to the point of exhaustion, until he finally slipped beneath the water, only to be discovered later the same day by the family, is a truly haunting image. For this very reason, Sophie joined Emily in swimming lessons with particular attention to the art of the exit. I need not have worried. Sophie demonstrated Herculean strength for her size, not only able to pull herself up the metal rungs but especially nimble when it came to mounting a flotation device such as a boogie board. This is not a natural movement for a dog, but Sophie had drive and determination in spades. Once up she would stand there, hanging ten, content to cruise around on the current. Seeing her there with limp hair clinging to pale skin, I realized I would have to be particularly careful to guard against possible sunburn. Reggie was a shade seeker, smart enough to avoid the heat of the day. Sophie needed to be taught. I didn't fancy lathering her up with SPF 45 for six months of the year!

When it came time to have Sophie spayed, I offered to do the job myself.

"Are you sure?" said Kathy.

I was stunned.

"What are you trying to say, you don't trust me to do a decent job with my own dog?"

She pursed her lips into a pensive kiss before adding, "Of course not. I'm just saying it's always more difficult operating on your own dog. If something's going to go wrong, it will go wrong with Sophie and then what will the kids do, especially Whitney?"

I thought about this urban legend, with its threat of inevitable doom — ignore the old wives' tale at your own peril. Over the years I have performed surgery, oftentimes minor procedures, on the pets of veterinarians because the owner felt unable to put scalpel on skin when it came to a member of the family. Conceivably it might feel like a conflict of interest, too personal. Perhaps some vets fear the quality of the judgment calls they might make if faced with a crisis. Not me. If something were to go wrong with Sophie's spay, the kids would never forgive me if I was *not* the one in control. And fortunately, Sophie's surgery was uneventful.

Given Sophie's apparent desire to learn, I was quite surprised to discover Jack Russell terriers lie outside the top ten most intelligent breeds of dog. How could that be? Even as a young dog, Sophie excelled at predicting when my wife or I were coming home, sensing the arrival of a car in the driveway minutes before one appeared. Moreover, on one occasion, she demonstrated her superior intellect with some quick thinking, ultimately saving me thousands of dollars.

We taught Sophie to sleep in her crate in a large mudroom off the kitchen, quite a distance from our bedroom. Slumber parties with Whitney had been attempted, but as a young dog Sophie refused to settle; you know the type, the kid who eats too much candy and won't shut up and go to sleep as she rides a sugar high into the wee hours. The crate door was left open, but there was a kiddie gate blocking her exit from the room, otherwise she would sneak a visit to

Whitney.

The mudroom housed our washer and dryer, and in the middle of the night a main water pipe to the washing machine burst. Sophie knew just what to do. She was too far down the other end of the house for her barking to be heard and besides, the AC was running in our bedroom, further muffling her cries for help. Gifted in the art of vertical takeoffs, she cleared the two-foot-high fence, raced into the bedroom, and leapt onto our bed, a distressed, soaking-wet fur ball. As unpleasant and unexpected as her nocturnal greeting was, I appreciated the fact that her prompt action had prevented some major flood damage to our home.

Despite my father's foreboding, Sophie turned into a receptive and accomplished lapdog. In fact, on several occasions, I have caught him in moments of weakness, conceding to her winning charm. Her innate kindness seems to overpower her flashes of independent spirit and I have found myself wishing I had made the time to train her as a therapy dog. Recently, however, I heard a story that reminded me why Sophie was probably not best suited for work in a hospice or elderly care facility.

Liz Henderson and her eight-year-old

golden retriever, Rommy, came to see me for a problem that was, according to the owner, the troubling ailment "hip displeasure." As we talked she informed me that Rommy had briefly been a therapy dog, and given the creature's vivacious personality I was not the least bit surprised.

"Unfortunately she got fired from the hospital," she said.

"What?" I said. "You're joking, right? Not this dog!"

Ms. Henderson smiled

"Let me tell you a funny anecdote," she said. "Rommy is your typical retriever, loves to retrieve — socks, sticks, and best of all, balls, especially tennis balls."

"Sounds like my Jack Russell," I said.

"She goes nuts for tennis balls. She had been doing great in her basic training, approved to go to the hospital and pay some of the elderly patients a visit, and they loved her."

What's not to love, I thought.

"It was all going so well, until she spied an old woman working her way along a corridor on a walker. Rommy saw her, saw the walker, and bolted. Somehow we managed to pry her off and thankfully the old lady didn't get bowled over and break a bone."

"I don't get it. Did the woman do something to make Rommy freak out?"

Ms. Henderson laughed.

"Not the woman. The walker," she said. "At the bottom of all four feet were tennis balls. Bright green tennis balls. Rommy just thought it was time to play."

And right there and then I realized why Sophie could never have made it as a therapy dog. She might not have the momentum to bowl you over, but one glimpse of a tennis ball and she'd never let go.

For a while, even before we acquired Sophie, a general unease had been brewing about raising our family in a desert environment. I am at pains to point out that the folks of Arizona could not have been friendlier; the place was brimming with well-meaning and warm hospitality. Heck, after my experiences in New England, I was taken aback the very first time I went for a hike down a desert trail and strangers stopped me to wish me well or to bid me a good morning instead of the familiar silence, glum faces, and downcast eyes. And this bonhomie extended into neighborhoods, to some of the most reliable, attentive, genuine people I have ever had the pleasure of knowing as part of my community. Yet, at times, particularly holidays, I started to realize how the hand of friendship only heightened my awareness of the absence of family.

Be it England, or New England, there is something about seasons, about grass and leaves, about snow and stifling humidity that just feels right. It is about what you know, what you grew up with, and wanting your children's experiences to parallel your own, creating opportunities to share memories. The alien desert environment made me feel so much further away from my parents and moreover this unaccustomed world seemed to offer new dangers at every turn. What was with all the sandstorms, flash floods, and plagues of killer bees? Were we irresponsible parents for nurturing our children in this land of peril? And, of all the hazardous pests we faced, none was more revered than the bark scorpion, a tiny translucent critter capable of inducing seizures in small children. I lived in perpetual fear that one would cross paths with Emily, and then, one morning at breakfast, my wife discovered the unthinkable.

"I knew it," she said, swatting the newspaper with the back of her hand. "It was only a matter of time."

"What was a matter of time?"

"Death due to scorpion sting. Right here. Killed a man."

344

The paper was shuffled across the table and I was directed to the appropriate article.

"What you neglected to point out," I said, "was the fact that the man was one hundred and two years old and in renal failure."

Kathy shooed away my pedantry, as though these additional facts were inconsequential. Scorpions killed people and therefore, knowing our luck, one of our children was likely to be next. Quite the leap, I know, but the very fact that these connections were being made told me it was time for us to leave this arid world and return to somewhere that resonated with our past.

Maybe this was why a phone call from my father helped me realize that the decision to head back east was right, confirmation of something I had known I had to do for some time.

Fifteen years earlier it had come in the middle of a school day, a call taken in a headmaster's office. Now it came in the middle of the night, a painful reminder of time zones, of distance and even abandonment. But there was my father's voice fighting for traction, the exact same pain as before, taking me back in time.

"I'm so sorry to wake you, son, but I needed to let you know. Whiskey had to be put to sleep this morning."

He began to bring me up to speed and as he spoke, instead of feeling involved and included, I felt detached and absent, as though this must be happening to someone else's father. For the first time since leaving Britain, I wondered if any of his friends in the village had asked, "Isn't your son a veterinarian? What does he think is wrong?" And that brought me to a far more disturbing question: What would Dad have said in reply?

"All of a sudden Whiskey became very unsteady on his back legs, so I took him to our vet, and he said he thought he'd had a stroke of some sort, gave him a shot, and for a couple of days he seemed to get better."

There was never a trace of finger pointing from my father. It was all in my head, in the inferences and the pauses where I could find my failings. How long had this been going on? Why didn't Dad call me when it first started? Did he feel as though I had nothing to offer so there was no point in even trying, forced to place his trust in "our vet" when all he had ever wanted was to place his trust in his son?

"Then it happened again, at least I think so, perhaps another stroke, leaving him completely unable to stand and worse, he seemed to have lost his sight. I couldn't see him suffer like that. You understand why I had to put him to sleep?"

I did, and I supported his decision absolutely. Whiskey was fourteen years old, a fine age for any dog, especially a golden retriever. But I couldn't help but think it should have been me delivering a dose of mercy.

"I'm sorry I couldn't have been there, to help I mean."

"I know you are. Of course. And I understand. It's just the way it is."

And I knew he did, but part of me wanted to argue, the self-destructive guilty part, the part that said I should have been a general practice veterinarian, working within easy driving distance. We all make choices, we chart a certain course, committing to it for better or for worse. Becoming a surgical specialist was right for me and so was living in America. But maybe I had begun to use this distance as an excuse, a subconscious justification for a hands-off approach to the animals in my parents' life, as though I was so remote as to be worthless.

"How was he, with the vet I mean?"

Knowing Whiskey, I imagined an ordeal, the need for heavy sedation, a rough-and-tumble battle to gain access to a vein. In

347

short, I worried it was something other than a graceful, painless goodbye.

Dad surprised me.

"He was good. Didn't growl. Didn't put up a fight. I think that tells you right there the kind of state he was in."

I heard him swallow hard and could imagine my father's proud smile, his lion-hearted little fellow finally behaving himself on this, his last visit with a veterinarian.

"Yes," I said. "If Whiskey wasn't trying to bite the vet's hand off he had to be in a pretty bad way."

For a moment the two of us were silent, comfortable with our memories — of the skinny puppy who beat parvovirus, the wayward Casanova using his charms to avoid getting neutered, the affectionate, loyal retriever that craved human touch.

Suddenly an important consideration crossed my mind.

"What did you decide to do . . . with his body, I mean?"

"He's going to be buried in a field up by Watery Lane. The property's owned by a friend in the village and there are a few other dogs buried there. It's a nice, quite private spot."

This was good. A resting place close to where they lived. Inadvertently, once again,

I found myself thinking about Patch, laid to rest under an apple tree in the backyard of a house now owned by a complete stranger.

"How's Bess holding up?"

"Ah, she's having a hard time of it. Been looking everywhere for him like the old days when he ran away, like she wants to tell him off for being naughty. It made me wonder if I should have let her be there, to watch him go."

I'd never thought about this. I'm not sure dogs are capable of understanding the concept of death, but they are sensitive to changes in their environment, structure, and routine. There must be confusion, a sense of upheaval, even loneliness. I hadn't thought to ask owners in this situation with multiple dogs whether or not they thought a member of the pack would benefit from witnessing a canine euthanasia and viewing their sibling's body after the fact. I see no harm in trying, if a grieving owner thinks it is the right thing to do.

"I'm not sure," I said. "It was probably going to be hard on her either way. The two of them were used to having each other for the last fourteen years."

"You're probably right. It was just a thought."

I tried to stifle a yawn, it being the middle

of the night, but Dad still caught it.

"I'm sorry, son. I'll let you go."

"No, no, it's fine. Look, I was going to call you over the weekend to let you know I'm going to take a job in Boston. Back at Angell Memorial. I know it's not England, but it is a single flight and literally just an ocean away."

"Ah, that's grand. That'll make it a lot easier to visit."

"And please, Dad, next time, if anything happens with Bess, feel free to ask me for advice. I know I'm not much use when it comes to everything outside of an operating room, but I can still get you answers. I'd still like to try to help."

"Right you are," said Dad. "I'll definitely do that from here on out. God bless, son. Get some rest."

But as I hung up and tried to go back to sleep, this goodbye replayed itself in my head and no matter how I tried to mix and edit the sentiment, I heard nothing new, the words lacking conviction. I realized I had forced my dad to write me off as his veterinarian. Even when seeking my support, he was the one making me feel better when it should have been the other way round. Just for once I wished I could be there for him when it came to the animals in his life. As I succumbed to sleep, trying to force the dream, I wasn't convinced I would ever get the chance.

11.
SAME DANCE, DIFFERENT SONG

When Reggie returned to the wilds of Massachusetts I imagine he must have felt like a lifer from Leavenworth spending a day at "juvie hall." Finally rehabilitated in what for him was his element, he headed out on a fresh tour of duty, working his latest backyard as if he had already planned a route using Google Earth. Head high, shoulder blades keeping the beat, tail up, he looked almost cocky, the new kid on the block, more than confident — defiant. What could possibly threaten this veteran of desert combat? The chipmunk? The woodchuck? A wild turkey? I imagined him coming across a garter snake and thinking, "Is that all you've got?" At the end of his first day Reggie came home with a little Ali shuffle in his stride, enough bluster to let us all know it had been a good day and it was good to be home.

For a while we had a run on classic

doormat offerings, which I put down to his desire to show me how much he approved of his new domain. However, it wasn't long before daily became weekly became monthly, and though Reggie defined feline freedom, it had become apparent that he was increasingly an indoor cat. Open a linen closet any time of day and there was Reggie, third shelf up, curled into a ball and fast asleep. With increasing frequency I'd find him on the children's beds, in front of the fireplace, at full stretch in a shaft of sunlight. Suddenly Reggie was all about leisure and relaxation. When I picked him up I could feel the extra weight of him. Then it hit me. Reggie wasn't being lazy or bingeing on too much kibble, he was simply getting old. Reginald C. Cat was starting to bask in his retirement.

"How old is he?" I asked Kathy.

"We'll never know for sure, but maybe fifteen, sixteen. Something around there."

I was surprised. He was already at a fine age for any cat. His choice of a sedentary lifestyle seemed to have come upon him so quickly, almost as if, now that he was home, he could let down his guard and succumb to a simpler, less stressful environment.

Sophie appeared equally at home in what, for her, was exotic territory. Unfortunately her comfort zone knew no boundaries, and the backyard was simply a gateway to a new world in which she could ignore all pesky name-calling and explore to her little heart's content. Improved (and costly) picket fencing took care of any possible aerial perimeter breach, but the terrier in her took full advantage of the rich loamy soil, burrowing for freedom like a prisoner in a World War II movie. Though the house opened onto dense forest and conservation land, the road out front was heavily trafficked. If Sophie was sufficiently motivated to cross the street, the stubborn terrier in her would defy all attempts to stop her getting there.

There are those who argue invisible fencing is a lazy alternative to appropriate training. For me, despite hours of training, it was a necessary alternative to the unthinkable. I could diminish the threat of a tunnel break. I couldn't make it go away completely. Besides, for Sophie, learning to use a shock collar was easy. She simply watched a bunch of Whitney's guy friends from high school, intent on mimicking their heroes on MTV's *Jackass*. Clutching the collar to their necks they would run into the danger zone, ignore the audible warning, and press on, screaming and visibly surprised to receive an electric shock. They may not have lit up the night sky but Sophie registered their distress. From there on out, the beeping noise alone would make her back off.

Though the assignation of Sophie to Whitney had always been unofficial, the passage of time only served to strengthen and clarify their connection, the two inseparable, like Paris Hilton and her dogs, long before she was a household name. Sophie was more like a girlfriend than a dog — trustworthy, receptive, and guaranteed to never join a rival clique, to never stab you in the back or turn into a bitch. She and Whitney even had the exact same taste in boys. She never hogged the remote because, like Whitney, she loved *Dawson's Creek* and *The O.C.* Now that Sophie was a little older and a whole lot calmer, every night had turned into a sleepover and on weekends she was more than happy to get her toenails painted hot pink. And Sophie loved to get pampered with a shampoo and blow dry, emerging from the bathroom like a greyhound out of the gate, feeling the air through her soft coat as she embarked on a mad dash around the house, cutting around furniture, her Day-Glo nails clicking out a wild staccato rhythm across the hardwood floors.

Contrary to my father's prediction, I was

happy to take her for walks — when she wasn't wearing nail polish — until one day she bared a side of her whose existence he had long suspected.

When Sophie was a puppy we had gone to great lengths to ensure she was appropriately socialized with both people and other animals. On her first birthday she had hosted (thanks to Whitney and Emily) a party to which all the neighborhood dogs were invited. There had been some chowing down of "cake" — a frightening concoction the kids cooked up out of dry and canned dog food — plus games and toys and swimming, all without gnashing of teeth. Okay, so one fine Saint Bernard named Chantelle plowed straight through a screen door in her excitement to join in the fun, but what I witnessed was a feisty terrier who integrated well with other dogs.

While Sophie maintained exemplary social graces with humans, so long as you consider rolling on your back and splaying out your crotch as acceptable, the wind was changing when it came to other members of her species. As part of settling into her new home, I anticipated she might become a little ill at ease, a little territorial and protective of the property entrusted to her care. I just wasn't prepared for her to take this attitude to the streets.

Funny how walking the dog can make you realize that it's not as easy to be a good pet owner as you thought. For years I had been criticizing my father over the way in which Whiskey and Bess insisted on dislocating his shoulder joints. And apparently I was no better as fifteen pounds of determined terrier drove me forward, angled low, ignoring all my attempts to bribe or cajole her to come to heel, fanning back and forth as if she were divining for water. Like so many dog owners who don't take enough time and make enough effort, I was held hostage to a dog determined to take me for a walk. If only my father could see me now.

They were at least a hundred yards away when I spotted them, headed in our direction, no more than stick figures. In seconds, distorted black lines in the fading daylight had transformed into a man and some kind of a dog, fairly large, I thought, perhaps something the size of a golden retriever. I knew Sophie had spotted them on her radar because she had stopped tugging on her leash and stood at rigid attention with her short tail sticking straight up, flashing a warning.

"Easy, Sophie."

I reached out to calm her, but as I did she

357

rushed forward again, stretching her leash, grumbling and growling, pawing at her collar. I always knew Sophie was smart, but I have never been able to find her opposable thumb or figure out what slick sleight-of-paw she used to get that collar off. Without skipping a beat she was charging toward the other dog, barking her head off with that insistent, determined, formidable terrier savagery. I don't think the dog, a chow chow, as it turned out, ever saw what hit her. One moment she's happily, innocently bouncing down a hill, her master at her side, the next she's hit by a furry white bullet. Naturally I offered chase, Sophie selectively deaf to my cries, the effect of my pursuit only adding to the drama as the two of us rushed toward the two of them. With hindsight, Sophie's lunge at the poor dog's neck was a tad theatrical, the action appearing to unfold with something of a *Matrix* slow-motion quality. Within seconds, I had grabbed her and pulled her off the chow and only then did I realize my dilemma. Oh, it wasn't the dog, who couldn't have been more passive. It was the owner, and it wasn't that I knew the owner, more that I knew *of* the owner. The man responded in exactly the appropriate manner, appalled and flabbergasted, attentive to his own dog as I secured Sophie, tethering her to a lamp-post. Strangely, the savage edge had left her, as if she had won the fight and wanted to make sure the other guy, KO'd on the canvas, was still alive. It was as if the terrier taste for blood had been satiated, only when I inspected her muzzle, there was no blood. I hurried over to the victim, embarrassed, and offering a sincere apology.

"You had best check her over," said the stranger, conveying the message: "Yes, I know what you do for a living, as well."

My knowledge of the man was gleaned through rumor, innuendo, and snippets of conversation overheard at girls' basketball games, on soccer sidelines, and at school plays. He was a lawyer, of course, inclined toward personal injury, and what he lacked in altitude he made up for in a grim sneer recognizable as his habitual facial expression. With minimal effort he tweaked his countenance into a frosty glare and I couldn't help but feel like he was already practicing for the moment when he called me to the stand, swore me in, and took my testimony apart.

The chow lay on her side, more out of choice than incapacitation, and, despite the assault, she was calm and remarkably easy to work on.

"The skin's not broken. There's no blood and I can't see any puncture marks."

By now the light was poor so I couldn't be certain, but I was hopeful Sophie had only aimed for a love bite and nothing more.

"I'm assuming that dog is fully vaccinated."

"Yes, of course," I said. The chow chow got to her feet, and out of the corner of my eye I could see Sophie starting to get agitated, but in a good way, doing the dancing deer move, eyes locked on their target, all four feet making small synchronous vertical jumps. She wanted to come over, this time to say hello properly.

"Look, if there's a problem you discover when you get home or over the next few days, don't hesitate to give me a call. My number's in the phone book."

"Oh, don't worry, I'll be sure to call," he said, and I sensed he enjoyed this last word, this open-ended possibility that the next time the phone rang at my house, he might be on the other end suggesting I speak to my insurance company or "lawyer up."

As it turned out, I called him. He may not have been a client, nor was the chow chow officially a patient, but professional experience has taught me that I often fare better after a thorny encounter if I use preemptive communication. My inquiry as to his dog's health caught him off guard but, begrudgingly, he sounded somewhat grateful for the follow-up.

"So far, so good" was as much as he would relinquish with regard to the lack of physical findings, as though there might still be consequences from which he could derive financial remuneration.

What disturbed me most was the unpredictability of Sophie's behavior and my failings as an owner of my first dog. Not only was I unable to rein her in on a walk, but now she was demonstrating the same kind of aggressive behavior I had witnessed as a kid with our German shepherd, Patch. I had been critical of my father's dog-training abilities and here I was committing the sins of the father myself. What next, getting up at four in the morning for walks to avoid meeting other dogs? All I needed was the flat cap and the walking stick and I was there!

While I was thinking about ways to address the problem, other, bigger pet quandaries came to light, the most devastating of which concerned Reggie.

All of us knew Reggie was getting old, slowing down, his neediness as endearing as it was unusual. Recon missions were still an integral part of life, but they seemed abbreviated, as though they were becoming a chore, a duty he no longer enjoyed. Then, one evening, at feeding time, the tinkle of dry cat food on metal failed to set off the lumpy thud of a cat dropping from a shelf upstairs.

"Anyone seen Reggie?"

The obvious answers ricocheted around the kitchen — "He's probably still asleep in the closet," "He might be trapped under the bed," "I thought I saw him outside." Common and uncommon hiding places were explored to no avail.

I called his name out the back door.

"Anyone notice anything wrong with him this morning?"

Head shaking and looks of confusion. None of us had picked up on any signs of sickness. He had eaten well and had been seen drinking from his water bowl, acting fine.

We let a couple of hours pass during which I imagined and investigated a number of improbable hiding places, places I had never seen him frequent but felt better checking out all the same. Then I grabbed a flashlight and hit the backyard, sweeping the beam back and forth, waiting for the glowing green dots to come bounding out of the undergrowth. But there was nothing. Though I told no one, I went out in front of the house, up and down the road, rooting around in the scrub and leaf litter along the sidewalk, just in case.

Nothing.

"He probably wandered off, got lost, and now he's working his way home," I told the kids. "Don't look so worried. This is Reggie. This is 'the Man.' He knows what he's doing. If he's hungry he'll just eat a cow. If he's tired, he'll hitch a ride or jack a car. Massachusetts is a cakewalk. There's nothing out in these woods for him to be afraid of."

The kids seemed troubled and upset, but they trusted their cat, the invincible daredevil who always escaped insurmountable danger, bursting into the spotlight at the last moment. He had always been a part of their lives. In the absence of illness how could that possibly change?

There was still no sign of Reggie the following morning, and by the following evening, after Sophie had eaten his food for the second night in a row, a fog of gloom and resignation was beginning to settle, with trembling lips, tears, and snappy emotional outbursts resistant to my fading optimism.

I checked in with neighbors, put in a call

to the local police department, but Kathy and I began to prime the kids for the possibility that Reggie wasn't coming home.

All the credible scenarios were considered. Attacked by a wild animal, maybe a raccoon or a coyote — possible but deemed unlikely. Reggie's feline reflexes may have been past their prime, but he never lost his street smarts. In the same way I found it hard to believe he was clipped by a car or mistimed a sprint across the road. I would have discovered evidence of trauma, his injured body by the roadside.

The kids favored a cat-napping, a theory I neither encouraged nor discouraged — disappearance with a remote possibility of return. It was always referred to in the manner of a mistake, not an abduction, as though some Johnny-on-the-spot had whisked him away just in case he was lost and Reggie was enjoying a temporary vacation, a brief retreat with "good people," from which he would return refreshed and revitalized, ready to play down all the fuss.

Personally, I had a different theory, but one I believed, knowing Reggie, melded perfectly with his independent spirit and innate dignity. I was thinking about the famous British explorer Captain Robert Scott, who led an ill-fated expedition to the

South Pole in 1912. Not only did Scott discover the Norwegians had got there first, but he and his men were not prepared for the challenge of the return journey and one by one the entire team succumbed to cold, starvation, and death. Notably, one particular officer, a Captain Lawrence Oates, suffering from severe frostbite, knew he was a burden, slowing down his colleagues, reducing their chances of survival. One day, in the middle of a blizzard, he turned to the others and rather famously announced, "I am just going outside and may be some time." Oates stepped outside his tent and was never seen again.

This suicide was always hailed as the mark of a courageous man and in the same vain I believe Reggie made a choice, took control of his destiny, took us out of the equation and chose to die on his terms. If I had been more astute perhaps I would have found a note in the form of a warning, of subtle clinical markers of failing health. Of course Reggie could have been injured, he could have suffered some acute illness, but I tend to think he had known something wasn't right for some time. I think he got his affairs in order and said his goodbyes, and we never knew it. He trotted off on his final patrol with no regrets, never once looking back, grateful to have lived as an independent spirit, and fully intending to die as one. This remarkable creature knew how to live. Why should I doubt his capacity for knowing how to die? If he had wanted to be nursed, treated, or cured, don't you think he would have asked for help? Reggie went old school, with pride and dignity, finding himself a cozy warm spot where it was quiet and safe. There he curled up, closed his big green eyes for the last time, and went to sleep — the perfect end to the perfect feline life. We never found his body because I believe Reggie didn't want it to be found. I think he discovered a way to leave behind one more reminder of how he lived. By going missing in action, he allowed us to believe he's still out there somewhere, still busy doing what he does best, using up lives and having fun doing it.

It would have been easier to have a body. With no burial or cremation, there was no formal conclusion to Reggie's life, no physical location where we could pay our respects, conjure his image, and recount memories. I recognized that Reggie's open-ended departure felt just as frustrating as being unable to visit Patch's final resting place.

It wasn't long after Reggie pulled his "Amelia Earhart" that I received another sad phone call from my father informing me that Bess had been put to sleep.

"She'd been declining for some time," he said, and I could sense he had seen this coming in a way he never had with Whiskey.

"It was the right thing to do, what with her incontinence, and then a stroke."

I hadn't mentioned it when Dad had been talking about Whiskey, but what we tend to think of as strokes in people are really quite uncommon in dogs. I hesitate to second-guess the diagnosis of a colleague, especially when I'm not there to examine the dog, but apparently lightning had struck twice. I don't doubt the severity of the ailment that floored poor Bess. I imagine the veterinarian used the term *stroke* as a way of helping my parents appreciate the abrupt and terminal impact of Bess's sudden deterioration. In the end, what does terminology matter? It was just semantics. Besides, once again I was in no position to argue, silently berating myself with "You weren't even there."

"I buried her with Whiskey. Back together at last. By heck, she missed him after he was gone." He drifted with the memory of the two of them and I could tell he took solace from knowing they were back together, as though losing Bess had been hard but offset by the certainty that she would be reunited with Whiskey. "Reckon we'll get a proper headstone for them both one of these days."

"Sounds good," I said, and then, without thinking, added, "Have you started asking mother about the possibility of another dog?"

Though it came out as a question, it was really a declaration of something we had both come to appreciate over time — for some of us, living with a pet can be a bit like finding religion; once you've been converted, it's hard to imagine life without them.

"Not yet, son. It's early days and you know what your mother's like."

I knew all right.

"Duncan," I mimicked, "that was our last dog and don't be asking me for any more."

"That's about the size of it," he said, and I could hear the smile in his voice.

"Thankfully," I said, "I've heard that one before."

"Me too," he said. "God willing, me too."

Perhaps the idea first crossed my mind when I was thinking back to the heyday of

Whiskey and Bess. Maybe it seemed like a possible solution to the problem of Sophie's antisocial behavior. Whatever the reason, the idea was already rattling around the back of my mind when my daughter exploited a moment of inescapable paternal weakness.

As I have mentioned before, Emily's CF required periods of hospitalization during which she was bombarded with an assortment of hardcore intravenous antibiotics. Ever since she was an infant, Emily's body has chosen to reject these medications in the form of allergic reactions ranging from unrelenting itchiness with disfiguring skin lesions all the way through to life-threatening blood-clotting disorders. In short, her body abhors the very drugs that help to keep her alive.

For this reason, these hospitalizations were always mingled with anxious anticipation and fear, not least when Emily was started on a new drug.

"Look, we'll begin in the ICU and desensitize her to the antibiotic. By increasing her dose in tiny increments we can fool her body into accepting the drug."

Her new pediatric pulmonologist spoke with the confidence of someone who had yet to discover the challenges of treating

Emily — in time he would come to realize who and what he was dealing with — but for now we played along, preferring his proactive rather than reactive approach. And so, one morning, at around 2 a.m., I found myself sitting beside Emily in the intensive care unit of Children's Hospital in Boston. Despite the hour, despite being entangled in the tentacles of wires and leads from so many monitors, despite the hubbub of noise and nurses all around, nine-year-old Emily in her pigtails and modest johnny was busy pretending to stick needles in my arms, ripping sticky bandages off my hairy flesh, savoring every wince and whine, thankful she could release her pent-up fears and pain on someone she trusted.

She had just convinced a passing nurse to photograph her tormented father with a Polaroid camera, when she said, "Daddy, do you think you could buy me a yellow Labrador?"

Her voice was so small, so innocent, the timing too improbable to feel anything other than spontaneous. It felt like a cry for help — a pure request for companionship, the stress of this moment, the anticipation of more untoward side effects, the need for unconditional security helping her find the words.

Ordinarily I might have offered my daughter a wan smile, reminding her that Daddy works for the Massachusetts Society for the Prevention of Cruelty to Animals, a facility with its own animal adoption shelter.

"Why would we purchase a new dog when there are so many abandoned dogs in need of a loving home?" I might have said, and that would be that, Emily nodding her understanding, looking a little bashful for being insensitive to the problem of pet overpopulation. Truthfully, I wish this had been the case, but at that moment in time, in that precise situation, watching your daughter being poked and prodded, with tubes and cables running in and out of her body, frightened about how her body will react, I defy most parents not to be vulnerable to a child's wish, no matter what it is.

"Of course," I said. "Once we get out of the hospital, we'll get you a dog."

What is it with children? Even soused with medication, at an ungodly hour, she still managed to spot the discrepancy.

"Not just a dog," she said. "A yellow Labrador."

"Sorry," I said. "Yellow Labrador."

"Promise?"

"I promise," I said, kissed her on the forehead, and melted as she smiled.

371

12.
AND MILES TO GO
BEFORE I SLEEP

Let me make it clear: there is no reneging on any promise made to a child in a hospital bed. It cannot be done. Don't even try to claim selective memory loss, distortion of the facts, sleep deprivation, or stress-induced delirium. Your child will be able to recount your promise like the Pledge of Allegiance, word for word, incontrovertible, and because it might as well be chiseled in stone, she will be irrationally impatient for it to be honored. Stat!

Instinctively I tried the customary conversation, the one in which you try to make the child see beyond cute and cuddly, trying to wear them down with the tiresome responsibilities: watching out for empty water bowls and filling when necessary, helping out with feeding and not just unwanted vegetables slid under the dinner table, thorough backyard seek-and-destroy missions to defuse land mines when on "poopy patrol," active involvement in all aspects of training including enthusiastic participation in walks regardless of inclement weather. But as soon as I started stringing sentences together I realized that inside my head I was actually hearing the words in my mother's voice before they came out of my mouth. It was exactly the same as when I was a kid begging for a dog, and like all kids before her, myself included, Emily would not be swayed, nodding her accord with stern and indomitable fervor, as if this dog would be revered like a deity, her loyalty and responsibility unwavering. And like most parents we nodded back and didn't believe a word of it.

To some extent, I was on board with the concept of a second dog and, more important, a dog that would be close to Emily. Whitney and Sophie were joined at the hip, so why not try to balance the canine budget, to see if Emily could develop a relationship that culminated in the same kind of devotion, dependence, and empathy. There were always times when Emily was sick and had to stay home from school, isolated from her friends. Here was a chance to have a constant companion, a playmate who never feared catching your cold, always cheerful and content just to share your space, guaranteed to make your down feel up.

Part of me hoped a feline addition to the family might fulfill my obligation. We all missed Reggie, and part of his legacy was a fresh appreciation of the powerful bond possible between a human and a cat. Emily's pulmonologist wasn't receptive.

"For someone with a respiratory condition, the effect of cat dander can range from problematic to downright dangerous. If you have to have a pet, I'd say stick with a dog."

Not that this kibosh on a feline replacement made the slightest bit of difference. Emily was not budging.

"Yellow, and Labrador."

"Why yellow?"

"Yellow, and Labrador."

"Why not something hypoallergenic, like a standard poodle?"

"Yellow, and Labrador."

"Okay," I said, "I get it. What about male or female?"

Emily canted her head to one side, as if to confirm that the dog's sex was not a significant consideration.

"Whichever will be best with Schmoopy. I'll let you decide." Sophie's name had become something of a movable feast — Schmoopy, Soapy, Sofa. "So long as it's yellow and a Labrador."

I thought about the prospect of teaming up a terrier with a retriever and it seemed to be an odd mix, like pairing together two contrary athletes, a scrappy featherweight boxer with a compulsive triathlete, and insisting they become partners in training. Terriers are independent, mischievous, clever, and feisty. Retrievers are team players, loyal, energetic, and desperate to please. Not exactly opposites, but hopefully different enough to attract. To be honest I wasn't worried. Every day at work I see all manner of bizarre canine combos. They all sort themselves out and find their natural rhythm. No doubt Sophie would assert herself, the archetypal example of "little dog syndrome," certain to point out her seniority and established position in the family dynamic. I knew Sophie would defend her private parking spot on the couch next to Whitney and gloat over the way she was swept away to Whitney's bedroom at night, thumbing her nose at the new upstart, but I had to believe Sophie would rediscover her social graces and not a recipe for Labrador tartare.

When it came to the sex of this yellow Labrador I was torn. I wondered if a male dog might be a better foil to Sophie, a little more yin to her yang. With Reggie MIA I now lived in a household of four females. I would enjoy the camaraderie of a fellow slave to testosterone, but sadly this thought led me to Whiskey, all dominant and prone to misbehavior and the temptations of the opposite sex. It was all the flashback I needed — a Labrador bitch made the most sense after all.

My quest began with a perusal of the animal adoption center at work. It's hard to wander around among the cages and runs, inciting the dogs into hopeful barking, drilled by eager and pleading eyes, and pretend to be "just looking." One of the volunteer staff was quick to pounce. There were too many dogs out there in need of a home, fine dogs, dogs that, in my opinion, would make the perfect pet for Emily. But this wasn't about my opinion and I needed to bear this in mind. Feeling awkward, I tried to phrase my inquiry as if I were asking for a friend, but it felt all wrong, as bad as asking your doctor about a friend's embarrassing sexual dysfunction when everyone knows you are talking about yourself.

"For some reason, this crazy person is after a purebred yellow Labrador. I know, it's so selfish and insensitive, I mean what's the chance of a pedigree dog like that being surrendered?"

I'm not sure she bought into the snobbish fanaticism of a third party as my excuse, and I can't say I blame her. She's working every day to place all manner of pit bulls and pit bull mixes in loving homes, fighting to keep them off death row and here's a veterinarian, who should know better, shopping for the perfect abandoned Labrador as if it were as easy as the point and click of a mouse on Amazon.com. And now that I had committed to my "friend," how could I clarify the demand with "But my daughter was in the hospital, and she was in the ICU and I promised"?

Sadly the shelter does receive a number of purebred dogs, including Labradors, but they are sporadic and, as you might expect, quickly snatched up.

I reported back to Emily, the furrowed brow and pouty frown letting me know what she really thought about Dad's "wait and see" approach to a shelter dog. Happy to remind me of the circumstances in which the promise was made, she suggested I might want to try harder, prompting me to contact our local Labrador rescue group.

"Do you ever rescue puppies?"

I thought back to the essential criteria for my mission — yellow and Labrador. Sex had been left up to me and age had not been stipulated. It was hard to imagine how a little girl could not see herself rocking a yellow ball of love back and forth in her arms, like a baby, but this vagueness had offered me a little wiggle room.

"Not often," said the woman on the other end of the line, all business, sounding as though she was used to calls from people who regarded rescue services as a cheap breeding facility. "Most of our dogs are adults. Some are elderly, some are puppies, but the majority vary in age from a year to ten years. Have you ever owned a dog?"

"Yes."

"So you have a sense of the responsibilities necessary to take care of a dog?"

"I think so."

"Because adopting a rescue Lab is quite different from selecting a puppy from a breeder or a pet store, you know."

"I understand."

"Do you?" she said, letting me hear the confrontation in her voice. I knew what she was doing and I couldn't blame her. I would be doing the same thing in her situation. Her MO was to filter out anyone less than wholly committed to rescuing a dog who had been abandoned or neglected, normally because the owner was lazy, selfish, and lacking in the most basic commitment to the dog in their life — time spent in each other's company. She had a wonderful product to give away, but a product that was not for everyone and a product she cherished and would not part with lightly.

"Go to a breeder and you start from scratch, a nice clean slate. If that's what you're looking for, we're not the right people for you. Our dogs are wonderful and in the right home you will be blessed and thankful to share such a creature, but some of them have had hard lives, difficult experiences. You need to see them, spend some time around them, because what you see is what you get."

I let her know I truly respected the valuable work she and the rest of her group were doing, while trying to convey my interest in a female yellow Labrador puppy. I felt like a fraud, the rescue mindset at odds with the wishes of my nine-year-old daughter, but I put it out there, gave her my details, and said I would be waiting for her call.

Reporting back to Emily led to a confession about the possible age of a rescue Labrador and clarification on her part. Of course she wanted a puppy, what was I thinking? There's no point in having a dog if you don't get to enjoy the cute and cuddly stage. Besides, she said, she wanted to enjoy all of this dog's life, not just a portion.

I suggested we keep an open mind, to which she responded, "I'm speaking to Mom," which I have learned is code for "I can see it's going to take collusion with a woman to get this job done properly."

Nothing happened for a couple of weeks and then I received a call querying my interest in a four-year-old Labrador named Max. Yes, he was a he, he was not a puppy, and as it turned out, he was black. But, as I pointed out to Emily, Max *was* a purebred Labrador. To her credit, Emily said she would be happy to meet Max, though she made it clear, this was just a date, nothing heavy, no commitment.

"That sounds good, Em. We'll just go and see what he's like. No harm in that."

For me, this attitude, this unwavering, effortless love for all creatures great and small, is one of the most delightful traits any father can witness in their child. I don't know whether it works its way out of her DNA or works its way in from her environment. I know my father looked for it in my sister, Fiona, watching it fade and disappear. I have been more fortunate. I knew Emily would gladly visit Max simply because it was an opportunity to befriend a new dog.

And so one Saturday morning, Kathy, Emily, and I took a drive about an hour north to Max's foster home. Truly, I had no great expectations of Emily falling in love, abandoning all those prerequisites, but I knew we could be in trouble from the moment we knocked on the front door.

"Kath," I whispered, urging my wife to follow my eyes down to the bottom corner of the screen door where a vicious rip at paw height left the material limp and peeled back.

Then the perpetrator appeared, chest bumping the thin mesh boundary between us.

"Come back, Max," said a female voice, her hand reaching out to a collar, a second hand required, the dog determined to make his greeting. "I'm Colleen, and this, as you might have gathered, is Max."

Once we were inside, Colleen released her grip, perhaps overcome by exhaustion, and Max exploded like one of those matchbox cars you rub along the floor several times before letting go, shooting forward, Emily buffeted and tossed about but smiling and happy as she tried to pet him.

"As you can see, Max is strong and determined. But he loves people."

I reckoned Max had to weigh about one hundred pounds, maybe a buck ten. Yes, he was overweight, but he was also tall and built.

"What's his story?" I asked.

"Oh, the usual," said Colleen. "Family pet with a family too busy or too distracted to give Max the attention he needs. He also has a tendency to wander. And bark. Not exactly a winning combination in a neighborhood."

We had excellent security with picket fencing and an electric fence, but I reckoned Max could break out of Guantánamo Bay in a heartbeat.

I looked for early clues from Emily. This was a huge dilemma for her. She loved dogs, therefore she loved Max, but was Max right for her?

"Would you mind if we took him for a walk?" I asked.

Colleen thought this was a great idea, so a leash was applied, the leather wrapped tight around my hand in the manner of a bull rider bracing for his eight seconds of glory, and the front door opened.

Sticking with the rodeo theme, walking Max was a bit like being bucked off a horse, getting your foot stuck in the stirrup, and being dragged around the arena. You went where he went and his motivation seemed completely random, across people's front yards, off sidewalks, making improbable detours at ninety degrees to where we wanted to go. How we got him back to Colleen's house I will never know.

"Good boy, Max," I said, having to physically shove him back inside. "Thanks, Colleen, for letting us meet him."

Colleen was courteous, but she recognized the tone of my remarks. She had been doing this job long enough to see we were not the perfect match for Max. Maybe she knew from the moment we met. But she was never humoring us or taunting poor Max. His was a tough case, nothing disastrous, nothing a little work, time, and affection couldn't cure, but a case that needed the right person and the right environment. Emily would never be able to take Max for a walk, it was as simple as that. We would be doing a disservice to this fine dog if he was failed for a second time, and I had no doubt Mr. Right was out there for Max, especially if he was a linebacker or professional bodybuilder who lived on one hundred acres.

Kathy had already given me the cold stare and the headshake that said "not for us," but I still had to feel out Emily as we walked away.

"What did you think, sweetheart?"

"I liked him," she said.

"But —" I said.

"No buts. I liked Max. I think Sophie would like Max too."

"Good point," I said. "But I'm not sure how Sophie would do around such a big strong dog. I worry she might try and fight with him."

"I'll drive," said Kathy, holding her hand out for the car keys.

"Really," I said. "You sure?"

"Positive. I have something else I want Emily to see."

And for the first time, I caught a whiff of something brewing, some flash of conspiracy, as though I was about to be literally and figuratively taken for a ride.

An hour later and without a single navigational hiccup — the "tell" that betrayed any hint of spontaneity — we pulled into a small and isolated farmyard, where our arrival was greeted with the faraway chorus of several dogs barking.

"There's no harm in looking, is there, Emily?" said Kathy, making as much attempt to hide her wink as Emily did to hide her smile.

Right here, right now, I should like to point out to any parent more gullible than me that "just looking" is not really an option for children when it comes to puppies. It's like sitting on Santa's lap and not being allowed to ask for a gift. It's like wandering around a candy store with a big brown paper bag and being told the bag must remain empty. Unless you want to subject your offspring to years of psychiatric counseling, unless you are one cold and heartless bastard and you are not afraid to wake up in the middle of the night and find your bed is on fire, chances are high your child is walking away with a dog.

A man stepped onto the porch to greet us. He was wearing shirts on top of shirts, plaid and wool over a white T-shirt, layer upon layer like a Russian matryoshka doll. His face was tan and leathery, the color of his jet-black hair at odds with all the wrinkles and furrows, and his mustache was black, full, and dastardly, tweaked to fine points at the tips. Not, I imagined, that Emily noticed, for at his side, tail wagging off the charts, was a pretty little yellow Labrador bitch.

"I called the other day," said Kathy, "about the puppy."

I never flinched. I already knew there had

been a plan and, by now, I realized it was probably a good one involving research, references, and the word of friends in the know and other veterinarians. This was a reputable breeder or we wouldn't have come this far. This was the solution I should have seen. If this had been a dog for me, I would have looked no farther than the adoption center. If this had been a Labrador for me, I would have been more than content with a rescue. But this was never about me. This was about a sick little girl in a hospital bed. This was about making a very specific promise come true.

"Sure," said the man, gently extending his right hand with a flat palm facing down. The yellow Lab read the signal, adopting a sitting position and a perfect stay as the man came forward to meet us. We all noticed the dog. A little different from poor old Max. "Why don't you follow me," he said. "I'll show you her mom and then I'll show you the puppy."

I appreciated the fact that he wanted to do business in this order. No hurry. He seemed to be saying, "Get a sense of the type of dog I breed, this facility, the appearance of the dogs, and in particular, their temperament."

Mom stood in a large dog run and

bounded over to meet us. She was remarkably similar in appearance to the dog that had stood by the man's side.

"You saw her sister when you pulled up. And as you can see, she's more English than American, a little more squat with shorter limbs and a classically thick tail."

The dog honed in on Emily, nuzzling, trying to lick her hands and face, working her hips like Shakira. I had to admit, the mother was strikingly pretty, her head broad but not masculine, her eyes expressive, her ears attentive.

There are many times in life when I choose to keep what I do for a living to myself — sitting next to strangers on a flight, garbled chitchat with my dentist, the overly familiar waiter — and this was one of those times. I was paying attention, digging for details about parent history, about specific health issues, and in particular seeking information pertinent to hips, elbows, cancer, and longevity, but I preferred to appear thorough rather than pushy or clever. No one likes the arrogant veterinarian looking for flaws, trying to score petty points, especially dog breeders who are respectful and good at what they do.

Emily tried to appear content during this preamble, but I was subject to many sleeve tugs, cupped little hands by my ear and whispers of "When do we see the puppy?"

"She was the only one in her litter," said the breeder as we walked into his kitchen, assaulted by the sleepy warmth of the room. The first yellow Lab we had met was still in a stay when we returned to the house, tagging along by her master's side when she received the command, released into another part of the house as we were guided toward a large dog crate near a fireplace.

"She's already used to a crate," he said, with his back to us, rustling the bed of newspapers as he reached inside. We sensed, rather than saw, something being scooped up, something sleepy and delicate, some fragile treasure that had to be moved slowly. Emily was losing it.

"Open your arms," he said, before turning around.

Emily knew the request was directed at her, and, as soon as she did, her arms were filled with a soft and stirring yellow creature.

I never felt taken advantage of. Kathy had told the breeder the story, told him who was going to be, at least on paper, this puppy's primary caregiver, and besides, I wouldn't have missed seeing the expression on Emily's face at that precise moment for anything in the world.

There is something different about the relationship between young children and animals. Perhaps it comes down to innocence, the honest exchange of emotions at their most simple and pure. Whatever the reason, when that little dog settled and snuggled into Emily's arms you could feel her excitement like an aura spreading from her body, an instant connection forming between two living things, a moment of silent intensity that says I am yours and you are mine.

I squatted down by her side and whispered, "Is this the puppy you were looking for?"

All she could manage was a tearful smile and a nod, her inability to articulate the words telling me all I needed to know.

13.

THE ENIGMA OF CANINE MOTIVATION

In contrast to the naming of Sophie, arrived at democratically after a lively debate over nominees among the whole family, the child strapped into the backseat informed Kathy and me that *she* had decided her dog would be called Meg.

I glanced in the rearview mirror. Emily remained in a state of rapt shock. She looked like a mother coming home from the hospital, clutching her newborn, her expression a mixture of concentration, excitement, and pride.

"I like it, Em, but why Meg?"

She didn't hesitate.

"It has to be an *M* word and 'Marmalade' didn't sound right."

Under certain circumstances, and this was one of them, there is no point in arguing with the carefully considered logic of a nine-year-old. Besides, "Meg" felt like a good fit — simple, monosyllabic, and feminine. Emily would go on to exploit variations on the theme — Meglet, Meggy-Moo-Cow, Meghan, Peghan, Peggy, and Peglet — but we were all happy with her choice.

As soon as we arrived home and pulled into the garage, Kathy pointed out a large cardboard box hidden away in a corner.

"It's a large dog crate. Collapsible. We should probably set it up."

She read my double take.

"What?" she said, unable to contain her iniquitous grin. "One way or another we were getting a second dog. I figured we'd need a crate either way."

"Well prepared, my ass," I thought, secretly impressed, searching mother and daughter for furtive smiles at having carried out their carefully orchestrated and perfectly executed plan. But the grifters stayed in character, and I went for the crate while Emily entered the house carrying Meg like a waiter delivering a large platter to a table, arms extended, a nutritious offering for Sophie.

Of course there was no savagery, drama, or hysteria. How could there be? Meg was a yellow five-toed sloth — irresistible, klutzy, doughy, huggable, kissable, and soft as a grape. The only thing we had to watch out for was Sophie mistaking her for a stuffed toy and wanting to give her a fearsome terrier shake. Naturally, Sophie was curious. She sniffed, licked, and at one point snapped out a clipped bark as if to say, "Just you remember who's the boss," but that was pretty much it.

It is in the nature of all gifts, birthday, Christmas, or otherwise, for most children to drift from a phase of undivided attention to comfortable familiarity to neglect and even rejection. To Emily's credit, she doesn't see dogs as gifts. She doesn't see them as friends. To Emily, dogs are family and thus you have no choice but to love them and be there for them. There followed an extended period during which Emily became a helicopter parent to her dog, placing me on permanent call for professional consults regarding every possible physiological hiccup from "Is she still breathing?" as Meg slept to hollers from the backyard insisting, "Dad, come see if her poop is okay."

There were some tears, primarily over sleeping arrangements.

"It's not fair. Whitney gets to sleep with Sophie every night."

She was right, it wasn't fair, though I had never been a fan of these slumber parties. Despite a childhood in which Patch, Whiskey, and Bess all made it onto the parental bed, communal spooning wasn't for me. As with most respiratory disorders, Emily's existing problems were exacerbated by horizontal recumbency during sleep, and huffing on dog fur — for I was in no doubt that Emily would be snuggling up tight — was the last thing she needed. And besides, as the breeder had pointed out, the crate was Meg's security blanket. It felt like home to her and she sought it out, and also being downstairs helped with the practicalities of toilet training.

Funny how I don't remember Sophie's discovery of the "little girl's room." Probably this selective amnesia is the mark of a receptive student. Then again I had failed to appreciate the excretory advantages of owning a small breed of dog. Minimal amounts of food in mean minimal amounts of waste out, and what Sophie lacked in ladylike technique — to this day she favors a bowel movement while on the move, walking forward, as though she might distance herself from the unsightly process somewhere back there — she more than makes up for with neat, tidy packages that are a breeze to clean up. When we lived in Arizona, these discreet nuggets practically turned to dust as soon as they hit the scorched earth, instantly vaporized by the power of solar radiation.

How had I managed to forget the digestive prowess of the larger breeds of dog? It was as though my experiences dodging backyard sloppy joes and tributes to Mister Whippy, courtesy of Patch, Whiskey, and Bess, had never happened. Inexplicably, I found myself horrified by the inordinate amount of stool generated by young Meg.

If you ask a veterinarian to think of a breed possessing a powerful oral fixation — driven, nay, *compelled* to ingest, unable to resist inappropriate or excessive amounts of food — the Labrador will instantly come to mind. There is a reason for this breed's badge of honor when it comes to eating. I myself have been guilty of this unfair and sweeping generalization, but when Emily made it clear she wanted a Lab, I held fast to the idea that there are exceptions to every rule. And I'm sure there are; the trouble is, Meg isn't one of them. From the start, Meg ate as though she was headed for the chair. She would never try to steal from Sophie, heaven help her, but if Sophie lost interest, even for a second, Meg's chops were all over the bowl, all but licking the glaze down to dry ceramic. And it wasn't just dog food that caught her attention. It was anything that could fit inside her mouth and therefore it was anything and everything. We used to have an antique Persian rug in our living room. I say used to. I'm not sure of the nutritional value of tassels nor what constitutes their flavorful irresistibility, but Meg worked hard and systematically to suck the goodness out of every corner before it was eventually consigned to the trash.

Early on, we realized the importance of teaching Meg not to jump up on the kitchen table or kitchen counters where she might graze on something inappropriate. To our surprise, she appeared to grasp the concept — until I discovered Meg's restraint was rooted in laziness, the acquisition of leftovers abandoned by Emily on low-lying coffee tables and couches requiring far less effort for a curious dog.

Still, I found it hard to understand how much was coming out of Meg relative to what was going in. Her weight seemed appropriate, she was growing at a normal rate, not too thin, not too fat, but her propensity to crap was disproportionate to her intake, even taking Sophie's stolen rations into consideration. The kids swore they weren't giving her table scraps. So where was all this output coming from?

This question lingered over the following months, but the answer remained elusive until the early hours of one morning when I awoke to the sound of something solid but hollow rattling back and forth downstairs. By this time Meg was no longer in her crate, having transitioned to a cozy dog bed near the kitchen, and from here she was perfectly positioned to go on sentry duty as our guard dog. Sure, she was still a puppy, and there was almost no chance of her biting a stranger, however, she had one incredibly useful asset on her side — a ridiculously masculine, booming, and intimidating bark. She sounded like some big old wrecking-yard guard dog. When strangers registered the origin of the bark, it was like the canine equivalent of that moment in the movie *The Crying Game* when you discover "she" is really a "he," only the other way round and, in Meg's case, based on her vocal cords and not her naughty bits.

But back to the strange sound from somewhere below me, making me wonder if someone was trying to break in. I raced downstairs and there was Meg on her bed, considering me with what looked like guilty chocolate eyes. I might have suspected a sleepy "What's got into you? Chill out, if someone's breaking in, I've got it covered." Instead I read, "Now I'm done for."

I snooped around all the same, checking

doors and windows before noticing that the trash can was partially pulled out of its usual position, away from the wall, sitting askew. I looked at the trash can. I looked at Meg. She kept her eyes on me, neck outstretched, chin on her bed, beating her tail three times. I looked back at the trash can, back at Meg — three more beats. It was like she couldn't help herself, unable to lie, begging me to stop embarrassing her by looking at the trash.

The trash container was made of heavy plastic, fitted with one of those flip-top lids. I stuck my hand inside like a curious snout, and rattled it around. It sounded about right. Clearly the flip-top was way too easy for Meg to negotiate — note to Labrador owners: they may play dumb, but when it comes to the acquisition of food, they are cunning and sharp. How long had Meg been grazing around, topping off her stomach when she got hunger pangs, emptying the excess in the backyard the following morning?

The next day I purchased a sturdy metallic trash container with a foot pedal. Only by depressing the pedal could you flip up the lid and access the trash.

"Okay, Meg, let's see you get past this."

A few days later, to my delight, there was

already a noticeable decline in the number of backyard landmines. I had solved the mystery and found a solution. My little yellow piglet's nights of sampling in the trough were over. I felt vindicated and masterful. Not even Pavlov himself could teach a dog how to open our new trash can.

And then, after a week or so, I began to notice that Poopy Patrol was suddenly revealing ridiculous quantities of stool once again. I would find myself lying awake at night, listening for the squeak of a foot pedal being depressed somehow, the lid flipping back, a preamble to dumpster diving. Then I would berate myself. Then I would think about setting up a doggy cam to catch her on tape. Then I would berate myself. Only when I worked on the logistics of a camouflaged observational blind from which I would scream "Ah-ha!" when I caught her in the act could I fall asleep.

Thankfully, Meg was eventually, undone by a turkey carcass.

The juices, the aroma of irresistible, bony, grisly, greasy leftovers wrapped in aluminum foil — I should have known better than to leave them overnight in my new Fort Knox trash can in the kitchen. I should have taken them out to the garage and deposited the remains in the regular trash, where they would have lain beyond temptation. Still, the bait had the food addict in a frenzy, and I had only just hit the pillow when I heard the sound of something hollow and metallic rattling around. I raced downstairs to witness the impossible, a foot on the pedal creating just enough lift in the lid for a nose to pry it the rest of the way open, the carcass and accompanying aluminum foil gone, nothing left but smiling greasy chops and a pink tongue busy licking them clean.

"Bad girl, Meg," I scolded, spinning the trash can around so that the pedal was toward the wall and inaccessible. "Come here and let me feel your tummy."

Remorseful, she stood perfectly still as I palpated her abdomen, stomach distended but soft and nonpainful.

"No more," I said, tapping her nose, her eyes still glistening with guilty pleasure. "Let's hope you did a good job of chewing your food."

She trotted off back to bed and so did I, anxious about what the morning would bring.

I am always the first up in the morning at our house, and even before I reached the bottom of the stairs I knew I was in trouble. Typically, when all is well, Meg greets me with a yawn and a downward-facing-dog yoga move, a prelude to the excitement that is breakfast. That morning I received no greeting, something I had time to register only milliseconds before I was accosted by the smell. Meg sat by the back door looking forlorn, but between the bottom of the stairs and where she sat were pools of foul-smelling watery diarrhea.

"Oh, Meg," I sighed.

I was in boxer shorts and nothing else and I wished I had a gas mask and a HazMat suit, but I let her out the back door and began the odious task of trying to clean up the kitchen floor before the rest of the family emerged.

There can be few things more unpleasant than waking up to the pungent aroma of puppy diarrhea and trying to scoop a brown and sloppy liquid into plastic shopping bags while working your way through mounds of paper towels and Lysol. And it was everywhere, as though Meg had thought it might be less noticeable if she had spread it around the kitchen island, under the kitchen table, and in front of the back door. When I was finished I had two bags precariously full of biohazard and I didn't want to touch anything with my hands for fear of contamination.

My plan had been to double-bag my collection, toss it in the trash in the garage, go check out Meg, and keep her away from food for the morning, giving her GI tract a break. Later, she could have something bland for dinner, maybe scrambled egg and rice or boiled chicken and rice. But to my horror, Meg had decided to find an alternative breakfast. She had correctly assumed that her usual dry food was off the menu and had therefore gone for the only alternative readily available, one of her own backyard turds!

There I stood in my boxers at the back door, diarrhea-laden bags in hand, screaming her name to absolutely no avail. I couldn't put the bags down. What if they leaked? What if they toppled over? Only one thing to do: run outside, carrying the bags, and shoo Meg away from the breakfast of champions.

I'm pretty sure that if what followed had been recorded on video and downloaded onto YouTube, it would have gone viral overnight. You see, it wasn't that I slipped or tripped, it was the fact that I was charging toward Meg, trying to make her stop by swinging one of the bags in her direction, only to find her focused if not mesmerized by her prize, holding her ground, remaining perfectly still as the bag bumped into her back end and, like a brown paint bomb, exploded, covering me with an enormous splash of the diarrhea I had just finished cleaning up.

It had the desired effect. Meg did desist from eating a stale poop. In fact she skittered away from the paralyzed, half-naked man who looked as if he had just emerged from a mud-wrestling contest.

"God damn it, Meg!"

"What's going on?"

The question came from Kathy, who stood at the back door in a bathrobe, coffee cup in hand, and in that speechless moment, I could see her trying to fathom the scene, her husband wandering the backyard in his underwear, his face a pinched mask of revulsion, and what on earth was he doing with those plastic bags?

Meg trotted over to greet her, apparently seeking the sanctuary of a sane member of the family, and like the Swamp Thing or the Creature from the *Brown* Lagoon, I inched my stiff body toward them, wincing with every slick, squishy crease in my joints, trying to hold my breath.

"I can explain," I said, hearing the whine for vindication in my voice.

But Kathy was petting a remarkably unsullied Meg, and to my horror, for an instant,

I thought I saw the two of them staring back at me, unified by their disgust, appalled by my unhygienic indecency, as though they were in collusion, as though, as I advanced, this crafty Labrador had whispered, "How do you live with this guy?"

I have heard it said, "Never trust a veterinarian who doesn't own a pet." I'm not sure I agree with this observation, but I will say, having a pet of your own does offer the veterinarian a different perspective, a view from the other side of the examination table, if you will. Sometimes, spending your working days with other people's cats and dogs can feel a bit like being a tourist in a far-off capital city. Sure, you tick off the major sites, you get a taste for what it is like, but ultimately the experience can only ever be superficial, a taste, a smattering of the highlights. Having your own pets is like living in this foreign city for an extended period of time. It is your chance to integrate, to immerse yourself and discover all the fine details, all the magic you might otherwise miss or overlook. There is no shortcut. Buying the T-shirt and mailing off the postcard just isn't the same.

One of my biggest failings as a veterinarian who shares his life with cats and dogs at home is a desensitization to their everyday health-care issues. And please, I choose my words carefully. Desensitization is not the same as negligence or avoidance when it comes to looking after the family pets. You can get so caught up in the big stuff at work, you become inattentive to the little stuff at home.

"Dad, Sophie's been scooting on the rug for days. When are you going to empty her anal sacs?"

"Don't forget to bring the nail clippers home!"

"What do you mean you never noticed the skin rash on Meg's belly?"

I know for a fact, many of my colleagues are a little slow on the uptake when it comes to their own pet's health. And it's not just veterinarians. Take my sister, Fiona, and her husband, Pete, a nurse and pediatrician, respectively, who live in Western Australia with their four kids. Recently their eldest, Jack, injured his knee playing Australian rules football. Pete reckoned his son would be fine with a bag of ice and a couple of Advil. It was not until the afternoon of the following day that they finally went to the emergency room, where an orthopedic surgeon remarked, "Your son has one of the most severe knee injuries I've seen in twenty years." If I'd have done the same thing with Meg, the women in my household would have eaten me alive, and using the line Pete employed — "Ah, Nick, we breed 'em tough down under!" — would certainly not have got me off the hook. Thankfully, when it comes to our pets, each and every member of my family provides real-time, in-your-face Post-it notes that will not wane, be silenced, or tuned out until the crisis, however trivial, has been averted or resolved.

Over the years, relative to so many of my clients, I realize we have been remarkably lucky with respect to our pets' health. I find myself constantly checking out Meg's hips, elbows, and knees, ensuring there are no early markers of orthopedic weakness. In fact Meg's most troubling medical disorder to date resulted from that meddlesome, unstoppable impulse, so rampant among her breed — oral curiosity.

It occurred shortly after the war-paint-diarrhea incident. With the trash can emptied every night and turned around, making it truly inaccessible, Meg turned elsewhere for relief from her craving for midnight munchies. I imagine she tried the refrigerator in vain. However, one night, among the various kitchen cabinets, Meg discovered a lazy Susan. Unbeknownst to us, the opening to this revolving shelf, unlike the cabinet doors with small porcelain handles, was amenable to a strong, persistent muzzle. To Meg it must have seemed like she had come upon one of those carousel snack-vending machines, only she required no cash and there were no plastic windows holding her back as the samples spun around before her awestruck eyes.

Unfortunately for Meg, the lazy Susan predominantly stored baking ingredients — flour, baking soda, brown sugar, confectioner's sugar — most of which were safely sealed inside large plastic containers topped by sturdy lids. Ultimately Meg's choice of snack may have been dictated by a lack of amenable alternatives or the only unfamiliar olfactory stimulant to her curiosity. Whatever the reason, Meg singled out two items, chewed open their plastic wrappers, and devoured their contents — a two-pound bag of ground coffee and a one-pound bag of semisweet chocolate chips!

Yes, of course, I realize both items should have been locked away in a dogproof container, but we had seriously underestimated Meg's oral fixation. Both chocolate (containing the stimulant theobromine) and coffee (naturally packing caffeine) are common household poisons for dogs, with the potential for seizure, coma, and death. If you know or suspect your dog has ingested either item, you should call your veterinarian. And there's the rub when it came to curious Meg. Those who could help her, those who loved her, including a veterinarian only a matter of vertical feet from where she stood, all slept peacefully, totally unaware of the poisons trying to take hold of her body.

When I went downstairs the following morning, the absence of Meg's greeting had me bracing for another trash-can disaster. But what I discovered was very different. Meg stood trembling by the back door and all across the hardwood kitchen floor were lakes of brown vomit.

Even in his sleepy haze it didn't take Sherlock long to discover the remnants of the chocolate-chip and ground-coffee wrappers and realize what had happened.

"Come here, girl, let's have a look at you."

You know that feeling when you've seriously overdone your caffeine habit, that jerky, jumpy, unpleasant shakiness and heightened sensitivity of all your senses. Well, multiply this level of agitation by a factor of ten and you have a rough approximation of where poor Meg was at —

the worst trip ever with no chance of relief.

A few weeks earlier I had seen a ten-week-old pit bull puppy come through Angell's emergency service with an equally dangerous caffeine-related poisoning albeit from a more palatable source. His owners had passed out drunk in their apartment. They had been working their way through an assortment of beverages during the evening and, clinging to a measure of civility, had opted for a nightcap of Bailey's Irish Cream. Unfortunately the liquor had a powerful sedative effect, husband and wife falling asleep on the couch, the bottle of Bailey's toppling over on its side, and the sticky, milky brown liquid pouring from its neck, irresistibly sweet to a curious puppy. For those who have tried the drink, the manufacturers have overpowered the stimulant punch of the coffee flavor with a traditional depressant — alcohol, and plenty of it. The result was a couple of drunks turning up with a drunken puppy who required twenty-four hours of intravenous fluids and supportive care for alcohol toxicity.

When it came to Meg, I had no idea how long the various toxins had been in her system; however, she had managed to vomit, and based on the amount of artwork scattered across the floor, an awful lot of what she had swallowed had come back up.

She was trembling and her heart was racing, but her color was good and her pulses strong, and when I listened with a stethoscope I heard no abnormal rhythms or dropped beats.

"What did you do?"

Meg tried to look innocent but her eyes were so wild she could only manage manic.

I let her out into the backyard and she instantly turned into a greyhound, charging around, unable to stop, as though it was a relief to blow off some steam. I began cleaning up the mess in the kitchen. There was no way of knowing if she had purged everything. After vomiting, a dog is supposed to be fed activated charcoal to deactivate the poison. I didn't have any on hand, but I could get it easily enough. Then again, I wasn't sure at this stage whether it would make any difference. What to do, what to do? The critics' corner would be waking up soon. If anything happened to this dog because I provided substandard care there would be hell to pay.

I went outside to check on the patient. It was a brisk morning and I sensed Meg preferred to be outside, finding the cool air soothing. By now she had transitioned from a relentless gallop to intermittent bursts of energy, zipping across the lawn sprint-stop, sprint-stop, as if she was beginning to calm down but still unable to settle.

"I've got something that will help," I told her, heading back inside to my "stash" and returning with a sedative. I popped the pill in her mouth.

"You stay out here and I'll keep checking on you. I need to make sure you don't get dehydrated, and that means plenty of water and no more Red Bull, you hear me."

She was pathetic, with that look I had seen so many times when Emily was a kid, the pained expression that begs "Please help me."

For the rest of the day Meg stayed in the backyard, occasionally darting inside, scrambling for traction on the hardwood floor before bolting back outside. It took a good twenty-four hours for her to come back down and, to some extent, it would have been a whole lot easier to have taken her to work and have her admitted for a day. Emily stood vigil over her dog, her doctor at her beck and call, no variation in her condition too small to necessitate a consult. And there was no way to try sliding past her. I discovered there's only one thing more dangerous than having your own pet sick — dealing with this sick pet's owner.

In the end, I received little to no kudos for my nursing care of Meg.

"I think Emily blames me for Meg's caffeine experiment," I said to Kathy. "And she's probably right. I mean it's not as though a dog can suppress her curiosity."

Kathy offered another possibility.

"I think Emily never felt as though her dog was in any real danger. I bet she'd be different if Meg had been snatched from death's door."

Meg was watching us, curled up on her bed, tail beating the floor as I came over to give her a pat.

"You hear that?" I said. "Next time a little more drama might be helpful if I'm ever going to impress my daughter."

Meg just offered me her goofy smile, happy for the physical contact. Soon after, another incident would prove Meg had been listening, confirmation of that most powerful Labrador trait of all — "We aim to please"!

I have to credit my wife with taking on the biggest burden of living with a Labrador — the provision of adequate exercise. They may not be border collies or Australian cattle dogs or Irish setters, but they can run and run to the degree that you feel like you

411

might never fully satisfy their desire to exercise.

Over the years I have met a handful of Labrador owners who have astounded me with one confession over all others, that being "My Labrador doesn't like to swim." (You really thought I might say, "My Labrador's never hungry!") When I think about Meg and water I find it hard to imagine how any relative of hers, regardless of color, would not share the Labrador's innate ability and desire to swim. They make it look easy, their position in the water low, their movement economical and perfectly natural. Meg views an open body of water, no matter its size, as she does food, the attraction magnetic, irresistible, and steadfast. It could be a paddling pool, swimming pool, or a frozen lake in February — give her access and she will find a way to get her body wet.

Swimming has become an integral part of Meg's exercise, though it never felt as though we had much choice. When Meg was a little more than one year old, Kathy took her down the street to walk a footpath next to a large lake near where we live. Naturally, as soon as Meg was off her leash, there were playful forays into the water, little doggy paddles out maybe five or ten yards before turning for shore, followed by a shakedown and a mad dash to catch up before another dip proved irresistible.

There were no other dogs and no other people around; however, Meg discovered some new and strange aquatic playmates, the likes of which she had never seen before — two majestic adult swans.

They glided into her peripheral vision from behind some reeds, moving horizontally, keeping their tight formation despite a strong wind whipping up a choppy surface.

Kathy saw them too late, and saw the yellow blur charging down the bank. With a leap, limited air time, and a booming belly flop, Meg was in the water and paddling their way, eager to introduce herself.

"Meg. No. Come back, Meg. MEG!"

At that moment, screaming at Meg to return to shore was about as effective as asking her to chew more slowly, and in her defense, she had no idea who she was up against. The swans saw this lumbering yellow dog advancing toward them, glanced at one another, and set off toward the horizon. I don't know if swans can be mean spirited, whether they were simply trying to make good their escape or wanted to teach Meg a lesson, but the two white birds set off while maintaining a taunting distance between their tails and Meg's smiling snout.

Kathy continued to scream, but Meg had locked on to her target, either eager to play their game or incredulous that they wouldn't stop and say hello. Kathy stood on the shore, the lake stretching out before her, dense forest on all sides with a tiny island about a quarter of a mile off in the distance before the water disappeared around a corner. Meg was swimming into the wind, determined and unruffled. It's hard to imagine she could have heard much of anything at water level, and Kathy was hoarse from shouting. By the time Meg was five hundred yards out, all she could see was a yellow dot bobbing among the white caps.

For several minutes she felt certain that Meg would turn around any moment, that she would realize the futility of her mission, until it dawned on Kathy that both the swans and Meg had disappeared, the twinkle of the bobbing yellow dot extinguished.

Kathy didn't hesitate. Her mind focused immediately on Emily as she pulled out her cell phone and dialed 911.

"My dog's gone chasing swans and she's disappeared and I'm pretty sure she's drowned. It's my daughter's dog . . ."

This was where she began to lose it, the guilt beginning to trickle in as she imagined

414

Emily's reaction when she broke the news.

". . . my daughter has an illness and . . . the dog means . . . I guess I was hoping you could help me recover the body, so at least she would have something to bury."

Kathy had been patched through to the local fire service, a fine group of men and women who knew Emily professionally, having whisked her away to the hospital in the middle of the night when she came down with a bout of the croup. They assured Kathy they would be right there, and in under five minutes two fire trucks had arrived.

"Any sign of her?"

The question came from an older gentleman, barely clinging to enough gray hair to make his military crewcut worthwhile. He appeared to be in charge, perhaps a captain, and he exuded unruffled calm, efficiency, and, most of all, empathy. Whether he was a dog owner, dog lover, or just someone who knew the importance of a dog to a sick child was never clear, but he approached Meg's situation with the exact same measure of professionalism he might demonstrate for a drowning child.

Kathy shook her head in response to his question.

"I'm guessing it's been about fifteen

minutes since I can say I could definitely see her."

The captain pondered this detail and turned to his crew, ordering them to get set up. From the back of one of the trucks emerged an orange inflatable boat, a Zodiac, and Kathy watched as a couple of the men began pulling out wet suits, gearing up with scuba equipment.

"Oh, God," she thought, "I wonder if this is going to be a rescue or a recovery."

Around this time Whitney appeared. She was at home, on break from college, and Kathy had called her while she waited for the emergency services. Whitney arrived in tears, carrying a large blanket, anticipating the need to have something in which to wrap Meg's body.

"Let me get my binoculars from the truck," said the captain, while Kathy and Whitney hugged, consoled one another, and thought about what they would say to Emily, still at school and blissfully ignorant of the unfolding drama.

He returned by way of his crew, who were completing their final preparations before launch, all manner of equipment finding its way inside the craft, including, Kathy noted, something long and hook-shaped, like a fishing gaff.

"They're almost done. We're treating this like any other genuine drowning emergency. Besides it's good practice." And then, bringing his binoculars up to his eyes, he said, "Let's have one last look."

Kathy and Whitney strained to see something on the horizon, willing a distant whitecap to turn yellow, but there was nothing out there.

A full minute passed, and then, "I think I see the swans."

Still, there was nothing definitive to the naked eye.

Thirty more seconds.

"Yeah, there they are." And finally the crest of a wave maintained its whiteness, a smudge split into two that acquired shape and turned into tiny bobbing birds.

"We're all set" came the cry from one of the men in wet suits, a tank of compressed air on his back as he waded into the water, spitting into his face mask. His buddy was about to launch the Zodiac.

"Just a second," said the captain, working the focus between his hands.

The second passed, no one looking at the water, everyone looking toward the captain. And then, his expression deadpan, slowly shaking his head he said, "She hasn't got a brain in her head, has she?"

"What?" said Kathy, trying to follow his line of sight and still unable to see anything meaningful.

"Trust a Labrador." He was laughing now. "Here she comes and she's still trying to catch those damn swans." He handed over the binoculars and turned to his men. "It's okay, fellas, we won't be needing you."

It took Kathy a while to work the magnification, but eventually she had Meg in her sights — the two swans up front, cruising back toward the shoreline and looking mighty pissed off by the relentless canine in tow, Meg smiling away, still convinced she was about to catch them.

Five minutes later and Meg was within shouting range, but to Kathy's horror, Meg remained just as oblivious to her calls as she had when she first set off.

By now, the captain and his entire team were on the shore with Kathy and Whitney, whooping it up like a crowd at the finish line, waving and shouting, trying to get Meg to look their way. For one frightening moment, it seemed as though they would have to make a water rescue after all as the two swans veered off and headed back out toward the island with Meg, once more, eager to follow. Seeing this, fearing this, the crowd picked up the intensity of its screams

418

and somehow got through to Meg. Maybe she thought everyone had come out to see how well she swam, that she had acquired an appreciative fan club, because finally, after being out in the water for over half an hour, she made an abrupt change in course, clambering in to shore before collapsing on the bank, exhausted.

Whitney wrapped her up in the towel, Meg panting away, eyes darting everywhere as if asking her entourage, "Did you see me? Did you see me?"

"I wonder if she took a break on the island or kept on going around the corner," said Whitney.

"All I know," said the captain, "is it's a good job those swans decided to come back this way. Otherwise I think she'd still be out there."

Kathy thanked him and his team, promising to drop by with some cookies, and after a while, a stiff wooden puppet dog that used to be a Labrador plodded her way back home.

Like any kid would, Emily enjoyed the tale, relishing her mother's fear, knowing there was a happy ending and another fine reason to love up her dog, another memorable childhood story, this one beginning with "Do you remember that time Meg chased after some swans?" My involvement came in the aftermath of the adventure, Meg "Phelps" succumbing to an ailment common among dogs that swim excessively in cold water.

"Dad, I think Meggy's broken her tail."

Emily's assessment was perfectly reasonable, the busy beefy otter tail suddenly painful and apparently paralyzed, hanging off her back end like a limp windsock on a still day.

I checked her over, and finding no fractures let her history help me make the diagnosis.

"It's not broken, sweetie. She's got something called 'swimmer's tail' or 'limber tail' or 'cold tail' or 'dead tail' or, the best name of all, 'broken wag'! The muscles to the base of her tail are not used to working so hard, acting like her rudder in the water. They're swollen and sore, but they'll get better in the next few days and I'll give her something to get rid of the pain and inflammation. She'll be swimming again in no time."

Emily didn't look happy.

"But no more swans, right?"

I wondered about this, thinking about how to keep this dog away from water. It would be like an act of cruelty for a Labrador, a "no-water torture." Then again, knowing

Meg, I was sure she would get right back in the saddle, if not chasing swans, then ducks, geese, bass fisherman, Jet Skis, anything or anyone who would potentially play with her in the water.

As it turned out, I need not have worried. I don't know what transpired between dog and swan out in the wilds of that roiling lake, what threats were made and what oaths were sworn, but Meg has never chased a single water bird since.

14.
THE GIFT OF
SECOND CHANCES

Meanwhile, in a country far, far away, an old man finally broke the magic spell that had left him bereft of canine company for almost two full years.

"Her name's Sasha," said my father, during one of our Sunday morning phone calls, the announcement taking me completely by surprise, and in the pause before he could continue I was all over this snippet of information. Dad had said "her name," i.e., a bitch and not a male dog. Admittedly this had been my suggestion during one of our previous clandestine discussions, when I caught Dad alone, Mum away at one of her spinning classes (referring to the lost art of spinning wool and nothing to do with spandex and stationary bicycles), unable to overhear. Of course I have nothing against male dogs, and I realized this was sensitive territory, but I felt as though my father had been, for want of a better word, overpowered by two strong alphas in Whiskey and Patch. He had struggled to rein them in, yet with Bess, things had been different. Tactfully, I homed in on the special connection that exists between fathers and daughters, mothers and sons, the undeniable magic between opposite sexes. Secretly, I believed a female was my father's best bet for having a dog he could handle.

The name "Sasha" hit me like a mental hiccup. My brain jumped to "Russia" and I figured that before I knew it, Dad was going to announce he was the proud owner of either a Samoyed or a Borzoi.

"Like you said, we went through a rescue group."

Though it was the right thing to do, my suggestion was also rooted in my own guilt for not following through when it came to Meg.

"Sasha and her brother needed a new home."

Oh, no, I thought. Here we go again. A new dynamic duo to strike fear into Yorkshire's sheep population and the local veterinary community.

"The owner was an officer in the military and was posted overseas. For some reason she was unable to take the dogs with her."

The word *military* flashed in brilliant green

neon, smacking of order, discipline, good manners, and solid basic training. Then again, what if Sasha was a former attack dog?

I could stand it no more.

"So what is she?"

It was my father's turn to fall silent for a second, before replying, "She's a Labrador. A black one." And then, "You're not pleased?"

In fact I was more than pleased. For the first time in my life, my father had chosen a dog in which my input had guided his decision in a very specific direction. He had crossed off every box: female (smaller, easier to handle as she grows older); mature (avoid the difficult puppy years); rescue (do your part to find a permanent home for a good animal who needs one). In my professional opinion, the old man in a flat cap and Wellington boots, hiking Herriot's countryside, had finally done good.

"Not at all," I said. "I think she sounds perfect."

It would be a while before I met her and by then Sasha was experiencing her first significant health problem.

I had been invited to lecture in England, the venue conveniently located for me to make a detour into the Dales for a few days. For a little over three years I had been regaled with tales of Sasha's accomplishments and impeccable manners, but to be honest, based on previous experiences I was skeptical. I had heard it all before. My father's track record did not exactly fill me with confidence. I fully expected to be set upon by a morbidly obese black blimp who never tired of barking, jumping up, and helping herself to my dinner as I ate.

In fact, the encounter was like stepping into a parallel universe in which everything is a mirror image of what you expect. For starters, Sasha was a perfect weight, her body slender, toned, and shiny. She greeted me with enthusiasm and civility, and I noticed how her tail beat twice as fast as her legs moved, the movement calculated and precise as though she were thinking about her performance, giving me a measured amount of attention. Then she let slip the retriever in her, insisting on bringing me her favorite green frog, showing it off, seeking my approval.

"Wow," I said to my father, who was glowing with pride. "All the rumors and hype were true. She's wonderful."

The cottage in which my parents live is small — a "two-up-two-down" with one tight full bathroom upstairs. Throw in a few more bodies and it can quickly feel cramped, with barely enough chairs to go around. Now, as if for the first time, I noticed how by far the largest space in their sitting room was taken up by a blanket and bed for Sasha — positioned so as to be the center of attention.

When my mother beckoned us to the kitchen for dinner I reckoned all their carefully rehearsed pretense would come undone.

"Lay on your bed," said my father, addressing Sasha. His tone was casual, conversational, no hand gestures, and I didn't even bother to look, anticipating the familiar nudge from a wet nose looking for handouts as soon as I sat down at the table.

Mum and Dad joined me, their actions, their conversation, their expressions all unnervingly ordinary.

"Wait a minute," I said. I got up and walked back into the sitting room. I half expected the door to be closed, the lower third of the door panel scarred by scratch marks. Either that or Sasha had been shackled in place.

The black Lab curled on her bed looked up at me as though she had been warned this might happen, anticipating my double take.

I returned to the dinner table.

"Something's not right here. Dad's finally got a dog that does as she is told?"

Both my parents abandoned their illusory indifference and let loose with uninhibited grins.

"Your father has been working incredibly hard with Sasha, isn't that right, Duncan? He's finally got the time to devote to all the necessary training and it's really paying off."

Dad began shaking his head.

"Now then," he said. "Sasha just happens to be particularly smart and eager to learn. If you want to join me for a walk tomorrow, son, I'll show you what I mean."

The following morning, I asked if I could borrow a pair of my father's Wellington boots, his unrivaled collection over the years akin to that of Imelda Marcos, if not as diverse. He handed over a royal blue pair and said, "They should fit you," and then added, "It's been a while."

The statement came out as fact, not accusation, with no trace of bitterness, but it struck me all the same. The calculation was painfully easy, two lonely points in time, a glaring void between the dates, and I realized more than a decade had passed since our last walk together with our dogs.

Put it down to jet lag or sleep deprivation from a restless night on a top bunk in their spare bedroom, but right then, as we were about to set out, seeing my father so fundamentally content and his dog thrilled to be joining us, I felt the weight of my neglect settle in. Worst of all, it took this particular moment, in all its simplicity, for me to even begin to get it. It hit me like a knockout punch, whereas before, safely and selfishly lost in my own world, I had barely felt a tap. My pursuits had cost my parents dearly. Their son, their daughter, their grandchildren were all so far away. Time spent with family shouldn't be the stuff of big dreams, and here was a man savoring the moment, when what we were about to share was so natural and such a basic component of who he was.

"Ready?" asked Dad as Sasha reared up on both front legs before he opened the front door.

"Sure," I said with a smile, knowing the very least I could do was to keep the guilt to myself, to take it with me, wanting it there as a reminder to take nothing for granted, to open my eyes, to be receptive and find a way to make things right.

From the get-go the dynamic between

man and dog was different from any of my previous experiences. Dad and I walked side by side and, at his side, walking to heel, was Sasha. Without a doubt, for me, this wholly uncharacteristic demonstration of exemplary canine conduct was conspicuous, but I kept the observation to myself as we headed through the village, passed the Fox and Hounds, the village green, and the corner store and turned up a narrow lane between rows of stone farm laborers' cottages when we started our ascent into the high fields.

Father was cracking a pace, the old walking stick our metronome, encouraging me to keep time despite the steepness of the slope we had to climb.

"You rarely see a vehicle up here, except the occasional farmer on an ATV."

I nodded and stood there for a moment, hands on hips, catching my breath, pretending to take in the incredible scenery, vast open fields stretching to every horizon, black lines of stone walls like an enormous jigsaw, finished and perfect. Best of all I noted that my father was not the least bit breathless.

"Just a little further and then we're going to cut across that field yonder."

"Dad, who on earth says 'yonder'?"

"Now then, son, if you're in Yorkshire, you'd best learn to speak the language."

I smiled and shook my head, thinking, "He's still trapped in an episode of *All Creatures.*" But as I looked around, and took in this precious slice of England, his heaven and a place he never takes for granted, I thought, "Why not?"

It was only after I scaled the railings of the metal gate, a grossly uncoordinated maneuver, and stood facing the acres of lush grass that I realized our predicament.

Sheep! Dozens of them, ewes and lambs in clusters and woolly constellations in all directions.

Dad appeared to be completely unfazed, whereas I flashed back to memories of Bess and a farmer's shotgun. I noticed Sasha, still at heel but seemingly on high alert, her eyes bright and a little too jumpy for my liking.

"You sure you want to go through? There's not a way around this field?"

Dad scaled the gate with ease and proficiency as Sasha negotiated the gap.

"We'll be fine," he said and left it at that.

If you've ever walked through a field of sheep, you'll appreciate how your path is a bit like the parting of the Red Sea. There will be the occasional standout, chewing the cud or savoring a particularly flavorful blade, but for the most part they scatter like, well, a flock of sheep. In other words, their stop-start movement is the perfect temptation for many a canine.

I had been comforted by the excellent leash control Sasha had demonstrated to this point, but this had to be torture, all those buttery balls of wool eager to play tag. At the very least I expected Dad to have to hold her back, to grimace and strain as he tried to control a panting dog choking against the collar at her neck.

Twenty yards in and I was watching the reaction of the sheep, listening to the bleating message being passed around the field, their game of "telephone": "Let's tease the dumb dog who has to live on a chain."

Then, to my horror, I looked down and over to Sasha and saw something I would never have imagined possible in my lifetime. The three of us were walking across the field, all in a row, like three gunslingers walking into Tombstone, the crowd scattering on all sides, and the dog in our posse was no longer on a leash.

I met my father's eyes and found delight and even self-assurance, as though I shouldn't look so surprised.

"I don't believe it," I said. "You finally did

431

it. You taught her how to get along with sheep. After all these years, you have a dog that can go for walks and be free."

We walked a while, in silence — father, son, dog — completely tethered yet totally independent, and for the first time, in all our time together, after all the mistakes I had witnessed as a kid and growing up, I was incredibly proud of the dog owner by my side and what he had accomplished.

"You care to share how you did it?"

Dad turned to me, trying to look affronted.

"No one should ask the magician how he does the —"

And like that, the smoke and mirrors were gone. Something quick and white flickered in my peripheral vision and Sasha vanished in a moment of explosive acceleration, in pursuit, and all I could think was it must be a lamb, perhaps separated from her mother, the canine hunting instinct impossible to suppress. If we were lucky, there would be no farmer around. The lamb, however, was another matter.

But as I watched Sasha sprinting into the distance, I noticed how her path zigzagged, interrupted by a series of cuts back and forth, her target invisible or at least much smaller than the other lambs in the field.

"Sasha!"

It was the first time I had heard my father shout her name and the cry was packed with frustration.

The command went ignored and I remember feeling shocked, a phenomenon that shocked me in its own right, given the person delivering the order.

Dad was shaking his head.

"Rabbits! I've tried everything to stop her chasing them but she loves it."

Sasha had reached the perimeter wall, her prey spelunking its way through a crevice in the limestone and away to freedom.

"She never chases the sheep or the lambs, but rabbits . . . that's another matter."

"She ever catch them?" I asked.

"Aye," said Dad. "Sadly, from time to time she does."

Sasha was trotting our way, head low to the ground, looking forlorn, almost apologetic for her guilty pleasure.

"Still, for a dog in a field full of sheep, catching the occasional rabbit actually keeps her in good graces with the farmers."

I didn't say anything, wondering if, like me, a farmer might see a dog charging across a sheep field and jump to the wrong conclusion. Then again, in a village of a hundred or so people, you would think this particular duo would be well known to those who watch over the livestock, especially given the frequency with which the two walked the Dale.

Over another fence and we were back on a footpath walled off from the fields. In the distance we spied a man headed in our direction and, at his feet, a small dog that turned out to be a Cairn terrier.

This time I wasn't surprised by my father's control and Sasha's genteel response. He called her name, asked her to sit, and returned her to the leash before we walked forward.

"She won't pull," he said, as if he knew I was thinking back to the days of Patch, the nightmare exchange, the embarrassing tug-of-war, hanging on for dear life if he had to cross paths with another person, let alone another dog. "The leash is to reassure the other owner. She doesn't really need it."

Our parties crossed paths, the humans exchanging pleasantries, the Cairn doing the terrier thing, all brazen and potty-mouthed. Sasha ignored the taunts, glued to my father's leg, eyes forward, as if to say, "Some dogs have no manners."

When we were past them, I said, "Yet again, very impressive."

"Well," he said, flashing his graying brows,

"I confess there was one encounter with another dog that got me into trouble."

"Here we go," I thought. "For all her training and all his hard work, that little switch, the one that turns your dog from virtuous into diabolical, a switch dangerously easy to flip in my little Jack Russell, existed even in this exemplary dog."

Dad described an early-morning walk in which he and Sasha were accosted by a wandering Irish wolfhound, with no owner in sight.

"At the time I was training Sasha with a retractable leash and this thing the size of a donkey began to trot toward her. Now, you know how I feel about dogs, but this dog was intimidating."

In my experience, every Irish wolfhound I have ever met has been a sweetheart, a gentle giant, blessed and cursed with a big heart and a life expectancy guaranteed to make you cry.

"Sasha instantly backed up and hid behind my leg and all the while the wolfhound kept coming."

"And what were you doing?"

He looked at me as if I had asked him for guidance on how one responds to an attack by Cujo.

"Nothing. I just stood there, rooted to the

spot, thinking this Goliath could practically swallow me whole. Then he began to chase poor Sash. I hadn't thought to press the button to reel in the leash and so she was on a long line. Suddenly I became a human maypole, Sasha clinging to me, making tight circles as the wolfhound joined in the dance, the leash going round and around, first my legs, then my chest and arms, trussing me up like a cartoon mummy until I couldn't move even if I tried. By the time his owner finally appeared, Connor the wolfhound just stood there looking on at this writhing, six-legged monster. I'll say this, there are less embarrassing ways to meet a fellow dog owner."

I laughed, imagining the scene, imagining how differently things would have played out with Patch or Whiskey. Sasha was an entirely different dog and my father was now an entirely different dog owner. When I think back to those devastated owners who are unable to move past the loss of a beloved dog, left numb and incapable of a future with a different animal for fear of falling in love again, I can now point to my father as an example of what is possible. Every dog is unique — their quirks, their impact, the way they interact, and the emotions they draw from us exclusive and unparalleled. Admittedly, love and loss may be universal, but as my father will attest, it's never the same, you are not being unfaithful, and, however much it hurts, it's worth it.

We carried on along the path, strolling now, and I was conscious of breathing in the moment — the fresh air, the earthy green smells, the vistas, and the sensation of my father's happiness at being out with his dog and his son. He told me how he was keeping busy mowing lawns for friends in the village and how he was learning Morse code and taking classes in amateur radio. For a while I took him on a detour.

"You mean you're hiding in the basement getting all 'Broadsword calling Danny Boy. Broadsword calling Danny Boy.' "

My impersonation of Richard Burton in the film *Where Eagles Dare* wasn't very good, but instantly I had uncovered another bond, the movies of my childhood, the most influential years of his fatherhood. And suddenly we were both infused with an easy wonderful lucidity and an excitement to contribute to the conversation as we ranted on about *The Guns of Navarone, The Good, the Bad and the Ugly,* and the best of the James Bond movies (only the ones with Sean Connery). When a pause in the conversation finally came I couldn't help but think how my father was finding things to do with his time, working to fill his day with alternatives to what he really wanted to do. He wanted to be around animals, manning a front desk at a veterinary practice, playing the role of the legendary Arthur Stone, the fixer, the liaison, a man who had the ear of a veterinarian, and that veterinarian would be his son. He seemed content with what he was doing, but once again, because I had focused on *my* path, I felt as though I had deprived him of something small and simple that was *his*.

When the trail met a narrow asphalt road, we turned for home, heading steeply downhill through a series of hairpin bends that would have tested the clutch and brakes of even the best four-wheel-drive vehicle. We had been gone for about two hours, keeping a good pace, and, for the most part, walking three abreast. Now I noticed Sasha was beginning to lag behind.

I wondered if she had learned it was safer to walk single file into the occasional oncoming traffic, until it became obvious she was actually having a hard time keeping up. Dad noticed my observation.

"Yes, I've been meaning to ask you about that. Poor Sash has been getting really tired by the end of our walk. It always seems to be about the same spot, as we turn for the village, she begins slowing down, and as soon as we get home I can guarantee she'll be straight to her bed and asleep for the next few hours."

We stopped to let her catch up, and I gave her a pat and in return received a smile and a wag of the tail.

"You need a rest, sweetheart?"

I hadn't thought to pack a stethoscope for this trip. Why would I? But as we stood there I lifted her lips and checked the color of her gums, laid my hand over her heart, and felt for the pulses in her back legs. As far as I could tell everything seemed to be fine.

"Maybe you can give her a proper once-over when we get home?"

I said I would. Would I ever stop thinking about Whiskey whenever my father said "once-over"? I didn't think so.

Back at the cottage, I did the examination under my father's watchful eye. Sasha did seem pooped and eager to lie down, but as I knew she would, she allowed me to squeeze and kneed her muscles, joints, and lymph nodes before digging my fingers deep into her belly, tickling for lumps or bumps or anything abnormal.

Watching me work as I look for clues,

hunting for disaster, is a difficult time for any pet owner. Sometimes the silence becomes oppressive and overwhelming.

"What are you finding?"

"Was I right?"

"Is it what you thought?"

I'm not trying to be mysterious or needlessly theatrical. I'm trying to be thorough and, moreover, certain before I speak.

This time, however, the silence was different.

I kept glancing up at my father. It wasn't that I believed there was something more special about this dog than any other dog he had owned. Yes, he had taken the opportunity to put more time into training Sasha, but he had given no less of himself to Patch, Whiskey, and Bess. Maybe it was my present state of mind, the way I felt tuned in, but the silence closed in around us, crackling with anticipation. It was a personal silence, a silence that can only exist within a family. It had a history rooted in strife and understanding. Its presence said it all. It was a silence with a past.

"Sorry, Dad, nothing's jumping out at me. How long has this been going on?"

My father inhaled into a frown, but it was my mother who answered.

"The last few weeks, I would say. But I'd

be tired if I walked as far as he does every day. Poor dog never gets a break."

My father was beside his dog, knees cracking as he knelt down. Sasha was curled up on her bed in front of the glowing fire, and rather than stroke, my dad simply laid his hand on top of her head, as if to say, "Just relax, just sleep."

I took them in, my parents, their dog. My mother looked on, but I sensed, beyond her affected detachment, there was a flicker of anxiety because she also feared something wasn't right.

Here, for the first time in my professional life, I realized my father's dog had a problem and I had no excuses for not getting to the bottom of it. Sasha was the perfect patient. I was a fully qualified veterinarian. Finally, I could give something back. If I made the diagnosis and determined a cure, my father would have his inside track.

I gave my series of lectures in England and headed home, suggesting Dad take Sasha to his local veterinarian in order to check her temperature, listen to her heart and lungs, and obtain a sample of blood and urine for analysis. As soon as I got back to the States I hit the textbooks.

It would have been a whole lot easier if Sasha had slipped in the back door of my practice after hours, but I reckoned I had a pretty good handle on what was going on. According to my father she had never shown signs of a seizure, never had a fainting episode or complete collapse where she couldn't get to her feet. So long as her doctor failed to discover anything unusual about Sasha's heart with the aid of a stethoscope, I felt confident that I could rule out a cardiac reason for her weakness.

Based on her healthy and steady body weight I thought cancer highly unlikely. Sasha wasn't on any medications that might cause her to be lethargic as an adverse reaction, and I felt sure the pending blood and urine tests would pick up any kind of metabolic or hormonal upset if it existed. My examination discovered no underlying muscle or joint disorder. So where did that leave me? Truth be told, I knew exactly where: a place, sadly, I often liked to find myself — trying to uncover diseases of a weird and wonderful nature.

Somewhere, way back in my memory, I remembered a case, or a lecture, concerning an animal that showed periodic weakness due to an insulin-secreting tumor of the pancreas. Insulin is one of those magical hormones essential in regulating the amount of glucose in our blood. Produce too much of it at the wrong time and your glucose levels plummet, leaving you exhausted and ready for a nap.

Obviously I didn't want to be right about this — no one wants to give a pet a diagnosis of an insulin-secreting tumor — but that said, I did want to give my father an answer. Sasha's problem was subtle and tricky, the kind of niggling health issue you might be tempted to ignore or overlook. If I had uncovered the cause of her exercise-induced weakness, there would be heartache ahead, but wasn't it better to know sooner rather than later, to maximize our options, to avoid those critical second guesses that convince you you could have acted earlier?

I found the appropriate page in the gold-standard textbook of veterinary internal medicine.

"The potential for hypoglycaemia (low blood glucose) is great, and this fact is supported by the number of owners who associate symptoms in their pets with jogging, play or long walks."

Long walks!

Suddenly, there it was. It all seemed to fit. By the end of her long walk Sasha was demonstrating all the signs of low blood glucose. With luck, her blood work would confirm this finding. In the meantime, from three thousand miles away, I believed I could wow my father with a little veterinary magic that would have made James Herriot proud.

"Is everything all right, son?"

I was calling on a weekday morning because I couldn't wait until the weekend.

"Oh yeah, sorry, I just needed to ask you a few more things about Sasha."

"Be my guest. Ask away! She's with me right now, lying down at my feet. You know I'm always happy to talk about our Sash."

It's funny, living in America has made me notice how much the English, and I am sure I am included in this generalization, never answer with a simple yes or no when there's an opportunity to ramble.

"Her weakness after the morning walks, does it happen all the time?"

There was a pause on the line and I imagined a thumb and forefinger working a stubbly chin.

"No. Not always."

I smiled. This was the answer I was looking for.

"And when she gets up after her walk, does she get something to eat?"

"More often than not I'll give her a treat."

"And she'll be fine, yeah?"

"That's right. Maybe the next day she'll

444

do the same thing, maybe not."

Two for two. Now for the something magical.

"Okay, Dad, here's what I need you to do. Tomorrow morning, when you go for your walk, if, as you head down the hill, Sasha starts to slow down, like she did when I was with you, I want you to give her a treat, preferably something sweet and sugary. Will you do that for me?"

"Aye, I suppose so. I'm sure I can find something. Do you want to let me in on what's going on?"

"Just give her the treat and let me know how it goes. I'll call this time tomorrow. Got to go."

Perhaps it was unfair to keep him hanging like that, but most of what a magician does is about building up to a big finish. I wasn't able to be with him when Sasha made her miraculous recovery, but I could imagine the look of amazement on my father's face, the way it melted into a smile, imagine the bounce in their coordinated strides as they rushed home to tell my mom about what had happened. His son had come through for his dog. His son had finally delivered. It was almost as good as being there.

What I had done was apply the finishing touch to a diagnostic trifecta with the wonderful name of Whipple's Triad. In theory, for dogs with an insulin-secreting tumor, the clinical signs should resolve if the patient is administered a dose of intravenous glucose. Obviously, this was not possible on a hillside in the Yorkshire Dales, but I believed my father could do the next best thing by offering Sasha a sugary snack. To see the full effect using an oral route may take a little longer, but with luck, even before they got home, Sasha would be reinvigorated, even peppy, lying down the last thing on her mind.

A five-time-zone head start meant the test should have been concluded by the time I called the following morning.

"How's it going?"

"Great," he said, sounding buoyant.

I knew it. I had been right. But no sooner had I registered the rush of diagnostic success than I became aware of a responsibility infinitely more important. Getting to the bottom of a difficult problem can be a nice boost for the ego, but you need to direct the high into an explanation about what it all means for the patient and the owner. Rightly or wrongly, I liked to think I did a reasonable job of delivering difficult news. Here, for the first time, was my chance to show my father another facet of what it means to

446

be a veterinarian, and hopefully, a chance for him to be grateful the news came from his son.

"So Sasha bounced back after you gave her the glucose snack on the walk?"

There was a pause, and then my father said, "What? Oh, that, no, it made absolutely no difference."

I was speechless.

"You still there, son? Or do we have a bad connection?"

"No, sorry, I'm still here. But what about the blood work. What about Sasha's blood glucose level?"

"Normal, son. Her vet called me this morning and said everything looked normal."

Speechlessness topped with stunned silence. What on earth was wrong with this dog? Moreover, why did my father sound pleased?"

"Thing is, unbeknownst to me, the vet did one more test on her blood. He found out her thyroid's not working properly. Turns out Sasha just needs to take a daily supplement and she'll be right as rain. You know, Nick, he's just a new graduate, been out of vet school for less than a year, but he's right smart, very conscientious, and now, because of his quick thinking, our Sasha has a permanent cure for her tiredness."

All I remember was a pause, a moment in which I felt light-headed and vaguely lost.

"Son? Are you still there?"

15.
CONCENTRIC CIRCLES

Nearly a decade has passed since I was comprehensively bested by a young veterinarian who had paid attention in class and remembered that "common things occur commonly." Sure, I could blame my distance from the patient, point out that I was deprived of the feedback from Sasha's normal blood work, or I could blame my years of focus on the physical practicalities of surgery for weakening any aptitude I had for internal medicine. But I won't, because I was beaten fair and square by a doctor who reminded me how easy it is for clinicians not to see what is staring them in the face, to forget (which is not quite the same as overlook) certain characteristics of disease, and helped me to appreciate how we never stop learning so long as we never stop being receptive, no matter who's teaching the class.

On a personal level, however, I was

crushed. Naturally I told my father how pleased I was that *his* veterinarian had gotten to the bottom of the problem, playing down my diagnostic test as naive, a stretch, something to rule out, just in case. Dad never caught on to my disappointment and for good reason. If I told him how much it had meant for me to solve Sasha's problem, to feel like I was the son who had become the veterinarian and could finally help him out, it would have been an admission of how much I felt like I had let him down.

As I saw it, this opportunity had not been a complete waste of time. Even though I hadn't delivered, my father had witnessed my commitment. When I was a kid, Dad was the one who said, "It doesn't matter if you don't win. It does matter if you don't try." This was never about a vain quest for validation, about needing my father and mother to feel proud. Their love for my sister and I had said it all our whole lives. No, for me, this was about sacrifice, their sacrifice, their ability as parents to let go, to tamp down and conceal their own loss because they love so much. This was about the practicalities of being so far away, and wanting to give them the kind of special attention that only comes from being nearby.

As with so much in life, it takes seismic

shifts for us to see and feel what we should have appreciated all along. Perhaps that's why the shape of life is better suited to a circle than a straight line.

Whitney, our eldest, went off to college and then moved three thousand miles away to California. When I confronted her with how she felt about leaving the dogs she told me, "I hated the fact that I couldn't explain to them why I was gone. And it got worse because I would come home for a vacation, and then leave, come home and leave, over and over again. Sophie and Meg reacted in totally different ways. Meg is so sweet but she can be a little, you know, simple. She was all over me as though nothing had changed. Sophie refused to be around me for hours, sometimes the whole day. I could tell she was angry. Eventually she would forgive me and we would go back to being in love until it was time for me to leave again."

Emily is in her senior year of high school. I am another parent who watched his children head off for the first day of kindergarten, blinked, and saw them tossing a mortarboard into the air. Here I am, thirty years later, sitting in the exact same boat as my father and the boat hasn't changed one bit. Like all the best rides, it's over before you know it, but this time, when it's time to get off, you and your child must head in separate directions. I think most parents instinctively want to keep their children in their lives. Now, finally, I get to see through my parents' eyes. I wonder if I have what it takes to know that a child's pursuit of happiness, whatever it involves and wherever it takes them, must always supersede a parent's sense of loss.

No doubt, this is one more blessing, one more reason to give thanks for the animals in our lives. Their lives are like smaller, concentric circles within our own. Our pets are the kids who never leave home, and that's absolutely fine by us because these kids don't ask for the keys to the car, don't turn up drunk at two in the morning, and don't complain if you turn their bedroom into a home gym. Their presence in times of upheaval and transition acts as a touchstone, a reminder of normalcy, of comfort, and the certainty of a love that can get you through.

I would like to think our pets are not a replacement for the kids who leave home. Naturally I've caught my father talking to Sasha in a manner that sounds disturbingly like a two-way conversation by a bad ventriloquist, inducing looks of incredulity and head shaking from my long-suffering mother. But surely, that sort of thing won't happen to me? From time to time, my wife points out a mannerism, an expression that is textbook Duncan (enough for her to occasionally label me as "Duncan Junior"). On some sort of subliminal, ordained level, are Meg and Sophie destined to step up and play the role of surrogate children in my life?

Though it pains me to admit it, in this context, over the last few years, I have become closer to our dogs, more mushy and attentive to their needs. The timeline for this heightened connection definitely correlates with our children's journey through adolescence, in other words, for me, the appeal of our pets is inversely proportional to the angst and isolation of the teenage years. The pets want to engage and in their eyes we are always cool. For the most part, pet moods are predictable and pets revel in the status quo. No wonder we find solace in their company. They never give us cause to want to be without them, and maybe, on some level, this makes their absence all the more wrenching. We should be grateful for all the teenage 'tude, the sullen, moody, and independent posturing. It's just nature's way of enabling parents to let go. If our kids were like our pets, all sweetness and light, on the day they left home most of us would be checking into an institution.

Inevitably, the more I notice about Meg and Sophie, the more I remember about the other dogs in my life. Sometimes, when I take Meg for a leash walk, I may as well be walking Patch or Whiskey, smiling away my embarrassment, pretending the foot of leather tethering me and my Labrador isn't really all that taut. Occasionally Meg even manages to exhibit some antisocial shenanigans around other dogs. It is as if, by hanging out with a Jack Russell terrier, she has somehow become indoctrinated, "terrierized," molded into an unpredictable tyrant. Oh, it's just posturing — direct eye contact with another dog, mutual scratch and sniff followed by a show of hackles and a growl — but still, it makes me realize that for all my efforts to do a better job of socializing our dogs compared to the dogs of my youth, sometimes I didn't do so well. Or maybe, more important, my father didn't do so badly. Thank goodness Meg's veterinarian makes house calls!

Every so often, I am pleased to discover something new and unique about Meg or Sophie, a special trait to share with the children, trying to turn my observation into a smile and a memory. Recently, when I thought I had seen it all regarding Labradors and food, Emily made a startling discovery. As I have mentioned on numerous occasions, flavor is not a variable most Labradors care to consider. On this particular morning, Emily was in charge of feeding the dogs. Normally the mouth of "the Hoover" is placed over the dry food in the bowl, the waiter or waitress has time to blink twice, and presto, the bowl is empty. For some reason, Emily poured just a fraction of a normal kibble serving into Meg's bowl, stood back, and watched. I would have put money on the reaction being snarf, gone, and a bemused expression that said, "Where's the rest?" Instead Meg was stupefied. She looked at the offering, looked up at Emily, and refused to go near it. Let me state that again — Meg refused her food. As soon as the normal amount of kibble was added, the Hoover strapped on the feed bag and it was business as usual. When Emily told me I didn't believe her.

"Meg. No way. Put a little Tabasco sauce on her tail and there's a good chance she'll chew it off."

So I tried the experiment for myself and Emily was right. I got the exact same reaction in Meg. It was as though Meg was incredulous at the pathetic volume on offer, insisting we would have to do better, that she would not deign to ingest such a meager portion. What can I say; maybe Meg is fussy about her food after all.

Another unparalleled and enduring whim of my dynamic duo is their affinity for vacations. When we get away, they get away, their excitement palpable on the ride over to their "canine motel." Emily has been crushed by the fact that Meg leaps out the back of the truck, then bounds across the reception area and straight through to the back of the kennel, where life is one endless game of chase or tag. Meg never looks back, the pause to say goodbye a waste of precious seconds. Meg is the kid who loves going off to camp. She is the kid who never gets homesick. Sophie, on the other hand, enjoys these furloughs because she acquires a new and invaluable purpose in life. She's too old and too smart for all those asinine Labrador games. Instead she prefers manning the front desk, spending her days politely interacting with the new guests as they arrive, in the manner of a Wal-Mart greeter. When we pick them up, they are always pleased to see us, but they always make me feel like I'm pulling them away from the party too soon, as though I was the first parent to arrive.

Sadly, these days, what I notice most about Sophie is how she is growing old. She's fourteen, an age that gets your attention, an age at which you begin to wonder how much time she has left. She is no longer able to climb the stairs. It's as though she understands her new frailty, unwilling to risk a slip or a fall. I catch her waiting at the bottom, head angled upward, front legs trembling ever so slightly, hoping to be picked up. Her vision is not what it used to be, and over the last few years it has become apparent that she can no longer hear. When I call her name, nothing happens. If she doesn't see you coming, she flinches at your touch. I have stopped taking her for walks off leash because once she wanders off the only way to get her back is to physically chase her down.

Whitney has noticed too. When she comes home to visit, Sophie still rolls over and whinnies with the joy of seeing her again, but as I watch the two of them reconnect, the way Whitney cradles her first dog in her arms, the way Sophie settles into place, perfectly content, I watch a young woman's expressions pass through delight and pride to concern and dread. After her most recent visit, Whitney confided, "I definitely say a little goodbye to her every time I leave. Even though she's so tiny I think our house will feel really empty without her, and I hate to think how devastated Meg will be too."

I am reminded of another dog and another father delivering the devastating news of a broken bond. Once again, an animal from my past has reached through time and space because one day it will be my turn, instead of my father's, to make a difficult phone call, and it will be about Sophie, not Patch. Will I do as good a job as my father did with me? How do I help Whitney to understand how the connection she currently feels is, at its core, permanent? How can I explain that it may be different later yet just as strong, with ramifications beyond her comprehension?

If she doesn't believe me, I will know exactly what to do. I'll tell her a story about a former client of mine, a remarkable woman named Sandi Rasmussen, who has taught me many valuable lessons about loss since the tragic death of her Min Pin, Cleo. I've kept in touch with Sandi over the years, and not so long ago she was on vacation in Europe, standing at the check-in line at Frankfurt Airport, when a young couple with a dog caught her eye. The dog was a striking German shepherd, and as they all

458

stood at another counter, it was obvious from their collective body language and the expression of the woman working the desk that something was seriously wrong.

"I tried not to pay attention," said Sandi, "but this dog was such a love and so handsome, I felt like I had to go and find out what was wrong. The man was a soldier who had just received his deployment papers for Iraq. He and his wife had been stationed in Germany and he was going back to the States, home to his family in Pittsburgh, and there he would settle his wife and his dog in his grandmother's house before heading off to war.

"The airline claimed he had purchased the wrong dog crate for the flight and refused to fly his dog. They said he could purchase a new crate at a cost of 300 euros or they would have to miss their flight and pay another 200 euros to rebook. The soldier's name was Daniel and he was devastated, tears welling up in his eyes. They didn't have that kind of money. I've never had a shepherd, but it was obvious, this dog was special, incredibly well behaved, and obviously meant the world to this young man. How could he leave this animal behind?"

In a different era, given the circumstances,

a shrewd airline manager might have been summoned, and, sensing an opportunity, done the right thing, getting the dog on the flight, gaining a customer for life in the process. Of course, these days, there would be no such compromise.

"There was nothing to think about," said Sandi. "I gave them the money. Daniel hugged me so hard. He promised to pay me back but I told him it wasn't necessary."

Okay, I know what you're thinking, a kind and generous gesture from one animal lover to another, but so what. The thing is, it didn't end there. Though Sandi was content to have played her part in making sure a soldier prepared to make the ultimate sacrifice was able to keep his dog, it turned out they were all on the same flight, and shortly after takeoff, Daniel sought her out to thank her once again.

"He wanted to know why I did this for him and so I told him the truth. I told him about my Cleo, a dog who wasn't with me long enough but who is still there for me today. I wanted him to know that I got it, that I understood exactly how far these creatures can crawl into our hearts and I wanted him to realize that the feeling never really goes away. I was doing this for Cleo, and by the end of my story, this time Daniel really was crying."

I imagined a young soldier, all macho crew cut, square-jawed and muscle-bound in desert fatigues, blocking an aisle chatting to a fiftysomething woman, mesmerized by her story and unable to hold back the tears.

"He cried so hard and he promised to pay it forward, to do something worthy of my Cleo. Then he gave me one more hug and said, 'This is why I am proud to serve my country.'"

And for me, this was the best part, because here's the kicker. Sandi isn't American. Sandi is Canadian. She could have corrected the solider as he headed back to his seat to be with his wife, but she chose not to, because that's not who she is. Wisely, she left it at that — the soldier had his lesson, I had mine, and one day, when the time comes, it's a lesson I will pass along to Whitney.

During an all-too-familiar damp spell in July, I find myself spending a few days in the Dales checking in on my parents.

Of an evening, families in England might gather around a fireplace. Instead, we are gathered around a black Labrador on a luxurious foam dog bed, and as I study my father over a mug of milky tea, a part of me finally comes to terms with the fact that I will never be able to offer him a true James Herriot experience. I can accept this because I realize that what I have offered instead is no less affecting and personal. I wouldn't want you to think that I don't try to share my take on veterinary medicine at every opportunity. Over the years my father has joined me for consultations, observing my interactions with owner and animal with a kind of earnest concentration, before I force him into gown, cap, and mask in order to watch me perform surgery in the OR. It's a far cry from his dreams of ether and ungloved hands or the physicality of large-animal interventions amid the jabs of heckling farmers, but he has stood quietly by, watching every cut and stitch, insisting he has been fascinated. On the drive home, from the passenger seat, he asks all the questions he held back for fear of disturbing me at work, and when he gets to our house his first order of business is to check in with my mum. To my delight, I have overheard whispered conversations as he recounts our day. He rambles because childish excitement has got his tongue, words delivered in quick bursts, as he shares what he has learned. As I listen, all I can think is that he sounds just like me when I was a little boy, when I was first infected with the "animal bug," and I think back on my earliest experiences spending time with a veterinarian. Perhaps I haven't done so badly. Maybe, on some imperfect level, I have shown my father a window into my world, a different world, and, given his response, I can tell it is not so different from the version he had always imagined.

"Did we tell you about your sister?" says my mother amid the click of knitting needles. "She's gone and got herself a dog."

"What the . . ." is the best I can manage as my brain grapples with a notion so absurd as to be unbelievable.

"Now then, son," says my father somewhat sternly, "don't act so surprised. Fiona has always been a dog lover."

This claim helps me transition from speechless into the Twilight Zone.

"Are we talking about the same one-and-only sister who nearly got bitten in the face by a certain golden retriever named Whiskey when she was a kid and hasn't shown the slightest interest in anything remotely canine ever since?"

My father tut-tuts away my recollection with a wave of his hand, as though he refuses to entertain such a notion.

"Fiona was very fond of our Whiskey. So

much so she decided to get a golden retriever for herself. They've named her Lily."

Now I know I have been teleported into some sort of bizarro world where all my father's dreams come true. It isn't until I telephone my sister that I accept this outlandish about-face.

"It was the kids who wanted a dog," she says, "but Lily is great. She's the best. Yeah, so she digs holes everywhere and she's turned the backyard into a muddy battlefield but we all love her to pieces."

Have I dialed the wrong number? Where is the sister who always sided with my mother, protesting the acquisition of a new dog? How has she come to embrace a creature who is into trench warfare reenactments? I don't know, but there is no denying the sentiment in her words. This Lily has been inserted into her family, a canine stranger, embraced and already vital, in a way I would never have imagined possible. Feeling the glow of what she has discovered, it makes me wonder whether Fiona had sensed something important was wanting in all their lives. Whatever it is that my parents have passed on, be it written in DNA or upbringing, finally, both their children have become addicted to the companionship of animals.

When Sasha gets up, following my father into the kitchen, I tackle her and chance the obligatory "once-over." On her belly, slightly off midline and to the right, is a lump, firm, possibly fatty but well attached, not mobile. With great care I mention my finding.

"Yes, we know," says Dad, laying a hand on her head like a blessing. "Not to worry, I'm keeping a close eye on it."

I nod my appreciation but wonder how it might change over the next few months. What I keep to myself is my observation of Sasha's front paws. She has big feet for a girl, and I notice how her toes are a little splayed on the left, reminiscent of an elderly woman with rheumatoid arthritis, the joints and knuckles thick and gnarly.

"How's she doing on her walks?" I ask.

"Fine," says Dad, "she's a little slower than she used to be but then so am I. We still manage three walks a day."

"How far?"

Dad winces but I can still sense his mind pacing out the routes, tallying up the mileage.

"Eight to ten miles, I reckon, all told."

No wonder Sasha stays lean (despite all the treats I see him slipping in her direction). Then again, so does my father. He seems to be wasting away. Is there something wrong that he isn't telling me? Are the changes in Sasha's paws the result of all this wear and tear and is she about to break down, unable to keep up with the routine her master so dearly craves? If his dog can't walk, I am not sure how my father will cope.

Without my parents knowing, I had strolled up to the top of the village in search of their dear friend Vera, seeking her take on my father's health. She is a small, feisty woman and wonderfully forthright, as sharp as ever at eighty-five, with the hands of a farmer after years of gardening.

"He lives for that dog, doesn't he?" she told me and I had to agree.

"Last month," she said, "when he went off to Australia to visit your sister, he was acting all melancholy about not seeing Sasha for so long, and how would he cope and how would she be affected by the trip, and I said to him, Duncan, don't be so bloody silly! The poor dog will love it. She finally gets to have a rest!"

Before I leave them again, with Sasha pooped out and asleep on her bed, I ask my father to take me to the private graveyard on the hillside where Whiskey and Bess were buried, a place I have never been.

We walk down through the village, past

the cottages and farmhouses, turn right, uphill, and after a quarter mile find a footpath. It leads us through a dense copse and I become aware of a pungent odor in the air, like raw onions.

"What's that smell?" I ask, beginning to feel the climb in my chest, surprised the mission has changed from a quick visit to an actual hike.

"Wild garlic," says my father, pointing to the long grassy leaves blanketing the woodland floor. Once again, he is hardly panting. Nearly fifty years of walking dogs has paid big dividends with regard to his fitness.

"Perhaps we should take some home to mother," I say. "Spice up her cooking!"

I look back to register my father's smile but he tactfully says nothing as we make it to the top and a narrow gap in the wall built specifically for hikers, and thin hikers at that.

"This way," says Dad, striding out.

I am waiting for a "not much further now" but it never comes. We cross another field mined with cow patties, and another, over a stile and then into a field occupied by sheep and lambs.

"Head toward the top left-hand corner," he says and all I can think of is how on earth he carried Bess and Whiskey all the way up here. Bess must have weighed sixty pounds, Whiskey more like eighty. And there was no way my mother would have been able to help.

We leave the field, cross a lightly rutted trail that obviously provides access for small vehicles, open a large railed gate, and step into one more field. We are in a large pasture, the final neat rectangular plot before the land angles up steeply, rising and merging into a much larger hill dotted with sheep pretending to be mountain goats. I can see at least thirty miles up and down the dale in both directions.

"Here we are," says my father, and to be honest I am a bit surprised. Up against the drystone wall, adjacent to a small metal hut in which shelters a bay gelding, there lie a series of tombstones. There are sheep in the field, watching us, and the horse comes over to see what we are up to. I think I must have expected the shade from some mighty oak, something very private, and something far more accessible. But then this soft muzzle brushes up against my shoulder, a blast of warm horse breath blowing across my hand. As I rub the horse's nose, his friendliness strikes me as being so respectful, almost reverential, and I begin to appreciate the whole scene with a new perspective, how it

468

has a certain calm and natural quietness to it, a simple place that makes you feel part of something bigger.

"The first one is theirs," says my father, doing a little tidying up around the base of the stone.

I read the legend.

WHISKEY AND BESS, FAITHFUL FRIENDS.

"Looks good," I say.

"Aye," says my father, this small word and his gentle tone speaking volumes about their relationship.

"But I had forgotten they weren't alone," I add.

There are three other headstones next to theirs forming a little row. Each of these stones also has a name chipped into the rock. Another "Bess," "Penny," and "Jet."

"Other dogs from the village?"

My father just nods.

"I have to ask, how on earth did you get them up here? I mean it's quite a way, and getting over the walls and fences."

"It was," he says, "but you can get a car a bit closer. I'll show you on the way back."

We stand for a quiet moment, paying our respects, but I am secretly watching how my father handles himself. Duncan will always be vulnerable when it comes to animals, keeping his soft side close to the surface, and I wonder if my trip up here, with me about to head off to America again, might have made him melancholy. When I gauge that he appears to be fine, I chance a difficult question.

"So what about Sasha? Is this where she will be buried too?"

"No," says my father, and I wonder if the physical aspect of what he had done over a decade ago, the challenge of burying these dogs, was now too much, beyond his strength.

"She'll be buried in our small patch of land behind the cottage. That way, I'll keep her close by."

As I stand there, I think, how strange to have made a lasting tribute to two dogs and still feel as though it wasn't enough, as though they were still too far away.

When we get back to the cottage I take my mother aside.

"How's he doing?" I ask.

"Your father? He's fine. Fit as a fiddle."

I search her face for signs of deception or exaggeration, and finding none add, "What happens when he loses Sasha? How's he going to cope?"

"Nicholas," she snaps, her shrill tone instantly transporting me back to a childhood scolding, "it's not a matter of how *he's* going to cope. How am *I* going to cope, what with him getting all maudlin and getting underfoot, moping about the house? I've told him a dozen times, this is it; after Sasha's gone, *no more dogs.*"

This time, when I look, I see something give. Mum may have given it her best shot but she smiles back at me, all resolve weakening in her mischievous sparkly green eyes.

I have heard it all before. If and when the situation arises, I know exactly what will happen next.

And best of all, so does she.

ACKNOWLEDGMENTS

The word *acknowledge* feels wholly inadequate in the context of a son's gratitude to his parents. So much of what I try to achieve in life stems from the values they imparted and the sacrifices they made. There is comfort in knowing they have found a slice of heaven in the Yorkshire Dales, and in spite of the distance and times zones between us, I want them to know that they have not been taken for granted, that I am forever proud to call them "Mum" and "Dad." For the record, any inference that my mother's culinary skills were more Easy-Bake Oven than Julia Child was inappropriate and the work of a cheeky son!

In no particular order I would like to thank Beth Benson, Chris Dodds, Sandi Rasmussen, Vera Brown, Fiona, Pete, Jack, Holly, George, and Nick Richmond, Jack Shepherd, Ryan James, Arthur Stone, and my agent, Kristin Lindstrom. Once again I have been blessed and awed by the talent and commitment of the entire team at Broadway, in particular Ellen Folan, Jennifer Robbins, and my editor, Christine Pride. Somehow Christine manages to find the writer in the veterinarian. I thank her for her expertise and friendship.

At the heart of this book lies a desire to appreciate the attributes of those — on both two legs and on four — with whom we spend our lives. With respect to Meg and Sophie, they continue to be an entertaining, disparate, yet surprisingly compatible combo that feels just right. But as ever, it is my daughters, Whitney and Emily, and my wife, Kathy, to whom I owe everything. Thank you for allowing me to share this story and for your love and support. This book, this man, and this life would be nothing without all of you.

ABOUT THE AUTHOR

Nick Trout graduated from veterinary school at the University of Cambridge in 1989. He is a Diplomate of the American and European Colleges of Veterinary Surgeons and is a staff surgeon at the prestigious Angell Animal Medical Center in Boston. He is the author of two books, the *New York Times* bestseller *Tell Me Where It Hurts* and *Love Is the Best Medicine,* and has been a contributing columnist for *The Bark* and *Prevention* magazines.

Nick considers himself a runner (though his marathon days are behind him), an avid reader, and a passionate advocate for the Cystic Fibrosis Foundation. He lives in Massachusetts with his wife, two daughters, and their two dogs, Meg, their yellow Labrador, and Sophie, their Jack Russell terrier.

Visit Nick Trout online at
www.facebook.com/drnicktrout

The employees of Thorndike Press hope you have enjoyed this Large Print book. All our Thorndike, Wheeler, and Kennebec Large Print titles are designed for easy reading, and all our books are made to last. Other Thorndike Press Large Print books are available at your library, through selected bookstores, or directly from us.

For information about titles, please call:
(800) 223-1244

or visit our Web site at:
http://gale.cengage.com/thorndike

To share your comments, please write:
Publisher
Thorndike Press
295 Kennedy Memorial Drive
Waterville, ME 04901